Sparks of Fire

Sparks of Fire

Unknown Poetry of Ṭáhirih

John S. Hatcher and Amrollah Hemmat

Bahá'í Publishing
Evanston, Illinois

Bahá'í Publishing
1233 Central Street, Evanston, Illinois 60201

Printed in the United States of America on acid-free paper ∞

27 26 25 24 4 3 2 1

Library of Congress Cataloging in Publication Control Number
2024024618

ISBN 978-1-61851-253-6

Cover design by Carlos Esparza
Book design by Patrick Falso

Dedicated to Muḥammad-Ḥusayn and Shikkar-Nisá Ma'ṣúmí, a Bahá'í couple who were burned to death for their beliefs in the village of Núk near Bírjand.

(*The Bahá'í World,* Volume XVII (1979–1983), pp. 276–277)

Contents

Acknowledgments

We are grateful to the staff of the Bahá'í World Center for providing a high-resolution facsimile of the original manuscript. Our particular thanks go to Dr. Roya Akhavan, who, despite difficult circumstances, made copies of the manuscript in her possession available to us, and to Dr. Amin Egea, who provided us with a high-resolution and most clear copy of the manuscript. In addition, we would like to express our gratitude to Mr. Afshin Zabihian and Mrs. Sa'ídeh Forúghí-Zabihian, who typed the original handwritten manuscript into a digital format, and did so with such care that their scholarly insight proved extremely valuable for alternate and improved reading of certain words. Finally, we are indebted to Mrs. Parvin Djoneidi, Mrs. Pouran Eames, Mr. Ehsanollah Hemmat, and Dr. Behnam Rahbin, who reviewed certain poems to share their insights about interpretations of difficult passages and elucidation of various abstruse terms.

Introduction

The heroic life of Ṭáhirih—Fáṭimih Umm-i-Salama (1817–1852)—has long been celebrated by playwrights, historians, and Persian social reformers, especially those advocating women's rights in present-day Iran. Though a nineteenth-century poet of superb eloquence and variety, she is better known by most as a woman of dauntless faith, courage, and resilience, whether by the Persian community in general or by the followers of the Bahá'í religion, for whom she looms as one of the most memorable figures of the Faith's Heroic Age (1844–1921).

The followers of the Bahá'í Faith celebrate her as one of the Letters of the Living—the first eighteen followers of the Báb, the Herald of Bahá'u'lláh and a Prophet in His own right. Though she never actually met the Báb, she recognized in His writings and through a dream vision that He was the long-awaited Qá'im of Shí'ih Islam. She remained one of the most outstanding teachers and leaders of the Bábí religion from her recognition of the Báb's station in 1844 to her execution for her beliefs in 1852.

Most students of nineteenth-century Persian history are aware of Ṭáhirih, and in particular of her courageous actions in defiance of time-honored traditional limitations imposed on women, but few are aware of her exceptional intellect and erudition. She studied rigorously under Siyyid Káẓim-i-Rashtí, read the writings of Shaykh Aḥmad-i-Aḥsá'í, and later eagerly taught others about the Báb as the advent of the promised Hidden Imám and the Prophet-Herald of a new Revelation. In addition, after recognizing the Báb as fulfilling these prophecies, she dedicated her amazing skills as a poet to praising the Báb and celebrating the long-awaited Day of Days, the Day of Resurrection, the

Last Judgment, the advent of which, she was firmly convinced, the Báb had fulfilled.

This volume—together with our previous three, all of which contain the original text of Ṭáhirih's poetry along with our English translations—is intended to provide both English and Persian readers with access to some of her amazing talent as a poet, as well as insight into her remarkable depth of knowledge about the teachings of the Báb. Her intimate familiarity with the writings and traditions of past religions—particularly Islam, Ṣúfism, and the wisdom and poetic traditions of Rúmí and others—is also strikingly apparent.

Because the poems in this volume are not always easy to understand, they may challenge even those familiar with Persian poetic traditions; with the cultural milieu in which she is writing; and with the spiritual, theological, and ontological theories she discusses and explains. For this reason, we have provided a substantial general introduction, extensive footnotes, introductions and endnotes for the more abstruse poems, and a glossary to assist the reader to become familiar with the more difficult and repeated allusions and tropes she employs throughout.

We are well aware that poetry, though ever the first literature to emerge in the evolution of a culture, becomes in time less popular because of its often indirect presentation of meaning through allegory, symbolism, metaphor, and other figurative tools. Nevertheless, one can hardly approach an understanding of the station, importance, or accomplishments of the heroic, talented, and learned Ṭáhirih without also approaching the focus of her life—teaching others about the Bábí Faith, its beliefs, and the religious traditions that form the foundation on which the Báb established His ministry. The poems in this volume, together with those in our previous three volumes, are a valuable resource for achieving such understanding.

In this fourth volume, the reader can sense a distinct unity of theme and purpose, albeit arranged in a series of motifs that result in a veritable symphonic structure. With the exception of the first three poems, the copyist has had access to and has been rigorously faithful to a manuscript in Ṭáhirih's own hand. Consequently, Ṭáhirih may well have intended a thematic structure to this collection, as opposed to the collections of miscellaneous poems she compiled at various times. Certainly, there are indications that the volume was designed by her to have a logical structure, as demonstrated in some of the obvious groupings of poems throughout. For this reason, with the exception of one poem and the omission of a few others we did not translate, the order of poems in this volume complies with the order in which they appear in the original manuscript.

We have pointed out some of the obvious instances where a sequence of poems within the volume revolves around specific motifs of the abiding themes of the work as a whole, though it is not our intent to impose our personal sense of her purpose on the reader. As you peruse this work, you may find other sorts of unity and thematic groupings in this remarkable demonstration of Ṭáhirih's stunning intellect and depth of understanding regarding philosophy, theology, ontology, and cosmology. It should be noted also, that the translation of poetry, and in particular abstruse poetry such as this, necessarily entails a level of interpretation. As the translators of this volume, while we have diligently striven to render Ṭáhirih's words as accurately as possible and provided context and analysis that we feel will enhance the reader's understanding, we cannot claim that in our interpretations and translations we have represented the poet exhaustively and flawlessly. What we offer is our best understanding based on rigorous study.

In general, this volume focuses on Ṭáhirih's very intricate understanding of how the advent of the Báb and His Revelation fulfills Islamic as well as Judeo-Christian prophecies about a turning point in human history—the Day of Days, the Ingathering, the Day of Judgment, the Second Coming of Christ, the advent of the Qá'im, and the return of the Twelfth Imám—all of which betoken the beginning of a new era so frequently alluded to in the Qur'án and in various ḥadíths.

In this vein, and unlike many of the poems in her previous volumes, the poems in *Sparks of Fire* tend to dwell relatively little on the dramatic events in Ṭáhirih's own memorable life. However, she does often conclude her poems with a plea to God for acceptance and relief from the tribulations of this earthly life. But the principal focus of the poems revolves around her observations about what is occurring both within and without the Bábí community as followers face grievous persecution from the religious divines and governmental authorities in Persia who are intent on eradicating the Bábí religion by persecuting and executing its followers, even as they executed the Báb Himself by firing squad in Tabriz on July 9, 1850.

If there is an abiding and ultimately unifying image employed to depict the fervor of the Bábí Faith and its significance, it is the fire of faith animating the fearless determination of those souls who eagerly sacrificed their lives rather than recant their newly found belief. And yet Ṭáhirih also observes throughout, and with an obvious irony, the dual implications of this metaphor—the sparks from the fire of that faith are matched with the equally unquenchable conflagration of hatred and cruelty of the Shí'ih divines in their determination to halt the rapid spread of this movement throughout Persia.

In addition to this overarching allusion to the sparks from the fire of faith and the flames of persecution, are deeper and more transcendental themes and creative applications of this variable symbol, the most frequently employed among these being the Sinaitic fire and the Burning Bush, which allude to God's Revelation to Moses in particular, and to the divine source of Revelation in general. In some of the poems in this volume, we also discover perhaps the most erudite expressions of Ṭáhirih's understanding and articulation of the heart of the Báb's expositions of the unity of God and of the exquisite and subtle process the Creator has devised to bring about the unity and advancement of humankind. These discourses are replete with allusions to some of the more abstruse Bábí concepts, which in time emerged in the Bahá'í writings.

Of course, we should not overlook the underlying allusions to Ṭáhirih's personal suffering, most particularly as noted at the end of many poems. In these instances, Ṭáhirih as narrator/persona pleads for assistance and expresses her longing to escape the tribulations she is being made to experience. In particular, she alludes to the solitude and torment of the imprisonment and isolation she was forced to endure immediately prior to her grotesque execution in which a guard is said to have forced a scarf down her throat until she strangled to death, after which he threw her body into an abandoned well.[1]

But the driving force of these poems are discourses, sometimes lengthy, about theological concepts, about the ontology of God and the Manifestations, about the Creator's use of timeliness and degree in portioning out guidance in such a way that it maximizes the need for the peoples of the world to exercise free will in recognizing this divine plan and in participating in promulgating its advancement. And among motifs related to this central and unifying theme are the challenges to the peoples of the world to recognize the advent of the Báb and to appreciate this turning point in human history as demonstrated by following the teachings of the Báb. Ṭáhirih likewise includes

1. See 'Abdu'l-Bahá, *Memorials of the Faithful,* no. 69.32.

dire warnings to those who reject His claims or, even worse, who persecute the Báb and His followers.

Intermingled with the seriousness of these observations are the joyous and ecstatic celebrations she shares with the believers. Indeed, many of the poems are replete with praise of God in gratitude for this Day of Days. Some contain prayers to God and sequences of epithets in praise of God as the Knower, the Exalted, the Omnipotent, the Eternal Beloved, the Everlasting, the Most Great Helper.

Also related to this central theme are Ṭáhirih's numerous allusions to "mysteries." In some instances, she is alluding to the overall abiding indirection with which God conceals the Manifestations and the subtlety of His methodology in enlightening and educating humankind by degrees. In other cases, she is referring to more specific verities concealed in abstruse verses and prophecies from religious scripture, and elsewhere she may be explicating some of the multiple levels of meanings in the verses revealed by the Báb. Some other "mysteries" have to do with the unity among the Manifestations; with the eternal Plan of God; and with the true meaning of "resurrection," not as designating the end of time, but as initiating the beginning of the collective enlightenment and unification of humankind.

Still another theme or conceit of many of the poems is Ṭáhirih's utilization of the language, tone, and imagery of Ṣúfí poetry. She particularly emphasizes the ecstasy experienced by those who are emboldened and empowered by their recognition of and allegiance to the Revelation of the Báb. Much of this sense of heavenly outpouring is stated in terms of the bounties descending from the cloud of 'Amá or from the Bird of Paradise singing about the advent of renewal, or, perhaps most frequent of all, images of sparks of fire emanating from the revealed Word causing the hearts to become aflame with the love of the Beloved. For while in some poems fire and flames and conflagration signalize a negative force testing the faithful, throughout this collection Ṭáhirih most often employs fire, sparks of fire, and the consuming spread of this spiritual force to represent the transformative effect of the advent of the Báb on Persia and on the world at large.

As with her poems in other works we have translated—*The Poetry of Ṭáhirih* (2001), *Adam's Wish* (2008), and *The Quickening* (2011)—the central emphasis in this volume is a thorough, almost exhaustive treatment of the emotional or affective indices associated with the consummation of the Last Judgment or Resurrection so often portrayed in the Qur'án.

THE MANUSCRIPT

The manuscript containing the poems in this volume includes several pieces that we have already translated in two of our previous volumes: *The Poetry of Ṭáhirih* and *Adam's Wish.* As such they are not included in the present volume, with the exception of one poem, which is different in several verses and which we feel is more authentic in this volume. However, this manuscript contains more than seventy previously unknown poems. Even though a few of the pages in this manuscript were at first not fully readable, as our editing of this volume proceeded, historian of the Bahá'í Faith Dr. Amin Egea discovered a copy of the manuscript that was clearer than the one originally available to us. This fortuitous discovery enabled us to revise certain parts of our translated poems as a number of words previously unreadable were now legible.

The manuscript itself ends with a note that indicates the date of completion of the transcription as the month *Rabí'u'th-Th̲ání* of the year 1339 of the Islamic lunar calendar (between mid-December 1920 and mid-January 1921), around seventy years after Ṭáhirih's martyrdom in August of 1852. The manuscript originally in our possession, consisting of 150 pages in length and including letters and poems, had been preserved in the Library of the Archives of Bahá'í Material of the National Spiritual Assembly of the Bahá'ís of Iran, which was established in 132 BE (1975 CE). A stamp of the library appears on the cover page and on page 80. A handwritten note by the archivist on the cover page, dated [25]35/7/26 of the Islamic solar calendar (October 18, 1976 in the Gregorian calendar), states: "This collection of poems of her holiness Ṭáhirih are images of the photocopy existing in the possession of the honorable Colonel Yahyá Shahidí, a relative of Ṭáhirih."

This date, brought to our attention by Dr. Egea, refers to the year 2535 according to the Shahanshahi calendar, a calendar that replaced the Hejri Shamsi calendar for a few years. While the Hejri Shamsi calendar was based on the year of the Prophet Muḥammad's migration from Mecca to Medina, the new Shahanshahi calendar was based on the reign of the ancient Persian king, Cyrus the Great. Established in 1975 by Muhammad Reza Shah Pahlavi, the new calendar was not long lasting or commonly employed. After the Islamic Revolution in 1979, it was replaced with the Hejri Shamsi calendar.

The clearer manuscript provided by Dr. Egea should have been the original copy given to the Archives of the National Spiritual Assembly of Iran because the two copies are identical, except that Dr. Egea's copy lacks the cover page that includes the NSA of Iran's Archives Library note and the aforementioned stamp imprints of the Archives Library.

The transcriber of the manuscript has compared certain poems with other transcriptions available and has made some notes on differences between them. It is obvious that compared to other transcribers—who, while having been talented calligraphers, let themselves or others occasionally alter certain poems by modifying some words here and there, or else by occasionally adding or omitting one or more verses or by changing the order of a few verses—the transcriber of this manuscript was conscientiously dedicated to maintaining the authenticity of the work and fidelity to the original.

We have followed those same approaches by translating as closely as possible words in the original manuscript, even in those cases when a slight change seemed to improve the poem, ostensibly making it more meaningful or adding to the beauty of the original Persian or Arabic. We believe the original style and wording of the poems have important historical significance, and we have therefore decided to preserve and represent the original as faithfully as possible, particularly for those scholars and students of the work of Ṭáhirih who may want to utilize this translation in discerning more lofty meanings contained in Ṭáhirih's exquisite art and thought. We have identified, in the endnotes to the poems in the original language, those cases where a word in the manuscript is unclear, is in need of minor modification, or where an alternative word for it is indicated in the manuscript, as explained below.

If, in rare cases, a couplet is missing a half-line (also called a "hemistich"), or a verse in its original form does not rhyme perfectly, these may possibly inform scholars about Ṭáhirih's circumstances when the poem was composed, or, more likely, she may have employed these devices to draw attention to certain meanings or tropes. Nevertheless, the rhyme and rhythm of the original poems impose limitations on the English rendering in terms of the beauty and style of the translation, and they may seem to detract from the creativity that is normally exercised in composing or translating poems. There are cases where an alternative wording appears on the top of a verse. Considering the transcriber's particular care in replicating what is in Ṭáhirih's own handwriting, these seem to have been inserted by the poet herself. Since it is not clear which wording was preferred by Ṭáhirih, we took the liberty of choosing language that, to our understanding, seems best in conveying the intended sense of the poem.

There is a very short poem on page 33 of the manuscript and another on page 93 that we have not translated because in these Ṭáhirih employs symbolism based on the alphabetic letters forming a specific word. Translation of these might be extremely ambiguous for the reader, and some may have been intentionally veiled by Ṭáhirih into coded tropes or culturally based allusions that cannot be effectively understood or translated into a distinctly different language and culture. It is our hope that in the future, other researchers might discern the full meanings of these obscure verses and translate them effectively.

Another poem (pages 98–101 of the manuscript) has been only partially translated (verses 34–43 on page 100) because a number of the verses are repetitive, at least insofar as the meaning is concerned. It is, however, a repetition that is acceptable in the original language because the rhythm and rhyme in these verses enhance the poetics and are in accord with her style. A fourth poem (pages 108–11 of the manuscript) has not been translated because around ten verses are missing in the transcribed manuscript. According to the transcriber's note, this part of the original manuscript has been torn off and lost. Therefore, he has left blank space for this part in the hope that it might be recovered at a later date.

A large part of the manuscript has been taken from the original handwritten work of Ṭáhirih herself, as emphasized by the transcriber in multiple places in the document. The transcriber is clearly knowledgeable about Persian and Arabic and has been careful to make copious notes in the margins of pages regarding his full compliance with the original. For example, he leaves a few lines blank to emulate the original.

In this same vein, on page 56 of the manuscript (before poem 4 "Arise, O Pen!" in our volume) the transcriber writes: "It should be made clear that whatever is written after this point is from the handwriting of her holiness Ṭáhirih herself. If rarely it happens that a verse is not rhymed melodiously, or there is a *siktih* [a short silence in the rhythm or short pause that some might find unpleasant but others find pleasing], or if occasionally a word is left out, or a word has been modified, since the present manuscript has been transcribed exactly with utmost care from the handwriting of that noble maiden, no alterations have been made."

The transcriber has included two versions of poem 11 in our translated volume, one from a manuscript transcribed by others and one directly transcribed from the handwriting of Ṭáhirih. Regarding this poem, the transcriber writes on page 66 of his manuscript: "What has been inserted on the margins of the pages [by others] also exists in Ṭáhirih's handwriting, and since they had modified some of the verses, I am writing them here the way they exist in Ṭáhirih's handwriting, without alteration." And on page 137 of the manuscript, the transcriber writes, "It has been transcribed from the handwriting of her holiness Ṭáhirih herself. Since she has omitted the letter *alif* indicating plural form, this humble one has also omitted these."

This note, an indication of the familiarity of the transcriber with Arabic grammar, is written after a couple of cases in which such omissions occur in a letter by the Báb transcribed by Ṭáhirih in her manuscript. This evidence would seem further to confirm the authenticity and accuracy of the transcribed manuscript. Yet, unlike our previous two volumes also subtitled "Unknown Poetry of Ṭáhirih," the handwriting of this transcriber is not calligraphic and occasionally not clear enough to be comprehended. Therefore, we have included a typed version of our reading of the manuscript, and that by itself imposes inevitable, albeit minimal, interpretation on our part. However, the unclear words in the manuscript are pointed out in the endnotes to the typed version.

Ṭáhirih's vast range of knowledge—so evident in her understanding of philosophy, religion, and religious traditions, as well as in her familiarity with esoteric gnostic and Shaykhí beliefs—is demonstrated in her choice of words, terminology, scholarly practices, and intentional violations of grammar, as well as her creation of neologisms and novel words. In this regard, she is following the practice of the Manifestations of God Who have tested people through violation of customary social conventions and in their innovations with language.

If the reader finds these poems difficult at first reading, it is understandable. It is apparent to us that Ṭáhirih is speaking to an exclusive audience, and it may be that, even with the various introductions and extensive notes we have provided for assistance to the reader, only students of theology and the Bábí teachings will comprehend some of the more obscure and difficult concepts. But Ṭáhirih's poetry works at various levels, and the reader, regardless of background, will most certainly appreciate her art on some level, and will also likely discover other layers of meaning with each successive reading.

The point is that we feel compelled to make it clear to the reader that Ṭáhirih—most often known for her daring, her beauty, and heroism—was a highly trained scholar and is speaking to other scholars at the level of learning of her Shaykhí students in Karbala. She thus expects her audience, as do all the great poets, to ascend to her standards. She does not deign to avoid elliptical imagery or sometimes abstruse allusions to befit any but the most learned, industrious, and persistent readers.

This aspect of her erudition calls to mind her ironic remarks to Vaḥíd—considered one of the most learned scholars in Persia at the time—demonstrating her lack of tolerance for those who deemed themselves to be learned in some formal sense. The occasion was her escape from authorities when she was being safeguarded at the home of Bahá'u'lláh. 'Abdu'l-Bahá, Who was but a child at the time, later recounts the incident in *Memorials of the Faithful:*

> One day the great Siyyid Yaḥyá, surnamed Vaḥíd, was present there. As he sat without, Ṭáhirih listened to him from behind the veil. I was then a child, and was sitting on her lap. With eloquence and fervor, Vaḥíd was discoursing on the signs and verses that bore witness to the advent of the new Manifestation. She suddenly interrupted him and, raising her voice, vehemently declared: "O Yaḥyá! Let deeds, not words, testify to thy faith, if thou art a man of true learning. Cease idly repeating the traditions of the past, for the day of service, of steadfast action, is come. Now is the time to show forth the true signs of God, to rend asunder the veils of idle fancy, to promote the Word of God, and to sacrifice ourselves in His path. Let deeds, not words, be our adorning!"[2]

In effect, she knew when it was time to write, when it was time to teach, and when it was time simply to remain stalwart in her unstinting fortitude and constancy in her beliefs. Consequently, her poems are filled with terminology and allusions discernable to Islamic and Bábí scholars. As such, decoding the entirety and depth of her symbolic allusions, her references to Qur'ánic verses, to ḥadíths, to Shaykhí texts, or to the Báb's writings, is beyond the scope of this volume. Indeed, such explication would be well worth a volume unto itself. Yet to the degree possible, we have included introductions to some of the more difficult poems, footnotes wherever we feel such annotation might be helpful, and endnotes where we feel even more information would prove valuable for the more scholarly readers. But it should be kept in mind that as important as is the knowledge of these intertextual relationships, we think it

2. Ibid., no. 69.24.

most valuable to approach each poem independently, even though as one traverses the sequence of poems, the elusive meanings concealed by veils of tropes and conceits begin to assist the reader accumulatively, and each successive piece informs us about the previous poems in this collection.

Most certainly one derives from studying these poems a sense of the personality, wit, and the sometimes brazen character of this remarkable woman. And yet there is also a prowess contrapuntal to her sense of humility before God and her frequent references to her personal anguish and her ardent desire to be rescued from this life. But most prominently, she is aware of and anxious to share her insights into the advent of the Day of Days as indicated in the multitude of eschatological passages she cites from the Qur'án that allude to this singular turning point in human history.

ABOUT THIS TRANSLATION

As mentioned above, classical Persian verse is often written in half-lines in which each verse forms a couplet. The first half of the line is followed by a caesura, but the two halves constitute a single poetic verse or unit. Most often each couplet constitutes a complete sentence, though this is not always the case. Occasionally, the sentence will continue for several verses, even though each verse in that sentence will most often constitute complete clauses or parallel phrases.

In adhering to the fidelity of the original, we have in our translation of Ṭáhirih's poetry, both here and in our previous volumes, remained true to the original by almost always translating half-line for half-line, and also, to the extent possible, word for word, except in those cases where switching the word order has proved necessary for purposes of coherent syntax.

We have not tried to emulate the meter or the rhyme scheme because we have found that this practice imposes such constraints that accurate rendering of meaning is virtually impossible. We firmly believe that conveying the beauty of the ideas and utilizing Ṭáhirih's imagery wherever possible are of greater value than attempting what is most often inadvisable when translating from one language to a distinctly different type of language. For example, sometimes Ṭáhirih (as well as other notable Persian poets writing in the classical form) will create beauteous sound effects by employing a number of words derived from the same root, but which have variable nuances of meaning or are utilized as different parts of speech. It would be impossible to replicate this effect in an English translation.

Stated more fully, we find that in the case of some related languages, it is clearly possible to translate meter and rhyme from one language to another. Among some of the Romance languages, for example, the structure, cognates, meter, and inflections are so similar—as is the case between Spanish and Italian, for instance—that a translator could successfully recreate meter and rhyme. But with languages so different in sound and structure as Persian and English, the attempt at discerning poetic meaning suffers severely if one attempts to impose a set rhyme scheme or meter. Therefore, we have focused our translations on two central features—rendering an accurate or literal English sense of each verse or half-line, attempting as best we can to choose those words that capture the poetic feel of the original, and retaining as completely as possible the various figurative images, allusions, and symbols.

USING ORIGINAL WORDS AND TERMS

As with the translation of any language that contains loaded contextual meaning or complex allusions, we have found that some words in Persian and Arabic have no worthy counterpart in English. Therefore, with certain recurring terms and phrases, we have chosen to use the original words, both for accuracy and because poetically it would be extremely awkward to try to capture the meaning of these loaded and complex terms and phrases in translation.

These are explained in footnotes when they first occur, and those that are repeated frequently are also included in the glossary we have provided at the end of the text. It is our hope that one will quickly become familiar with these repeated terms and their variable connotations as one proceeds through this collection so that it will not be necessary to refer constantly to the notes or glossary.

To give an example here, let us cite the word *'Amá*. This term in its most common usage refers to a metaphysical poetic notion of a cloud in the celestial realm from which emanate the divine bounties of God. These bounties descend upon humankind like drops of rain, as explained more fully in a note from an authoritative translation of Bahá'u'lláh's poem "Rashḥ-i-'Amá," translated in the published poem as "The Clouds of the Realms Above":

> "*'Amá*" is defined as an extremely thin and subtle cloud, seen and then not seen. For shouldst thou gaze with the utmost care, thou wouldst discern something, but as soon as thou dost look again, it ceaseth to be seen. For this reason, in the usage of mystics who seek after truth,

> 'Amá signifieth the Universal Reality without individuations as such, for these individuations exist in the mode of uncompounded simplicity and oneness and are not differentiated from the Divine Essence. Thus they are individuated and not individuated. This is the station alluded to by the terms *Aḥadíyyih* (Absolute Oneness) and *'Amá*. This is the station of the "Hidden Treasure" mentioned in the Ḥadí<u>th</u>. The divine attributes, therefore, are individuations that exist in the Essence but are not differentiated therefrom. They are seen and then not seen. This, in brief, is what is meant by 'Amá.[3]

As the reader can readily appreciate, with such a breadth and abundance of meaning, a single word or phrase in English could hardly capture the full impact of this word. Consequently, we have chosen not to translate the term with all its possible connotations but have instead provided a more complete understanding of its symbolic meaning in the footnotes and the glossary. We trust that the reader will, after several encounters with the term, begin to infer the fullness of what Ṭáhirih intends.

Several other terms we have chosen to keep in the original are no less complex and subtle in their meaning. For example, throughout the poems in this volume, Ṭáhirih has on numerous occasions employed various forms of the command that we also find frequently in the Qur'án and later in the works of Bahá'u'lláh: "Be and it is!" The sense of the original is that God as Creator has but to wish or desire for something to come about, and it is preordained to become accomplished. The phrase also relates to the following notion from John 1:1 in the New Testament: "In the beginning was the Word, and the Word was with God, and the Word was God."

The Logos or the Word of God, whether representing the Manifestation or alluding to the function of the Prophets as the means by which the Word of God is conveyed to humankind, is replete with meaning. For example, in one of the obligatory prayers of Bahá'u'lláh, we find the affirmation that the Manifestation is the means by which God brings forth all that He desires to occur in the spiritual and social evolution of humankind: "He who hath been manifested is the Hidden Mystery, the Treasured Symbol, through Whom

---

3. Ibid., from a previously untranslated Tablet, quoted in Bahá'u'lláh, *The Call of the Divine Beloved*, note 8, p. 105.

the letters B and E (Be) have been joined and knit together."[4] The conjoining of the letters "B" and "E" in English (other letters are used to form this same command in other languages) forms the imperative "Be!" And when issued forth from God through the Manifestations, whatsoever the Creator desires will come to pass. We have thus chosen to use the original *kun fa yakúnu* (Be! And it will be!), or, in the case of something that has already been consummated by the Will of God, *kun fa kán* ("Be! And it was!").

We feel our previous translations of Ṭáhirih's verse will also prove valuable for the reader interested in the life, mind, and written works of this remarkable woman who in the future will doubtless assume a major role in religious and literary history. However, we are not suggesting that our works must be read in sequence or that we have captured the chronology of her life and work. As her manuscripts have become available to us, we have eagerly proceeded to indulge ourselves in the joyful discovery of precisely how learned, courageous, and phenomenal Ṭáhirih was.

As we reflect on this and the other two volumes we have designated as being "Unknown Poetry of Ṭáhirih," and compare the wording, language, style of composition, and commonality of expressions, symbolism, and theological and philosophical concepts contained within them—many unique to Ṭáhirih's poetry—we become further confirmed in our conclusion that, with the exception of a few poems composed by Bihjat (a poet with whom Ṭáhirih corresponded), the poems in these volumes are composed by one poet and that this poet is indeed Ṭáhirih. While this conclusion may fly in the face of the opinion of some scholars that most of the poems attributed to Ṭáhirih were composed by others, we feel we have provided quite sufficient proof to support our conclusion, much of which we have included in introductions to the poems, the footnotes, and most comprehensively in the endnotes.

While we readily acknowledge we have hardly scratched the surface of all there is to discern in her work, we trust that our work over the years will, at the very least, constitute groundwork whereby future scholars can probe further the insights Ṭáhirih has provided as she analyzes some of the most important theological issues that characterize the advent of the Báb and Bahá'u'lláh. Clearly these two Manifestation were well aware of her value and importance, as demonstrated by Their acknowledgements of her station and utilization

4. Bahá'u'lláh, *Prayers and Meditations,* no. 183.10.

of her talents in carrying out Their ministries. The Báb chose her as one of His Letters of the Living—the only female to have such an honor—and Bahá'u'lláh went to great pains to rescue Ṭáhirih from imprisonment and conceal her at His home, as well as consult with her and Quddús to plan the dramatic events surrounding the famous conference at Badasht.

Finally, the reader should note that, unless otherwise indicated, all citations from the Qur'án are to Abdullah Yusuf Ali, *The Holy Qur'an: Text, Translation and Commentary* (New York: Tahrike Tarsile Qur'an, Inc. 2001). In addition, we have employed italics where the original words and phrases are common Arabic terms or where Ṭáhirih has written a whole sentence in Arabic.

THEMES AND MOTIFS

As one final addition to this introduction, we think it might be a helpful head start for the reader if we share a few of our observations about some major themes that are interwoven throughout this volume. As mentioned, we get the sense that after going through the poems in this collection, the reader may well infer that the volume constitutes a single, unified opus.

True, sections of poems are interwoven occasionally within sections of prose, prayers, and letters that we have not translated and included. Likewise, the poems are varied in arrangement—some lengthy discourses are followed by short emotional lyric pieces. But there are several sections where a sequence of poems is clearly united by a particular train of thought. And while we have in the introductions to the poems tried to point these out as the volume progresses, it may prove useful for the reader to be aware of a few motifs that recur, because it often feels as if Ṭáhirih is having a conversation with her readers that traverses various strains, themes, and affects. Some poems are joyous and celebratory, achieving a pitch of delight and ecstasy, while others lament the recalcitrance of humankind in being persistently oblivious to the bounties of God and unconcerned with or uninformed about the underlying logic of His eternal plan.

The imagery of fire, as the title implies, is one of the most prevalent metaphors. And as we have also already mentioned, this can represent either positive or negative forces. But the predominant use of this conceit is in the positive sense, even as *'Amá*—with one exception—always represents the heavenly source of divine bestowals. As any student of literature knows, images of fire and burning are common in mystic prose and poetry, regardless of what religious tradition or culture is involved. For example, in Zoroastrian symbolism, fire and light play an important positive role. Similarly, among the medieval English Christian mystics, Richard Rolle of Hampole (1300–1349) is well known for his work *Incendium Amoris* (*The Fire of Love*), in which he explores the ecstatic sensations and experiences associated with his intense meditation. Likewise, in the Báb's writings and Ṭáhirih's poems the images of fire as one of the four cardinal elements, and allusions to the fire on Mt. Sinai that attracted Moses, have a particular spiritual significance.

Another major motif interwoven among these poems is imagery relating to veils, curtains, concealment, and how these deterrents to understanding become removed through spiritual insight and the acquisition of knowledge, especially the learning related to deciphering metaphorical and symbolic meanings of prophecies regarding this Day of Days. An extension of these conceits is the more complex idea of the veils of physical reality that can interfere with our ability to recognize the spiritual purpose latent in the totality of creation.

However, it is crucial to mention that Ṭáhirih also frequently employs the image of veils in a positive sense. For example, in poem 11, verse 6, we find: "With verses of the Revelation,\ Manifest the Point cloaked in veils of light." In verse 21 of the same poem, Ṭáhirih writes: "Is this the hidden Mystery or the cloaked name \ That has become revealed from behind threefold veils?" Likewise, in verse 39 of the same poem, we read: "That which He desires was concealed in the veils of *Th̲aná'!* \ Now is it nigh in the sphere of "fulfilment"! Again, in verse 2 of poem 44, we read "Gaze with unblemished eyes at the veil of fire— \ The mystery of certitude that hath appeared from the book of justice and light!" And these are but a few examples.

In this regard, we often find Ṭáhirih talking in terms of the antithesis of God and Godliness as being "other than God," everything that is not of God. In employing these phrases, she is not necessarily speaking of evil thoughts or actions, but simply the fact that the ultimate force governing creation is the Creator Himself. Consequently, human history and purpose can only be properly understood and advanced by humankind when we become aware that everything else in one's life should be understood as subservient to, or else a pathway to, the divine purpose of creation and our participation in facilitating that divinely guided process.

A more elusive and abstruse motif throughout relates to Ṭáhirih's repeated efforts to make clear the distinction between the essential reality that is the divine essence of the Creator, and His independence from His creation, even though He is ever aware of and always promulgating creation through

His will. In relationship to this process by which the created world of existence emanates from God, Ṭáhirih speaks often about the Manifestation as the Primal Point, the source, the functionary by Whose means the Creator brings existence into being. In other words, the Creator's process is indirect, instigated by the actions of the Manifestations, Who operate at the level of Command and Who are ontologically distinct from and superior to ordinary human beings.

Related to this theme, and integral to it, is the concept of Divine Unity, which Ṭáhirih speaks of frequently, a concept perhaps best explained by Bahá'u'lláh when He observes,

> The essence of belief in Divine unity consisteth in regarding Him Who is the Manifestation of God and Him Who is the invisible, the inaccessible, the unknowable Essence as one and the same. By this is meant that whatever pertaineth to the former, all His acts and doings, whatever He ordaineth or forbiddeth, should be considered, in all their aspects, and under all circumstances, and without any reservation, as identical with the Will of God Himself. This is the loftiest station to which a true believer in the unity of God can ever hope to attain. Blessed is the man that reacheth this station, and is of them that are steadfast in their belief.[5]

Finally, we feel it worthwhile to repeat that one of the most dominant concepts and oft repeated terms in the context of Ṭáhirih's informed representation of Bábí theology relates to the concept of "mystery" and "mysteries." While her use of these terms is often derived from her allusions to the ḥadí<u>th</u> of the Hidden Treasure and the mystery underlying God's purpose in bringing about creation as a result of His desire to be known, Ṭáhirih also uses these terms more generally to refer to the myriad spiritual verities that—while formerly "mysterious," unknown, and considered by many divines to be largely unknowable—are in this Day being unconcealed, unveiled, unravelled, and made accessible, even to the ordinary believer.

To conclude, we can note how this theme is explicitly and beautifully expressed in poem 62—"Behold Once More!"—where the speaker

5. Ibid., *Gleanings from the Writings of Bahá'u'lláh,* no. 84.3.

(presumably Ṭáhirih) exhorts the Bird of Paradise (presumably the Báb or the Holy Spirit) to sing about the "Hidden Mystery":

19
O Bird, chant a verse for those who delight in hearing again the name of God
That Thou mightiest behold the veil removed from the Desired One!

20
Sing about that Hidden Mystery with a melody about God the Creator,
Disclosing how God hath indeed created a new creation to praise the Hidden Mystery!

POEM 1

A Prologue Prayer

(The original poem begins on p. 495)

1
O Thou by Whose grace the spirit of faith hath reached the mystic knower,
Thy verses[1] supply the light of elucidation for the sincere ones.

2
O Exalted Lord, each and every one hath soared to such a height
That in their flight each hath attained nearness to paradise itself.

3
Warmed by this light, their faces beam with rapture
They achieved the station of "or nearer!"[2]

---

1. *Dhikr,* "mentioning," is also a title for the Báb.

2. A reference to the Qur'ánic verses describing Muḥammad's Night Journey, or Mi'ráj, as portrayed in Súrih 17:1 and alluded to in Súrih 53:8–9: "Then he approached and came closer, And was at a distance of but two bow-lengths or (even) nearer." This verse relates to the point in the narrative when Muḥammad approaches God as near as was possible. This and all future citations to the Qur'án are from *The Qur'án: Text, Translation and Commentary* by Abdullah Yusuf Ali unless specified otherwise.

4
They each have divine verses concealed within their bosoms;[3]
Each illumined the swooning one among the plains of Paran[4]

5
They each are honored with a crown by the Exalted Creator;
Each approacheth the station of "nearness" while reciting "Alláh!"

6
And those whom the kindness of God from His benevolence swayed
In their search for God attained nearness to the near ones!

7
O God, O Creator with new creation, such a wondrous world Thou hast wrought
That through its appearance the Fire hath been set ablaze!

8
Whosoever hath been encompassed, by the invisible attraction of Your love,
Such a one hath become the target of thunder bolts of grandeur from all four sides.[5]

9
Such a one will be utterly engulfed by fire of rapturous love!
So utterly consumed by flame wilt such a one be that no particle of self remaineth!

---

3. A reference to Qur'án 27:12, when God tells Moses: "Now put thy hand into thy bosom, and it will come forth white without stain."

4. Reference to Moses, who swooned when God revealed His glory at Mount Sinai (Qur'án 7:143).

5. This hemistich can also be read as: "Such a one hath become the target of rounds of bullets from all four sides."

10
O God, how wondrous the world Thou hast made manifest!
All the grandiose ones have been humbled and cast upon the earth.[6]

11
O God, from Thy mere glance hath appeared to me
that which consumeth my very being!

12
O God, a myriad knights appeareth in the midst of a sea of fire!
God's allusion to each of these hath appeared in Qur'ánic verses!

13
O God, their station is lofty beyond descent!
O Exalted Lord, in every respect their station hath excelled!

14
The inhabitants of the heavenly realm are illumined by a light,
That most great effulgence which hath shone on them from paradise.

15
O God, all the venerated ones stand row upon row!
They give thanks to the King, the most pure One, the Assayer, for what He hath done.

16
The angelic hosts are exulting in the refulgence of their glory!
All have approached the throne of grandeur with songs of praise.

---

6. "Cast upon the earth" (*ṭarḥán*) and derivations of it—such as *ṭarḥí, maṭrúḥ, and inṭiráḥ*—refer to Qur'án 12:9: "Slay ye Joseph or cast him out to some (unknown) land. . . ." These words appear in many verses of Ṭáhirih in this and other volumes. We also find the word "fallen" (*maṭrúḥ*) in the Báb's Súrih of Naḥl (the Bee) in the Commentary on the Súrih of Joseph. The word often alludes to the confinement of the reality of the Manifestation of God to material existence.

17
Towards this lowly one fallen on the dust,
The world itself approacheth like the blast from a storm!

18
O God, with glory have so many tents been pitched
That from every quarter effulgence hath come to Paran!

19
With purity of heart, heavenly hosts are assisting!
For their sake doth Jesus encircle them on high!

20
O Creator, doomed are the earthbound ones, doomed indeed!
For they advance toward purehearted ones with oppression and dissent!

21
O God, by the certain truth of these kings among kings!
O God, by that same grace that creates and is beneficent!

22
No limit is there to Thine unconditional love
Which surely permeateth all those endowed with a soul!

23
Since He desires only the Lord, the Beloved, the Omnipotent, the Eternal,
In His sight all else is abolished and charred.

24
O God, O Creator, by Thine inviolable truth!
O Lord, through Thy benevolence, only Thou art the remedy for this ailing soul!

POEM 2

Do Not Grieve

(The original poem begins on p. 492)

This melodious poem is composed in the style of a famous ghazal by Háfiz,[1] in which all lines of the poem conclude with the phrase "grieve not" (*gh̲am makh̲ur*). The poem from Háfiz begins with: *"The lost Joseph will return to Canaan. Grieve not! / This abode of sorrows will become a garden one day! Grieve not!"*

The poem from Háfiz is a consolation for the suffering ones, a quest for patience because in due time, all sorrows will be followed by happiness. However, Ṭáhirih's poem is far more sophisticated. In addition to dealing with theological and philosophical problems, her style is not nearly as simple and obvious as that of Háfiz. Often, she artistically combines the causes of sorrow with that which will provide hope. She implies that, in fact, these are but two aspects of the same cause, rather than being sequential in time.

For example, the new and wondrous flame gets obscured, but by light and glory. Similarly, the pure water flows, but in rivers of fire. And later, Abraham beholds God, but while sacrificing His son. The sum total of these enigmatic observations can be stated as a theological verity that when we become truly enlightened, we will be able to perceive wisdom in all afflictions.

---

1. See Sahba Shayani, "Literary Imitation in Three Poems Attributed to Ṭáhirih," *Hawwa,* vol. 21, no. 4, pp. 308–9, for this poetic device employed in other poems of Ṭáhirih.

Yet, Ṭáhirih's poem is not merely about consoling the grieved or explaining the wisdom of calamities. She is making important theological points in relation to the Báb, describing His mission, life, and station by making references to all major Abrahamic Prophets—to Adam, Noah, and Abraham. (See endnotes for further information about this poem.)

1
Whatsoever should descend to thee from Paradise will come. Do not grieve!
What befitteth thee will come to thee from the countenance of the Beloved! Do not grieve!

2
O thou who art consumed with passion for us, behold what we behold!
Observe the grandeur and majesty of that illumined countenance. Do not grieve!

3
Indeed, hearken to the verses of the exalted Lord intoned by us,
Descended from the fourth among the elements[2] Do not grieve!

4
The first of these, endowed with flames of Fire
Descended from the apex of exaltation onto the desert below. Do not grieve!

5
With a new enkindling, He ignited the entire creation
Which became obscured by beams of light. Do not grieve!

6
The second of these was like unto the first, but pure water
Flowing forth from rivers of flaming fire. Do not grieve!

2. This refers to the earth, which is the fourth added to the three archetypal elements of fire, water, and air. It is a reference to the Báb, as explained in the introduction to this poem.

7
The third of these, like unto the second, was delirious from the dawning of light,
Spirited with the giddy glee of children. Do not grieve!

8
The guileless acceptance from these three stations
Was concealed in the Temple,[3] O illuminating Sun. Do not grieve!

9
O my soul, Glad Tidings from the Creator descended for thee;
From mere dust,[4] the perfection of the elements became palpable. Do not grieve!

10
Indeed, behold how all the Celestial Kingdoms[5] are descending!
The universe itself hath become enlightened by the rays of these flames—do not grieve!

11
Behold how in the land of *Tá* the throne is exalted to the highest;
The face of God doth dawn from the mysterious cycling of day and night.[6] Do not grieve!

---

3. This is most probably a reference to the qualities hidden in the reality of the Manifestation of God, yet not revealed.

4. The fourth element, the earth. Qualities of the elements became manifest by the appearance of Adam, Who was made of earth and appeared on earth. In this dispensation, it refers to the Báb.

5. "Celestial Kingdoms" (*amlák-i-samávī*) can also be read as "the angels of heaven." In Rúmí's poems it is an allusion to spiritual powers (Siyyid Ṣádiq Gawharin, *Sharḥ-i-Iṣṭiláḥát-Taṣavvuf*, vol. 1, p. 278).

6. This would seem to be an allusion to the sequence of Revelations.

12
Behold that panorama when the Creator doth appear!
Discover how this eternal system endures no change![7] Except for this, Grieve not!

13
In the beginning, His creation is perfected[8] and His affairs ordered;[9]
He appeareth in the realm of grandeur and benevolence. Do not grieve!

14
Thereafter, so that He might render perfection and completion,
That creation of the Bestowing One trembles. Do not grieve!

15
If over the expanse of the earth He is quavering[10] and wailing,
Questing for that Living Judge to return Him to its original form, do not grieve!

16
Questing to be released from the need for cycling, whilst enduring the weight of calamities,
To apprehend the meaning underlying the mystery of cycling days and nights, do not grieve!

17
Suddenly, wondrous assistance cometh to him from the Creator;
He will return him to the loftiest paradise! Do not grieve!

---

7. A reference to Qur'án 33:62 and 48:23: "no change wilt thou find in the practice (approved) of Alláh."

8. A reference to the creation of Adam, a symbol for the reality of the Manifestation of God or the Báb Himself in perfect form and in the image of God.

9. Qur'án 32:5. See endnote to poem.

10. The image of a whale quavering on the expanse of the earth appears in the Báb's Commentary on the Súrih of Joseph. In reference to His condition among people, He sees Himself as a lonely fish quavering on the surface of the earth, as if He has been killed by the swords of people (Suratu'l-'Abd).

18
Indeed, O beloved one gazing into the Mirrors of Perfection!
O behold! Behold the aid and benevolence of God. Do not grieve!

19
The way[11] of God is not a design subject to change or diminishment!
His way—so new and illuminating—becometh manifest before our very eyes.
Do not grieve!

20
Behold Adam, who had been in the presence of God,
and then with Eve,[12] so blissful and delightful. Do not grieve!

21
When suddenly he descended, trembling from the heavens
Fallen onto earth below, miserable and naked.[13] Do not grieve.

22
Until he discovered that the same One beside him had always been near,[14]
God Himself, besides Whom is naught but vain imaginings and falsehood.
Do not grieve.

23
Even so was Noah, supplicated for the drowning of the base ones!
When he received the command,[15] the sea grew stormy. Do not grieve.

---

11. *Sunnat*, "method," "manner," "customary practice," a reference to the subject of verse 12, referring to the Qur'ánic verses mentioned in the footnote.

12. Eve here would seem to be an allusion to the "soul" of Adam when He becomes manifest on earth.

13. An allusion to the fall of Adam.

14. A reference to Qur'án 50:16: "It was We Who created man, and We know what dark suggestions his soul makes to him: for We are nearer to him than (his) jugular vein."

15. A reference to Qur'án 11:40: "At length, behold! there came Our command, and the fountains of the earth gushed forth!"

24
Indeed, in the direction of the Ka'bih, behold him[16] who built it,
How he appears as one possessed by the ecstasy of the Creator. Do not grieve.

25
He fashioned the Ka'bih in the form of a cube that from it,
The mystery of the pilgrim's pilgrimage might be understood. Do not grieve.

26
He was raised aloft from his station that he might offer a sacrifice for the Beloved;[17]
While sacrificing, he bore witness to the Living Judge. Do not grieve.

27
He then became prostrate, completely miserable, sick, and weak,
Conversing secretly and in private with his Beloved. Do not grieve.

28
Ṭáhirih, arise from your station! The mystery of manifestation[18] hath become visible!
Behold Moses of the family of Imran on the heights of Paran. Do not grieve.

29
Behold how Jesus, son of Mary, hath descended from heaven!
Aḥmad[19] hath once again been made manifest. Do not grieve.

---

16. An allusion to Abraham, Who, according to Islamic belief, constructed the Ka'bih. See Qur'án 22:26 and 2:127.

17. A reference to Abraham and His attempt to sacrifice His son.

18. "The mystery of manifestation" (*sirr-i-shuhúd*) or "the mystery of witnessing (God)," which has now become disclosed, is perhaps a reference to what the Báb describes in the Panj-Sha'n (pp. 17–19). In previous dispensations, people were too limited to understand that they could witness God in the Temple of the Manifestation of God; therefore, such knowledge was not bestowed except to a few, such as Mullá Ḥusayn.

19. Aḥmad refers to the reality of the Manifestation of God that repeatedly appears in the world as different personages, in contrast to Muḥammad, Who was the appearance of Aḥmad in the Islamic dispensation.

30
O my Bihjat, discern in these lines the mysteries of creation.[20]
Discover and apprehend in them everything concealed in veils. Do not grieve.

20. "Creation" is a translation for *fiṭarí,* an allusion to Abraham's contemplative insight (see Qur'án 6:74–79).

POEM 3

Guidance for Bihjat

(The original poem begins on p. 489)

This beautiful poem is reminiscent of certain ghazals by Rúmí, not only in style, but also in the way in which it freely violates poetic conventions, a clear indication that Ṭáhirih is not concerned about being considered an accomplished poet in any traditional sense. In fact, like Muḥammad and the Báb, she seems to be testing and possibly remonstrating those whose minds are bound by traditional rules of language and grammar, or those who take pride in what she perceives as their superficial accumulated knowledge.

For Ṭáhirih, such adherence to poetic conventions parallels her daring abandonment of conventionality in regard to the attachment to outworn religious traditions and systems of belief. In verse 9 of this poem, for example, Ṭáhirih violates the rule of complying with the rhyme established by the first verse of the ghazal. One strength of the poem, then, is her demonstration of how she has been able to modify this verse by breaking with commonly held traditions in a manner that is patently obvious to all.

1
Most surely will I go mad from concealing my adoration for Thee,
For if I behold Thee disclosed, I will be obliged to become prostrate before Thee.

2
Thou who art my most beloved, assist me with Thine incomparable benevolence!
Desperate and fallen am I; none is betrothed to me but Thee.

3
The enlightened letters[1] have come to Thy quarter!
From Thy palpable enthrallment, they have been cleansed of every defilement.

4
Bestow but a glance, and the immaculacy of thine eyes gazing on me
From the precincts of the Living One will absorb all my imperfections.

5
O Beloved, none consumes or entices me but Thee;
None exists for me *in the heavens or earth* but Thee.

6
With thy newly disclosed benevolence, assist me that I may become adorned
With the length and breadth of the robe of Glory descended from the Celestial Grandeur!

7
Then, O my Beloved, assist me with Thine infinite benevolence
To shoulder the burden of Thy Trust[2] bestowed from the realm of command.

8
By virtue of that trust, I perceive not a command, but rather being adorned
With the honor of pure light, the honor of the charge of the Living One.

---

1. Letters, "*ḥurúf,*" has been used by the Báb, not only in reference to the Letters of the Living, but to the believers in general as in "the Letters of the Gospel" in *Selection from the Writings of the Báb,* no. 83.

2. A reference to Qur'án 33:72: "We did indeed offer the Trust to the Heavens and the Earth and the Mountains; but they refused to undertake it, being afraid thereof: but man undertook it; . . ."

9
I know that my incomparable Beloved cometh to heal me
With a medicinal inscription from the region of Iraq.

10
Begone! For He is my solace with Divine assistance!
The prescription and evident command from Him suffice in the blinking of an eye.

11
My Bihjat, if what is befitting me fails to come,
Then certainly a bestowal to me will become thy task!

12
By lucid Truth of Thy Creator, that same gift hath been bestowed on thee!
There is none but God Who can make such a command.

13
Ḥamd!! He is the Beloved of God! There is no He but Him!
By His effulgence did all creation become wholly illumined!

POEM 4

Arise, O Pen

(The original poem begins on p. 487)

Transcriber's Note: "It should be made clear that whatever is written after this point is from the handwriting [of] her holiness Ṭáhirih herself. If rarely it happens that a verse is not rhymed melodiously, or there is a short silence in the rhythm [*siktih,* short pauses that might be pleasing to some but unpleasant to others], or if on occasion a word is left out, or a word has been modified [in other available manuscripts], since the present manuscript has been transcribed exactly with utmost care from the handwriting of that noble maiden, no alterations have taken place."

1
O Pen, arise with sparks and ecstasy!
From the mystery of *Qadar,* let flow onto tablets

2
the ensign concealed behind veils of light
that it might become glistening, illumined, and manifest!

3
Recount the indisputable Signs of God!
Disclose the mysteries from behind those veils

4
That the proof may become fulfilled
Before all living things—even as it should—

5
That all might discover the most hidden mystery
That all might become aware of the mysteries of *Qadar*,

6
That perhaps from overflowing light, the One Who
Should appear with the attraction of the Forgiving One

7
Might release everyone from vain imaginations and doubts!
Then from letters B and E, issue forth His command[1]

---

1. The letters *káf* and *nún* forming the word *kun,* meaning "Be," representing God's command for creation to come into being that thereby He might become known and loved.

POEM 5

A Prayer of the Manifestation

(The original poem begins on p. 487)

1
O Thou, warbling on fiery branches,
Issuing forth the concealed and exalted verses,

2
Disclose the veiled and hidden mysteries
That the secrets of "*kun fa yakún*!"[1] might become revealed.

3
The wondrous Ensign[2] descendeth
From the station of Command of the incomparable God,

4
An Ensign Which hath existed since the day that hath no beginning,
Immovable, unyielding, independent of the deeds of men.

---

1. "Be and it is" (*kun fa yakún*), a phrase appearing in many places in the Qur'án such as in 2:117: "To Him is due the primal origin of the heavens and the earth: When He decreeth a matter, He saith to it: "Be," and "it is."

2. "Ensign" (*áyih*) is a reference to the Primal Point, the first creation of God, which, in turn, bestowed existence and life to the world of being.

5
Whatsoever is distinct from God is illumined by Its light!
The faces of the Prophets are aglow with Its light!

6
All are humble before It. Everyone!
The concept of servitude was made evident by Its station.

7
From eternity It had been concealed in the origins of creation;
The glory of the realm of Unity had not yet become revealed.

8
Nor had appeared the dawn of revelation and the effusion of verses,
That precious gift of bestowing an abundance of knowledge.

9
It was devoid of all conditions and degrees
Until Its light became divulged through the command "Be" and "Is"

10
From it emanated every particle of existence,
Each a sign alluding to the mystery of creation!

11
If even for a moment they[3] deprive themselves of this verity,
Instantly they are transmuted into nothingness because of their separation from the Creator!

12
Because all dwell in the world of creation,
All are but expressions of its bestowals.

---

3. Those who are separated or remote from God in the realm of creation—that is, in physical reality.

13
The Mystic Knower is He Who doth discover in the Bayán
The mystery of Unity from the Lord of the Bayán.

14
He it is Who also doth behold mysteries upon mysteries,
And thence apprehendeth the secrets and songs.

15
He perceiveth the entire creation replete with lights!
He beholdeth the cup of purest of wines!

16
He is enabled to observe what cannot be seen!
He apprehendeth the mystery that words cannot express!

17
He can no longer be found in the material world,
But findeth Himself in the banquet of honor and exaltation.

18
"O God, Thou the powerful, the living, the kind,
But for Thee, kind Lord, there is none other.

19
Because I am in tears, rescue me with Thy benevolence.
Because of my abasement, I am afflicted and astray.

20
O Creator, the world and the totality of existence
Have suffocated me with its surging flames!

21
O Thou exalted Lord, since Thou art my objective,
Release me from stratagems, O sublime Countenance.

22
There is no helper or sustainer for me save Thee
Since all my affairs derive from Thy behest, O Thou the Omnipotent.

23
What is best for me hath been concealed by Thee;
Wherefore disclose it from the station of "*Kun fa kán*"!

24
O God, I do not discern what is the best for me,
being in the hands of those Thou has created.

25
O Beloved, Bounteous, Exalted One
Because Thou hast fashioned me and brought me forth again,

26
They have through their resolve and schemes, O Thou Creator,
Perceived me as naught throughout Thy realm!

27
In the same manner, O My wondrous Lord,
That Thou hast so often bestowed Thy bounteous grace,

28
Have mercy on me, O merciful Lord!
Assist me, O Thou eternal God!"

POEM 6

God's Methodology for Instructing Humankind

(The original poem begins on p. 485)

This poem deviates from Ṭáhirih's usual practice of having each line be a complete sentence, though sometimes the sentence encompasses two lines. But this poem has more of a narrative quality. For example, lines 21–28 function as one sentence in which Ṭáhirih (the presumptive speaker) advises the seeker how to attain nearness to God through the Manifestation by discarding concerns for "self" and focusing instead on supplication and devotion.

The theme of this poem is a straightforward depiction of God's methodology in advancing civilization and educating humankind. This piece contains relatively minimal imagery and allusions commonly found in her shorter poems. The result is a wonderfully detailed and complete depiction of progressive revelation, God's purpose in bringing about creation, and the imperative that everyone discern for themselves the advent of the new Manifestation. It also alludes to the wisdom of the seeker studying the revealed word rather than being swayed by the opinions of others or spurious interpretations of certain ḥadíths.

After further advice and a lucid depiction of God's methodology in teaching humankind by sending Manifestations to guide the peoples of the world through example and, most importantly, through Their revealed words, Ṭáhirih ends with a touching plaintive prayer in lines 43–50, beseeching God for assistance as she undergoes rejection and persecution.

1
O Thou transcendent and bounteous God,
Thou the Omnipotent, the Self-subsisting, the Eternal, the Benevolent!

2
O Thou, besides Whose essence, naught else doth exist;
Thine essence doth endure, while all else is evanescent.

3
From the beginning that hath no beginning,[1] Thou wast alone,
O Thou besides Whom nothing else becometh manifest!

4
O Thou the Most Hidden of the hidden, whosoever hath perceived aught but Thee,
Hath tumbled into the fire and become instantly consumed.

5
But perceiving, O my God, is not a practice
That words can depict nor whose path portray.

6
Thy transcendent essence is exalted and eminent!
It is exalted beyond all syllables and sounds!

7
Whosoever hath breathed so much as a hint
That I have unfolded aught of Thy station

8
Hath thereby become consumed by the fire of blasphemy
And hath fallen from the celestial realm!

---

1. A reference to the ḥadíth: "There was God and with Him there was no other thing" (*kána'lláhu va lam yakun ma'ahú min shay'in*). A variation of this ḥadíth is attributed to Imám 'Alí and mentioned by Siyyid Káẓim-i-Rashtí in his *Sharḥ Khuṭbah Ṭutunjiyyah* (see Ishráq-i-Khávarí, *Qámús-i-Íqán*, pp. 1287–89).

9
None knoweth Thee except Thyself!
None could portray Thine essence except Thyself!

10
Thy sublime essence transcendeth the grasp of imagination!
It is sanctified beyond the attributes of human hearts!

11
Indeed, the light of knowledge of Thee descended solely from Thy Pen,
And naught from *'Amá*[2] is manifest save Thee!

12
My sole desire is the appearance of the Mystery of *Qadar*,
That same One by Whom both fire and light are ignited.

13
That same One Whom Thou didst designate as Thine own Self
Thou didst create by means of the command "*kun fa kán*!"[3]

14
He was thence adorned with robes of light!
He declared Thy praises, O Thou Forgiving One!

15
He came forth in the station of transcendence
With the illumination of Bayán in His person and speech!

16
O God! His Grandeur!
His resplendent radiance!

---

2. See glossary.
3. Referring to the creation of Adam mentioned in Qur'án 3:59. Here it alludes to the reality of the Manifestation of God.

17
Through Him the world of being was made manifest!
He hath appeared to disclose secrets and unveil mysteries!

18
Whosoever beheld Him became detached from self,
Beheld Divinity unveiled and without concealment,

19
Regarded all other than Him as mere nothingness,
Became prostrate before Him in the manner of *innamá*![4]

20
O Thou who doth attend to these wondrous verses,
Hearken indeed to the quavering of ecstasy from their rapture!

21
And shouldest thine eyes attain not a capacity
Capable of observing the Benevolent Living One,

22
Then must thou needs purify thyself from all but Him,
Then cleanse thyself from all the remote ones.

23
After which—nonexistent and completely selfless—
Approach thou the Gate to the abode of the Placeless,

---

4. *Innamá*: "Indeed." This term appears several times in this volume. As is the case with verse 12 of the first poem in *Adam's Wish,* this Arabic word is perhaps a reference to Qur'án 48:10 in which it is made clear that the Manifestation of God is God's representative and thus speaks and acts on God's behalf: "Verily, those who were swearing allegiance to you, were indeed swearing allegiance to Alláh." Here, it can refer to Muḥammad's servitude and manner of worship, as He used to prostrate in prayers according to a variety of ḥadíths.

24
Writhing and twisting in devotion and supplication
So that the ecstasy of the wine of Grandeur might emerge,

25
So that the Living, Bountiful, Exalted One might provide,
O thou who hast longed for reunion,

26
Most surely and plainly from the station of Command
Eyes for thee that can discern the Truth in the world,

27
After which thou willest arise, beholding, as did Aḥmad with His own eyes,[5]
Ascending to the zenith of the realm on high,

28
Beholding in that realm of the placeless that which cannot be seen,
Hearing that which cannot be heard!

29
O Thou who art oblivious to the mysteries of *qadar,*
By attending to the words of mortals and mere ḥadí<u>th</u>,

30
That transcendent state will ne'er appear in thee!
Thou willest not know the joy of nearness made manifest.

31
Thou must needs detach thyself from all save Him!
Become prostrate on the earth like a corpse at *Mana!*[6]

---

5. A reference to Muḥammad's night journey. Alternatively, the verse can be understood as "you ascend to an exalted spiritual station when seeing with the eyes bestowed by God."

6. The place in Mecca where pilgrims offer sacrifices.

32
Thou must needs be earnest in thine entreaty
That thou mightest discern the pathway to Our traces.[7]

33
From eternity hath God's method[8] been the same,
That naught beside Him canst bear any similitude to Him.[9]

34
He Who doth bestow perception and doth beckon with His command
Is the Creator, He who deviseth the world of being, He Who doth engender it!

35
The Prophets were all resounding,
Their breasts smoldering with the ecstasy of Oneness!

36
They appeared that a new creation might descend;
There is no God except the Lord of the throne of 'Amá.

37
O My dear one, none of Them was concerned for Himself!
Each was merely a herald for the exalted Lord!

38
They conveyed the heavenly command, became Messengers;
Became immaculate, without defect or deceitful intent.

39
But from eternity have Their tongues been proclaiming
That the Eternal Lord alone is our Mentor and Guide,

---

7. *Áyát.* See glossary.
8. *Sunnat.* See glossary.
9. A reference to Qur'án 42:11: "there is nothing whatever like unto Him."

40
So that whosoever with purity of heart approacheth
Might behold the countenance of the Lord of the Worlds.

41
Whereas for him who hath been found to be base
And hath sought out the lies of the deceivers,

42
For him, no pathway leads to the Creator's feast!
Rather will he fall, afflicted into the depths of despair!

43
O Thou One True God, O Thou answering Lord,
O Thou Who doth answer every cry of sorrow and sadness,

44
I call upon Thee by the subtlety of Thy succor,
With my very bones shaking from fear of Thee,

45
How long shall I remain fallen into the depths of agitation?
How long must I behold my orisons unanswered?

46
O God, through Thine ever-enduring troth,
Rescue *Zá*[10] from the sorrows of her affliction,

47
And lift her up, O my God, with a decree
And cause her to become seated in the banquet of *innamá!*

---

10. An allusion to Zahrá (a title for Fáṭimih, Muḥammad's daughter). Inasmuch as Ṭáhirih's given name was Fáṭimih, she thereby fulfills the prophecy of the return of Fáṭimih during the time of the End.

48
Cause her to drink from the chalice of wine
And let her feast upon Thy divine fruit!

49
O Lord, until such time as Thou dost behold her state
And doth find pleasure in her plaint,

50
Then, O God, the True One, give me patience, O God!
O God, for my sake, hasten! Hasten, O God! O my God![11]

11. These closing plaints might seem overdone to anyone who is not familiar with the actual suffering that Ṭáhirih was made to endure, all of which concluded with her being strangled and tossed into an abandoned well. In short, in view of her personal history, these pleas are well warranted.

POEM 7

The Day of God

(The original poem begins on p. 482)

This poem is about the station of the Manifestation of God and the Revelation taking place during what Bahá'ís regard as the "Day of God"—a fulfillment of Islamic prophecy. As in poem 3, the Arabic word *ḥamd* (meaning "praise" or "thanks"), the name of the first Súrih of the Qur'án, is employed by Ṭáhirih in this piece as an allusion to the first creation of God, the reality of the Manifestation of God, and its appearance in Muḥammad as indicated by the appellation "*Aḥmad.*" In this context, the Manifestation is not only the first creation of God, but also the source of the creation of both the spiritual and material realms. It is in this sense that the Báb (Whom Ṭáhirih had recognized as the Qá'im) is called "the Primal Point," a title that rightly befits each of the Manifestations inasmuch as each is like a perfect mirror manifesting flawlessly all the attributes and powers of God, even though the essential reality of God is unknowable.

The concept of the Primal Point being the source of all levels of reality is emphasized in this poem by contrasting in verse 6 the realm of the transcendent divine (*láhút*) with the realm of manifesting God in the earthly kingdom, the latter being symbolized by the "ruby rod" (*qaṣabiyi-yáqút*). Ruby is associated with the color red, and the "crimson rod" (*qaṣabiyi-aḥmar*) is a term the Báb equates with the realm of *qaḍá*—the fourth of the seven stages of creation,[1] representing the appearance of the Báb Himself.

1. The Báb, "Interpretation of Bismilláh," p. 16.

This station, compared to the transcendent realm of *láhút*, is the closest to the realm of being and the most direct way for humankind to relate to God. Shaykh Aḥmad-i-Aḥsá'í also uses the same term, the "ruby rod" (*qaṣabi-yi-yáqút*), that Ṭáhirih has employed in this poem. In his hierarchy of the six realms of existence, descending from transcendence to immanence, Shaykh Aḥmad associates the "ruby rod" with a realm very close to the material existence, the realm of Fire (*al-kawnu'n-nár*). This level, which he also calls "the Universal Nature," is associated with the color red.[2]

Therefore, praising the transcendent divine—the exalted and inaccessible station that cannot be described by words—is in essence praising the divine perfections and attributes reflected in the perfect Mirrors that are His representatives, the Manifestations of God. As such both the word *ḥamd* and its synonym *thaná',* in addition to meaning "praise," also allude to the reality of the Manifestation of God. In this sense, these two words can be represented by the word "Praise." Thus we observe that the Báb in His Commentary on the Súrih of Joseph (the Qayyúmu'l-Asmá') refers to Himself with appellations such as "the Point of Praise" or "*Nuqtatu'th-Thaná*" (section 28), and (section 4) as the "Gate of Praise" or "*Bábu'th-Thaná',*" and (section 93) as the "Glory of Praise," "*Saná'u mina'th-Thaná'.*"

This poem presents the idea that if one surveys and contemplates the panorama of the universe, one can behold the "lights" of the Creator's actions in each of the realms of God, whether in the celestial realm of *'Amá,* or in the created or physical realm of the earth; whether in the love and inherent attraction of creation for the Creator, or in witnessing God's majesty, especially as revealed in the "Temple" or physical presence of the Manifestations of God.

Thus Ṭáhirih sees the Pen—a symbol she employs in various poems to refer to the reality of the Manifestation of God—present at the banquet of God. However, she observes that the Pen is not active, but seems to be reclining, unconscious, as if drunk and reposing on a lush, divine bed. Because the Pen has not yet been raised up by the Creator, Ṭáhirih, as the persona/narrator of the poem, urges the Pen to become engaged in writing. She asks it to reveal the divine mysteries, and to shed light on the verses of God and explain the nature of existence because the Day of Resurrection has at long last arrived, that time designated for the Pen to arise and reveal verses similar in tone and style to the verses of the Qur'án.

---

2. Shaykh Aḥmad-i-Aḥsá'í, *Sharḥu'l-Favá'id,* vol. 2, p. 280.

1
O Bird of Paradise, return with Thine eternal song!
Return and free me from every sorrow!

2
Rehearse for me those wondrous runes!
Recite again the secrets of sanctity!

3
Bring forth those flagons of fragrance
From the flames of Paran!

4
First sing about the *Ḥamd* of the One
By Whose radiance the world was made to glisten!

5
Since His *Ḥamd* became the source of life,[3]
It was among the first creations to become manifest!

6
By Him did the world of *Láhút*[4] take shape,
And the ruby rod[5] didst become imbued with its grace.

7
Through Him the realm of sublime glory hath been established!
By Him, *'Amá*, the summit of loftiness, was fashioned!

---

3. This is implicitly explained in the ḥadí<u>th</u> of the Hidden Treasure in which it is the wish of God to become known that He might be loved, not for His sake, but for the benefit of humankind and creation as a whole.

4. Divinity.

5. "Ruby rod" (*qaṣabi-yi-yáqút*) represents the perfections of the divine manifested in the material realm.

8
Because the *Ḥamd* of God portrayed Him flawlessly,
Like a mirror reflecting the face of the Transcendent One,

9
The essence of eternal *Ḥamd* is beyond the power of words,
Thereby barring the path by which words can depict Him!

10
His reality transcendeth fancy and thought!
Portraying Him defies the power of words!

11
Employing proofs of His reality induces silence!
The Inaccessible One transcendeth the attributes of the realm of time and change!

12
Such a task doth presume to portray the Eternal, The living One,
Whilst the shadow of the shadow faileth to betoken the Shadow of God![6]

13
O Bird of Paradise, behold the panorama before Thee!
What beholdest Thou in that unsullied setting?

14
It is the flame of *Ḥamd* ignited before Thee!
It is the very countenance of *Ḥamd* in motion!

15
He hath become reflected in the mirrors of deeds
So that the light of His beauty might shine forth.

---

6. "Shadow of God" alludes to the Manifestation of God and "shadow of the shadow" to the created realm. See endnotes to poem 11 for further explanation.

16
In whatever stratum of the degrees of Glory
His countenance will shed forth its light for that station.

17
In each one of the tablets I behold Him manifest,
Portraying the mystery of His radiant face shining forth!

18
In *'Amá,* in the midst of that rarified firmament,
It doth become a cloud flashing with lightning in the sky!

19
The earth itself is illumined by His light!
Worlds within worlds are brightened by His glory!

20
Good God, such a rapturous condition this is!
Every particle in existence is praising Him!

21
I behold it cycling ever more luminous, like the moon
Is His face as it traverses each and every dawning place.

22
From it doth the glorious sun acquire its light!
It doth secure receptive souls from fading away!

23
O Lord, His home is Thine Empyrean!
O God, Thy countenance is His paradise!

24
From His letters hath emanated the world of worlds!
From the rays of His light hath the *ḥúrí* and paradise itself been sustained!

25
O God, from adoration of Thy face doth the "H" of *ḥubb*[7] itself derive,
Whilst "M" testifieth to the magnificence of His majesty.

26
Its "D" is for adding the fourth of the four pillars;[8]
It hath appeared with the light of grandeur.

27
To portray Him, the entirety of creation intones His praise;
Through union with Him hath his Holiness Adam become everlasting!

28
O Lord, naught but Thy *Ḥamd* hath become manifest
From the exalted station of the action (*fi'ál*)[9] of "*kun fa kán*!"

29
I behold wholly illumined the robe of *Ḥamd*
From which proceedeth the grandeur of all verses from the past!

30
O hearer, hearken to the verses of *Thaná'*[10]
That thou mightest comprehend the mystery of creation!

---

7. The three letters of the word *ḥmd*, the Arabic written form of *ḥamd* (Praise), each allude to a certain word or letter: *ḥ* to *ḥubb* (love), *m* to *majd* (majesty), and *d* (verse 26) to the letter *dál* with its *Abjad* numeric equivalence being four, alluding to the four pillars.

8. The fourth of the four elements—fire, air, water, and earth—completes and establishes the process of creation. The earth is an allusion to the Báb, the Manifestation of the transcendent divine in the earthly realm. See the introduction to poem 14 and footnotes for verses 4–6 of that poem for further explanation. Furthermore, "D" is a reference to the fourth and last letter of the Arabic spelling of the name Muḥammad, an allusion to the Báb Himself (see Nader Saiedi, *Gate of the Heart*, pp. 555–56 for further explanation).

9. "Action" (*fi'ál*) is a reference to Qur'án 11:107: "for thy Lord is the (sure) accomplisher of what He planneth. . . ." And 85:16: "Doer (without let) of all that He intends."

10. See glossary.

31
Cleanse thyself from the dust!
Release thyself from mere rocks and clay

32
That thou mightest behold the face of the Beloved made manifest
From the station of the majesty of the Lord of *kun fa kán*!

33
The entire creation is in commotion and exultation!
The Throne itself beholds the Unity of God and His grandeur![11]

34
All dwellers of the Throne are entirely ready!
All the peoples of the world are striving!

35
Verily, I behold the Pen plainly intoxicated,
Languishing on the carpet of "*kun fa kán*,"

36
As if the countenance of God were being manifest,
As if the strains of musicians were redemptive!

37
O Pen, this is the Day to become awakened!
The Day for regal robes of Resurrection hath come!

38
Commence declaring and examining!
Speak of exploring and exhuming!

11. The word *i'zizá* in the original is assumed to mean "grandeur."

39
Cause the entire world to become mindful of the mysteries of God,
The hidden mysteries and the "darkness of night"![12]

40
Say: *Ḥamd* to the Eternal Creator!
Verily, it is the flawless essence of Aḥmad, the Incomparable!

41
Ḥamd hath appeared for the sole aim of portraying God,
The name of the Absolute, the depiction of the Absolute!

42
By virtue of His station of descent from the celestial realm,
He hath been portrayed as a reflection of Aḥmad!

43
Come, then, if thou wishest to be informed about the hidden mysteries!
Ḥamd became Aḥmad to make the Call descend and become revealed!

44
He appeared with the stature of *Ḥamd*,
Became entirely illumined by sacred verses!

45
Truly the verse of *Núr*[13] bears witness to that which I utter!
From the totality of existence doth the splendor of Sinai become manifest!

---

12. "Darkness of night" (*layl-i-ghasaq*) is a reference to Qur'án 17:7: "Establish regular prayers—at the sun's decline till the darkness of the night. . . ." Darkness in mystical symbolism represents the transcendence of God.

13. The "verse of light (*Núr*)" is the title given to verse 35 of the Súrih of Light (24:35) of the Qur'án, which begins with: "Alláh is the Light of the heavens and the earth."

46
Through Him didst the spirit of the people of spirit become verdant!
Worlds upon worlds appeared glorious because of His radiance!

47
O Pen, become engaged in transcribing revealed guidance!
O Pen, I behold thee drunken and unconscious![14]

48
Through the title "Aḥmad" did you become unconscious.
Thou didst flounder, prone at the Eternal Banquet!

49
Verily, bespeak where lieth the mystery of sobriety!
From whence cometh the mystery of the Day of Resurrection?

50
Hast thou encountered a countenance like that of Aḥmad
Or words wherewith to portray the station of Aḥmad?

51
Hasten! Hasten, O Thou Source of Life for the world!
At last, after a millennium, I observe Thee awake![15]

52
In the manner of the *Ḥamd* of the Eternal Creator,
Recount the story of that which is most glorious!

---

14. Perhaps an allusion to the functions of the first and second trumpets. Now is the time for the second trumpet and the awakening of the peoples of the world through the Revelation of Bahá'u'lláh.

15. The passing of a thousand years alludes to the period of time during which the Shí'ih priesthood had "invoked the name of the Hidden Imám" (Shoghi Effendi, *God Passes By,* p. 4), and the Báb represents the appearance of the Qá'im or the Hidden Imám.

POEM 8

Awakening of the Qá'im

(The original poem begins on p. 476)

In surveying Persian poetry, one often encounters simple and stereotypical narratives, cliché agons, well-known characters, and antagonists and protagonists who function in culturally well-established roles: the nightingale in love with the flower, the female cupbearer being begged by totally intoxicated men to bestow on them more wine, and other similar conceits. In contrast, this brief lyric by Ṭáhirih, like many of her other poems, while including some of these traditional figures, is a complicated and multifaceted narrative. It contains symbolic allusions that require some study and reflection if the reader is to discern Ṭáhirih's intended meaning.

In this highly imaginative poem, the nightingale of Sinai is summoned to sing ecstatic songs, but the bird is also alluded to as a cupbearer whom the speaker beseeches to pour perfumed drink into the crystal cup. The objective of this request is to enable the immaculate honorable one to drink of it, and, while looking into the cup, to behold the image of the Beloved instead of his own reflection. Once he has imbibed this wine, he would exclusively behold the Beloved and would perceive no one as a stranger in whatever region they dwell. He would thereby function as Moses did when He miraculously withdrew His light-emitting hand from His bosom, and by that light, purified the totality of creation. Ultimately, He would sing like a bird, praising God for all these heavenly bestowals. (See endnotes for further information about this poem.)

1
O Nightingale on Sinai, warble Thy melodious songs!
Return with Thine entrancing charms![1]

2
Pour pure musk into Thy crystal goblet
That the Immaculate One[2] might imbibe,

3
That He might behold in the glimmering from that cup[3]
The splendor of the resplendent Beloved!

4
He would obliterate the lustrous panorama
So that He might behold naught else in the world but Him,[4]

5
So that the mystery of the Beloved might become conspicuously displayed!
There is none to become His rival.

6
He will bring forth from the sleeve of the robe
The captivating[5] essence of the Lord of the worlds.

---

1. Charm; literally "attraction" (*ja<u>dh</u>b*). See introduction to poem 16 for explanation of the word.

2. "Immaculate One" (*jínáb-i-mustaṭáb*) can also be translated as the "Immaculate Threshold," a reference to the Báb as the Gate.

3. Looking into the cup is seen in another poem of Ṭáhirih (poem 22 of the *Quickening*) in relation to Moses: "From Your bountiful truth, Moses beholds a drop in the cup of ecstasy; He has taken that cup and watches over it." This confirms that the "Immaculate One" in the present poem is an allusion to Moses.

4. The notion of seeing in a cup the mysteries of the universe is found in a famous poem by Háfiz, an allusion to possessing a discerning and pure heart. In Persian literature, the ancient king Jam<u>sh</u>íd is often associated with this fable.

5. "Captivating." Literally it means "attracting." See *Jazb* in glossary.

7
By its radiance will He cleanse the world of defilement
And embody the splendor of the Lord of the universe.

8
With the ecstasy of the benevolent One, He will begin chanting!
He will declare, "Praised be He Who is the Lord of existence!"

POEM 9

A Summons to the Bird of Paradise

(The original poem begins on p. 475)

This poem would seem to be a continuation of the discourse in the previous poem. Ṭáhirih calls on the Bird on the Tree of Paradise to describe what it beholds recurring—that the Primal Point, the Beauteous Beloved, as previously manifested in Adam, Noah, Abraham, and Moses, has appeared again, adorned with the same powers and attributes. Like Adam, His heart is burning with the love of God. Like Noah, He is sacrificing all He has in the perilous journey to God, and like Abraham He is constructing the Ka'bih, the place designated for adoration of God.

In the same way that the Ten Commandments were not the final purpose of the dispensation of Moses, so the laws brought by the "Lord of the Bayán" (the Báb) have as their primary purpose the preparation of the peoples of the world for the discovery of the "Hidden Mystery"—in this case the divine reality of the Báb. In this vein, Abraham arrived at the station of full enlightenment only after traversing three stages of understanding—first, beholding the ascendancy of God in stars, then in the moon, and finally in the sun. Yet after His detachment from searching for God's signs in the physical universe, He saw the mystery of creation in the transcendent reality of *'Amá*. Similarly, Ṭáhirih alludes to the same progressive unfolding of spiritual revelation and enlightenment in the Revelation of the Báb.

The Báb proclaimed three successively more lofty stations for Himself: He declared Himself the Gate to the Hidden Imám, then the Imám Himself, and finally a Manifestation of God. In this final station, He attained "Lordship" (*rububíyyat*), thereby paralleling Abraham's three progressive stages of enlightenment that concluded with His recognition of the divinity of God.

Ṭáhirih ends the poem by asking the Bird of Paradise to drink from the goblet and recount what it beholds—namely, the Beauteous figure of Moses appearing once more in Sinai, immersed in ecstasy and prayers. She then urges the bird to bring about the ecstasy of the Primal Point and manifest Its mystery, an ineffable mystery that is beyond the power of words to portray.

1
O Bird of Paradise, once more with glory and splendor
Behold what Thou canst observe amid the panorama!

2
Who is this beauteous and perfect Beloved
So wondrously adept in designing His intentions?

3
He hath caused the entire world to clamor with ecstasy!
The very breast of Adam is inflamed with love for Him!

4
He caused Noah to wander from door to door,
Bestowing for the sake of God all that He possessed!

5
All that Abraham generated was caused by His allure;
He fashioned the Ka'bih by virtue of His command.

6
When a meteor flashed from the Heaven of Bounty,[1]
Abraham circumambulated it at the behest of that Honorable One

1. "Bounty," literally "attraction" (*ijtidháb,* a variation of *jadhb*). See *jadhb* in glossary.

7
So that all created things in the universe can discern
That He is the Beloved and all but Him is nonexistent.

8
Indeed, O Thou Bird of Paradise,
What dost thou learn from the mysteries of God's perpetual method?

9
When Abraham became afflicted by God's test,
Without a word, the enigma of God's method became fully disclosed!

10
From the revelation of the Lord of the Bayán,
Abraham became aware of the Ten Commandments![2]

11
These ten are for providing order,
For cleansing and purifying the people

12
So that they become acceptable before their Creator
And thereby discover the Hidden Mystery made manifest.

13
Look again, O Thou Bird perched upon the tree of Paradise,
That Thou mightest behold sparks emanating from the countenance of the Hidden One!

---

2. Ten Commandments (*'As̲harih kalám*) in this poem alludes to laws in general and specifically to Abrahamic laws. "Ten" is a symbol for completion, and according to Qur'án 22:26–30, Abraham was commanded by God to implement pilgrimage laws capable of cleansing the hearts of the pilgrims. Qur'án 2:196 defines the law of ten days of pilgrimage for those who are afflicted and do not possess a sacrifice to offer.

14
Thus did the mystery of creation[3] once more become manifest
From the station of Command by the Beloved of the world,

15
But only after God's own Abraham examined
Wordlessly the three mirrors[4] reflecting the nature of creation.

16
And when He had become detached from all save God,
He discovered the mystery of creation in the bounty of *'Amá.*

17
Indeed, behold, O Thou Bird perched on the tree of Paradise,
How once again the proper order of things appeareth in the crystal goblet.

18
Who is this One becoming *Kalím*[5] through the fire of divine friendship,
So upright in the honesty of His bearing as He covenants with God?

19
Imbibe from the goblet and once more recount for me
Who is this One with such a beauteous visage, with a moonlike countenance,

20
He who hath ventured to Ṭúr with such ecstasy and rapture,
Whose sole orisons and accents are, "O Friend! O Thou Forgiving One!"?

---

3. "Creation": *Fiṭrí* and similar word, *futúrí,* in verse 16. See glossary.

4. The three mirrors are a reference to Abraham's search for God in the kingdom of heaven and earth. First, He assumed the stars are His God, not happy with that He took the moon and after that the sun as His God. Finally, He recognized that His true God is the creator of all three. See Qur'án 6:75–79.

5. A title for Moses, "He Who conversed with God." The Báb is assuming the station of Moses.

21

O Thou Bird of Paradise, usher me into the presence of His ecstasy
So that, wordlessly, Thou Thyself wilt likewise become His Mystery!

POEM 10

The Unity of God's Prophets

(The original poem begins on p. 474)

Tawḥíd or "the unity of God" is possibly the most important theological principle set forth in the Qur'án, as well as in the religion of Islam itself. In this poem Ṭáhirih provides an extraordinary interpretation of the Súrih of Tawḥíd, a very important but short Súrih in the Qur'án. While this Súrih is primarily understood as explaining the transcendence of God and that one should not worship idols or "join partners with God,"[1] Ṭáhirih brings attention to the unity of the Manifestations of God and to the fact that They all manifest the same reality. This interpretation of the belief in the unity of God is what we also find in the writings of Bahá'u'lláh, examined most prominently and completely in the Kitáb-i-Íqán (the Book of Certitude).

The unity of God is established by the fact that the Primal Point (*nuqtiyi'-úlá*) or the Primal Will (*mas̲h̲íyyat-i-avvaliyyih*), which is effectively the essential reality of the Báb, has manifested itself in the essence of all the Prophets of God, and, to some degree, in the essential reality of everything in existence. The designation "'Alí" in the first verse of the poem refers to the divine aspect of the Báb, which, when combined with "Muḥammad"—symbolizing the simultaneous station of prophethood and servitude—comprises the Báb's

1. Qur'án 4:48: "Alláh forgiveth not that partners should be set up with him; but He forgiveth anything else, to whom He pleaseth; to set up partners with Alláh is to devise a sin most heinous indeed."

given name: "'Alí-Muḥammad." In this sense, the Báb functions as a gate between the two realms, the transcendent divine unity and the kingdom of names or world of multiplicities.[2]

1
O 'Alí, the mystery of the eternal Lord,
He for Whom there is no semblance or comparison,

2
He Whose station from the beginning hath been *"begets not"*[3]
And Who till eternity will never be titled "*begotten*"!

3
Know thou that His essence is *aḥad*[4] and peruse
The Súrih of Unity in relation to this theme!

4
His origin is the source of the doctrine of unity!
The mystery of ecstasy is displayed in His creation!

5
His image became infused into the essence of reality itself,
Enveloping all created things, from minuscule particles to the cosmos.

6
He taught Adam the knowledge of every existent entity[5]
And set Noah free from worry and betrayal!

---

2. Physical reality as a whole. See Nader Saiedi, *Gate of the Heart,* p. 56 for further explanation of this symbolism.
3. Reference to Qur'án, Súrih of Unity (112: 3): "He begets not, nor is He begotten."
4. Reference to Qur'án 112:1 and 4.
5. A reference to Qur'án 2:31: "And He taught Adam the names of all things . . ."

7

How many a S͟huaib[6] He made enlightened
About all of the hidden mysteries!

8

Thus did He guide everything in creation to His Vicegerents!
Upon Mt. Sinai He chose[7] Moses to lead the way.

9

By means of His fragrant breeze was Jesus, son of Mary, brought into being[8]
So that the radiance from His spirit assisted all else in creation.

10

He didst propagate the glad tidings[9] of the advent of Aḥmad!
He was the source of His joyful revelation!

11

O my God, through the veracity of Thine essential reality,
Release me from worldly sorrows and attachments,

12

So that I might behold Thy hidden visage,
I would sacrifice my life for the Bayán![10]

---

6. According to the Islamic tradition, Shoaib (Jethro) was a prophet whose daughter married Moses and who was known for his extraordinary eloquence. Muḥammad called him the k͟hatíb of prophets (Dehkhoda: Shoaib). "K͟hatíb" of God means "a revealer of secrets," "a professor of the unity of God," "and an able orator" (Steingass: k͟hatíb).

7. "Chose" (iṣṭafá) is a reference to the Qur'ánic verses such as 3:32: "Truly Alláh chose Adam and Noah and the descendants of Abraham and the descendants of Amran above the nations."

8. See Qur'án 21:96: ". . . We breathed into her of Our spirit, and We made her and her son a sign for all peoples." And 66:12: "And Mary the daughter of 'Imran, who guarded her chastity; and We breathed into (her body) of Our spirit; . . ."

9. A reference to Qur'án 33:45, 25:56, and 17:105 where God designates Muḥammad as the bearer of glad tidings and as a warner.

10. There are variable possible meanings to the word "Bayán" here and in other poems. It can be a reference to the Báb, to the Báb's revelation of the Bayán, to the

13
O Lord, O Self-Subsisting One, O Ruler of this world and the next,
Resurrect me among the righteous ones![11]

Word made flesh (the Logos), or simply to divine utterance. Since Ṭáhirih does indeed sacrifice her life for her beliefs, each seems valid.

11. The righteous people, as in Qur'án 5:84.

POEM 11

Bringing Creation into Being

(The original poem begins on p. 473)

This poem appears as the latter half of the first poem in *Adam's Wish*. However, the manuscript we are using for the present volume consists of parts that were missing in the manuscript we had at our disposal for *Adam's Wish*. Conversely, there are verses in the same poem in *Adam's Wish* that do not appear in the present manuscript. Additionally, there are occasional differences in the wording of the same verse, or else, the same verse may be placed in a different line in this version of the poem.

Considering the differences with the *Adam's Wish* manuscript, we can conclude that the present manuscript in its totality is more authentic than the previous one. This conclusion accords with the claim of the transcriber of the manuscript who comments on the care he took to copy accurately the original handwriting of Ṭáhirih herself, starting with Poem 4 of this volume. This claim becomes even more plausible because this version contains parts that are absent in the manuscript we utilized for the same poem in *Adam's Wish*, and because those missing parts are quite essential to Ṭáhirih's discourse in the piece.

For example, several verses missing in the earlier version are an obvious continuation of the passages Ṭáhirih cites from the Qur'án. We believe this new version of the poem has helped us better understand and translate Ṭáhirih's intent for the piece. In this poem, through complex and imaginative symbolism and employing allusions to the Qur'án, to the writings of the Báb, as well as to Persian and Arabic literature and to the stories of prophets, Ṭáhirih addresses multiple layers of long-standing philosophical and theological questions. Among these are the relationship between God and His creation, and between physical reality and spiritual reality; the relationship between the divine and material nature of the Manifestations of God, and, similarly, the relationship between the spiritual and physical nature of human beings; and the glad tidings of the advent of this unique event in human history, the "Day of Days," when the full advent of the Primal Point has at long last arrived.

At the outset of the poem, Ṭáhirih addresses the Bird of *'Amá,* urging the bird to sing and reveal the eternal mysteries. While *'Amá* has been previously explained, Ṭáhirih often employs this term as an allusion to the reality that is intermediary between the transcendent divine and the human reality which is both spiritual and physical.

The "bird" (*ṭayr*) is a common image Ṭáhirih employs and has various meanings. We know that the Báb alludes to Himself as the bird (*ṭayr*) in His Commentary on the Súrih of Joseph. For instance, in Section 30[1] He alludes to Himself as the bird in the atmosphere of *'Amá* and similarly in Section 41[2] as the bird singing in the atmosphere of *'Amá*. The Bird of Paradise (*ṭayr-i-ṭúbá*)—the bird warbling on the tree in paradise—is a similar rhetorical device employed by Ṭáhirih in this and certain other poems.

Likewise, the tree of knowledge, at times in the writings associated with the Lote tree or the tree on Sinai through which God talked to Moses, symbolizes an intermediary station between the divine and the human reality. The Bird of *'Amá* and the Bird of Paradise can also be understood in multiple ways. They can refer to the reality of the Manifestation of God that appears at different eras in physical forms, to the Primal Point (the transcendental and the spiritual reality that is the source of the creation of the worlds of being), to the Báb, or in certain contexts to the spiritual station of Ṭáhirih herself, inasmuch as she is able to uncover divine mysteries.

1. The Báb, Qayyúmu'l-Asmá', Suratu'l-Tablígh.
2. Ibid., Suratu'l-Kitáb.

Because this poem is replete with theologically and philosophically esoteric terminology, we have felt it necessary to assist the reader with an abundance of notes so that terms and passages that would otherwise be utterly obscure and inaccessible to many readers might be comprehensible. Nevertheless, the poem, however beautiful and indicative of Ṭáhirih's remarkable intellect, still requires several readings and a great deal of reflection on the part of the reader. (See endnotes for further information about this poem.)

1
O Bird of *'Amá*, commence singing!
Pour forth in sparks Your pages of Thaná'!

2
Recount the Mysteries of the Eternal One,
Those incomparable hidden mysteries.

3
Make manifest from behind the veil the countenance of Bahá!
Render the world of creation unconscious through His attraction!

4
Make manifest in the Source of all power
The mystery concealed in the realm of the placeless!

5
Return Adam to His paradisiacal abode!
Return Him to the station of Truth[3] and Grandeur.

6
With verses of the Revelation,
Manifest the Point cloaked in veils of light[4]

---

3. "Truth" (*Ṣidq*). A reference to Qur'án 54:55 about the condition of the dutiful believers who are "In the seat of truth with the most powerful King."

4. "Veils of light" alludes to the glory of God that prevents human beings from directly knowing Him, based on the ḥadíth "God's veil is light (or fire). Were He to remove it, the glories of His face would burn away everything perceived by the sight of His creatures" (Sachico Murata, *The Tao of Islam*, p. 353, n41) or the ḥadíth "God

7
To purify the chosen ones from waywardness,
The command of the Lord of the World was revealed.

8
The blazing Letter[5] that had been hidden
Was a fire concealed in the veils of Divinity.

9
The time for its manifestation arrived, and it became light!
All else but God was illumined in Sinai by its splendor.

10
Through its realization, the realm of light itself appeared!
Then the "Hidden Mystery" emerged from behind the veil.

11
The guidance of the light emanating[6] from His face,
Caused the Sun of prophethood to face the Moon of vicegerency.

12
All light and shadow vanished and became concealed!
All approached the shore of the Most Great Ocean!

13
O God, O God, what is that shimmering light
that hath appeared from what Thou hast done!

---

has seventy thousand veils of light and darkness." Verse 8 of this poem refers to the same concept.

5. "Letter" (*ḥarf*), also means utterance and speech.

6. The word *'aks* in the Báb's writing is used to mean reflection of light (*ta'akkus*) (Panj-Sha'n, Persian section, pp. 46, 52). In Ṭáhirih's poetry *'aks* takes a positive meaning ("light" or "rays") while a derivative of the word, *'aksiyyih,* assumes a negative meaning in various contexts.

14
As if the mystery of unity had been disclosed
or else the world of creation had become the land of "*you shall never see me,*"[7]

15
As if the glistening veil had been removed
And the countenance of the Hidden Unapproachable One had dawned,

16
As if God Himself had appeared with glorious splendor
in sublime mirrors, with glory and *há*?[8]

17
Has Aḥmad[9] descended from the heavens?
From His countenance faces were illumined!

18
Or hath 'Alí once again become Resurrected?[10]
Or at the "Return"[11] have the Mysteries become manifest?

19
Or hath the "*cleft asunder*"[12] sky been created,
Ceaselessly streaming light from behind dark, thick clouds?

---

7. "You shall never see me!" (*lan taránī*). This is what God told Moses in Sinai according to Qur'án 7:143.

8. See glossary.

9. A title for Muḥammad alluding to the return of the Prophet's attributes in the person of the Báb.

10. Based on ḥadíth (Shaykh Aḥmad-i-Aḥsá'í, *Kitábu'r-Raj'at*, p. 151), 'Alí appeared and was martyred multiple times in the Day of Resurrection. Also, 'Alí had the title *karrár* (repeated) because he would attack the enemy repeatedly without fear or concern for his own safety.

11. A translation of the word "*raj'at*," an allusion to the return of the holy figures of Islam at the time of the Day of Resurrection.

12. See Qur'án 73:17–18: "Then how shall you, if you deny (Alláh), guard yourselves against a Day that will make children hoaryheaded? Whereon the sky will be cleft asunder?" Also see Qur'án 82:1–2: "When the Sky is cleft asunder; When

20
Is this the Promised Day? Hath the Mystery of manifestation
Shown its face from the place of the placeless?

21
Is this the Hidden Mystery or the cloaked name
That hath become revealed from behind threefold veils?[13]

22
The station of "*you cannot see me*" hath appeared among us!
The Face of God hath appeared with honor and nobility![14]

23
The Temple,[15] endowed with perfection and light,
Is gleaming and with longing is manifesting adornments,

24
Hath begun speaking, portraying the allure of the Most Beneficent One,
Thereby unlocking all the sealed portals!

---

the Stars are scattered. . . ." Two variations of the word *faṭara,* meaning "to create," appear in this verse.

13. Perhaps a reference to the first three stages of the seven stages of creation. In that sense, the verse refers to the appearance of the station of Decree (*qaḍá'*) from the stations of Will (*ma<u>sh</u>íyyat*), Determination (*irádih*), and Measure (*qadar*). Each of these represents a level of mystery (*sirr*), or a degree of veiling of the transcendent Divine.

14. Ṭáhirih now begins to affirm all that has occurred, thereby answering forcefully the rhetorical questions posed in the previous verses. The tone and purport of these verses is similar to Bahá'u'lláh's tablet entitled Muballi<u>gh</u>, originally part of a tablet revealed in honor of Hájí Muḥammad Ibráhím (See *Tablets of Bahá'u'lláh,* pp. 117–18) in which there is a series of rhetorical questions followed by thundering answers, all of which recite the fulfillment of proofs associated with the appearance of the Manifestation in the Day of Resurrection.

15. As in the Súriy-i-Haykal, the Temple represents the physical dimension of the Manifestation, the appearance of the powers and attributes of God in the form of a human persona.

25
With the revivifying call of "*hasten unto me*,"[16]
He hath removed the rust of unbelief, doubt, and wavering.

26
So many hints of love, one after another,
Have ushered forth intensely from Him in this very age!

27
Indeed, Behold, O Bird of Paradise, Behold!
The truth of my utterance hath assuredly come to pass!

28
The fire of Sinai is aflame!
It is the light of Paran blazing forth!

29
The Greatest Name hath appeared in all its purity,
And it hath caused all existence to become confounded!

30
It hath illuminated every name
And hath guided us to every name of God,

---

16. "Hasten unto me" (*háta lak*): A word-for-word translation of this would be: "Come forward. It is yours" (apparently, Arabicized from the Hebrew word *Hitalikh*). In Qur'án 12:23 this phrase is mentioned. When Joseph was living at the house of Potiphar, an officer of Pharaoh (Gen. 39:2), Potiphar's wife "seduced him and locked the doors and said: 'Come hither' (*hayta lak*), according to the story in the Qur'án. He said, "Alláh forbid!" This story has inspired Persian poets, and the love story of Yúsuf (Joseph) and Zuleikhá appears frequently in Persian literature. By "hasten" (*hayyá*) in verse 23, "Hasten unto me" (*háta lak*) in this verse of the poem, and by "unlocked all the closed portals" in the previous verse, Ṭáhirih might be alluding to this story in order to explain that the appearance of the true Beloved at this time has unlocked all the doors, bestowing you freedom, calling you saying, "Hasten unto me!" This understanding of verses 23–26 of the poem is aligned with the fact that the Báb alludes to Himself as the female figure of the Maid of Heaven.

31
To the holy, glorious, exalted station,
That station in creation beyond reckoning!

32
He hath colored all colors with the "color of God!"[17]
He hath caused the face of God to be witnessed by all![18]

33
O God, O God, such a station, such a destiny this is
that hath emanated from the letters *kun fa kán!*[19]

34
O Bird of Paradise, behold with Thine immaculate vision
that all mightest become evident to Thee,

35
How this is that same luminous lamp[20]
By which all of creation hath been enlightened!

36
This is that same illuminating "Lantern"
through which the human temple hath been filled with spirit!

37
The conveyer of this light was the mirror of Bahá
From the hidden treasures, concealed behind the plush veils,

---

17. Ṭáhirih is thus alluding to Qur'án 2:138. "Our religion is the Baptism (or Color) of God: And who can baptize (color) better than God? And it is He whom we worship." In this passage, the word *ṣibg͟hat* is used (meaning "color") because Arab Christians used dye in the baptismal water.

18. "Witnessed" (*Mas͟hhúd*); this word alludes to the Day of God or the Day of Resurrection. See Qur'án 11:103 and 85:03.

19. See glossary.

20. In verses 35–40 of this poem, Ṭáhirih refers to the "Verse of Light" in the Súrih of Light (24:36) of the Qur'án. See endnotes for this poem.

38
The same "Glittering Star" expounded in the Bayán,
The brilliant "Light" in the heavens of existence!

39
That which He desires was concealed in the veils of *Thaná'!*
Now is it nigh in the sphere of "fulfilment"![21]

40
Before it appeared as a "Tree" wrapped in raiment,
Because the flame of that Fire was encased in glass![22]

41
Neither can there be conceived a dawning or setting for Him!
Neither can luminescence nor branches[23] be assigned to Him!

42
Verily, He was a firm root[24] from the Day of Eternity,
So sanctified was He from all causes and limitations!

43
His bounty is embodied in verses of the Eternal!
Thereby is His name in the shadow of the Absolute!

---

21. The word *nashá'* ("fulfillment") literally means "growth" and "increase." It can also be read as "We desire," in contrast to the "He desires" (*yashá'*) of the first half of the verse. In this sense, the term refers to the appearance of divine authority at this critical period in history.

22. A reference to the word *zujájah,* meaning "glass," in the Verse of Light of the Qur'án.

23. The divine reality of the Manifestation of God, which is alluded to through images such as "Tree" and "Fire" in verse 40 of the poem, is in fact beyond any allusions. "Shining" is a reference to the aforementioned "Parable of His Light" in Qur'án 24:36 and "branches" is a reference to the parable in Qur'án 14:24, referred to in verse 42.

24. Qur'án 14:24: "Seest thou not how Alláh sets forth a parable?—A goodly word like a goodly tree, whose root is firmly fixed, and its branches (reach) to the heavens,—of its Lord. So Alláh sets forth parables for men, in order that they may receive admonition."

44
"Limits" or "limiting,"—attributes *other than Him*[25]—
are bound by separation from Him, as is their contingent reality.[26]

45
The Point of mystery hath now attained a loftier height
because His emanation is beyond limit or calculation.

46
Through His aid, the renewal of all ages hath been established,
Even as definition, classification,[27] and manifestation hath come into being.

47
In the process of elucidating, interpreting, and articulating,
It became the illuminating letters of the Bayán.

48
The perfect body[28] composed of the four elements,
Appeared in an unremarkable condition.[29]

49
O Bird of *'Amá,* harken to His mystery,
Which is concealed within His song and melody.

---

25. "Other than Him" (*má sivá*).

26. The terms separation (*'adá*) and contingents (*iḍáfát*) refer to anything that is not of the essence of God, in Ṣúfí terms, *a'yán kh̲árijih,* or external archetypes. Like shadows, they have only a contingent existence (*vujúd-i-iḍáfí*) (Syyid Ja'far Sajjadi, *Farhang-i-Lugh̲át va Ta'bírát-i-Irfání,* pp. 322–23, 482).

27. *Ta'yín,* a derivative of *ta'ayyun,* the term coined by the Persian philosopher Ṣadr'ud-Dín Qúnaví, sometimes translated as "designation," "determination," or "entification." It means to assume the character of an entity, a thing distinct from other things. (Sachico Murata, W. C. Chittick, and Tu Weiming, *The Sage Learning of Liu Zhi: Islamic Thought in Confucian Terms,* p. 185).

28. The "temple" or *"haykal"* that the Manifestation assumes when He is born into the material world, a process and significance that Bahá'u'lláh elucidates at great length in the Súriy-i-Haykal.

29. The Manifestations are not necessarily physically impressive, except to those who recognize in Them the spiritual attributes and powers emanating from Their metaphysical essence.

50
Behold the Divine splendor of His lights,
His sparks of fire from Paran!

51
Then He hid His face and became enfolded[30]
In a veil in the realm of the placeless.

52
Through Him did creation itself come into being!
When He beheld Himself, He infused Himself into the world of being![31]

53
Time came into existence by His ceaseless motion![32]
The world of being came into existence through His design.

54
The Glorious Sun of *Thaná'* assumed its proper orbit
that it might discover the mystery of *Há*.

55
Thus did the Moon reflect the Sun's light into the world of existence
as it traversed the constellations of the heavens.

---

30. The tropes that follow are similar to the analogies employed in a poem by the Persian mystic Shah Ni'matu'lláh Valí: "An existence made itself manifest in the whole world / but it became hidden from people's eyes. / In each mirror it shows a different beauty / in each constellation it appears in a new shape." (Syyid Ja'far Sajjadi, *Farhang-i-Lughát va Ta'bírát-i-Irfání*, p. 482.)

31. An allusion to the ḥadíth of the Hidden Treasure.

32. Though time does not exist in the metaphysical realm, this passage alludes to how time becomes an attribute of the physical realm through the revolution of the spheres (*tadvír*) and the design for and regulation of the affairs in the universe (*tadbír*).

56
And after the Sun arrived at each constellation, it moved to the next
Where it discovered a new reality and assumed a new station.[33]

57
The Star of Glory thus traversed the constellations
As it struggled arduously in arcs of ascent and descent

58
Until it resided in the shadow of the shadow[34]
And determined that the Mystery of Truth had descended to earth.[35]

59
It had traversed the orbits of the spheres
Because the mystery of *Há* had become concealed in the dust!

60
From there It witnessed the hidden mysteries of *Há*
With its ceaseless struggles.

61
By the splendor of *Há,* It discerned that Adam had become incarnate.
Adam seemed drunk, then conscious,[36] but groaning constantly

---

33. Ṭáhirih here may be describing how the reality of the Manifestation assumes different degrees of ascendancy and Revelation as humankind passes through successive stages of development, even though the Prophet is possessed of divine perfection from inception, as explained in the doctrine of the "Most Great Infallibility." Also, Ṭáhirih might be alluding to the process of gradualness or timeliness that occurs with the unfolding of each new Revelation, and, in the case of the Báb, with the disclosure of the Báb's true station.

34. As in poem 7, "shadow of shadow" refers to the world of creation. See endnotes for this poem for further explanation.

35. A reference to Qur'án 53:1: "By the Star when it goes down."

36. See Qur'án 22:2 regarding the intensity of the shock experienced in the Last Day or at the Time of the End when people seem to be drunk even though they are not.

62
Over the surface of the Earth, suffering, weary,
Like a waterless fish convulsing because of such calamity!

63
His sole preoccupation was endlessly sighing with regret,
And the mountain of Sar-andíb[37] had become the place of his descent.

64
In solitude and with complete humility he lamented,
"From what point will the Sun of Unity dawn?"

65
With his words, his predicament, his plight, and his reflections
He recalled how that day and that divine station cannot be portrayed

66
As he queried why this fish hath fallen sorrowful
Onto an expanse of indignity, of regret, and a stranger,

67
Lamenting, "Where are those sparks of fire?
Where are those heavenly ecstasies of the Creator?

68
Where is Paradise and where is the Garden?
Where is the Mystery of the Holiness[38] radiating from the Bayán?

69
Where is that noble and faithful companion?
Alas! Alas! He hath become hidden from me!"

---

37. The mountain on which Adam is believed to have descended. The name was used to refer to Sri Lanka. Some believe the mountain to be in that area, though there may be no connection between the source of the legend and the country itself.

38. An allusion to Quddús.

70
His sole effort and endeavor was lamenting
Until no traces of him remained.

71
As all his hope of companionship dissipated
and he was remote in a state of solemn humility,[39]

72
Suddenly the luminous face of the Creator
Appeared from distant places!

73
With thousands of glorious effulgences
and an endless flow of His boundless grace,

74
The Creator removed the veil from His face![40]

75
With a ceaseless, exhilarating, fragrant breath,
He exhaled over the outstretched bones,

76
Announcing to Adam, "I am the Merciful Lord,
Reviving the dried bones with my resplendence![41]

---

39. A reference to Qur'án 20:108: "On that Day will they follow the Caller (straight): no crookedness (can they show) him: all sounds shall humble themselves in the Presence of (Alláh) Most Gracious: nothing shalt thou hear but the tramp of their feet (as they march)."

40. According to the transcriber, this couplet has no half-line, possibly, it would seem, to emphasize the impact of the act of unveiling the Countenance of God.

41. A reference to Qur'án 36:78–79: ". . . He says, 'Who can give life to (dry) bones and decomposed ones . . .? Say, He will give them life Who created them for the first time! for He is Well-versed in every kind of creation!'"

77
Though My countenance be concealed in the heavens,
My majesty flourishes in *'Amá!*

78
Though My inscrutability be hidden in *huvíyyat,*[42]
It can be discerned through the veil of *váḥidíyyat.*[43]

79
My sanctified name doth not change from *Aḥad*[44] to *ḥadd:*[45]
My revelation is illumined from the realm of the *Ṣamad.*[46]

80
My glorious condition cannot be understood!
My sublime station is exalted beyond words!

81
With the power of Our own flame, we set thee aglow
and adorned thee with the Light of Honor.

82
There is not a particle of imperfection in thy creation!
Your animate[47] essence is a perfect creation!

---

42. *Huvíyyat,* "the Divine," here alludes to the idea that the mystery of the nature of the Prophet is ever beyond human understanding.

43. "Unity" (*Váḥidíyyat*). Though the nature of the divine is concealed, the evidence of His presence can be found in the intermediary station of the Manifestations of God, the realm of 'Amá, also referred to as "unity" (*Váḥidíyyat*).

44. The "One," the "Single" (*Aḥad*).

45. The "realm of limitations" (*Ḥadd*).

46. The "Eternal" (*Ṣamad*). As in verse 43 of this poem, Ṭáhirih uses the names of God (*Aḥad* or "One" and *Ṣamad*) in conjunction with each other to emphasize the transcendence of God. The Báb also, on multiple occasions in His Commentary on the Súrih of Joseph, uses the two terms together as "the Single Eternal" (*al-'Aḥadu'ṣ-Ṣamad*), as in Section 109 (Súratu'l-'Abd). This is also the case with a similar verse in the Qur'án (112:1–2) recited in the Islamic obligatory prayer: "Say: He is Alláh, the One and Only Alláh, the Eternal, Absolute."

47. Literally "active" (*fa"ál*).

83
Therefore, with utmost perfection and honor,
recount our attributes and grandeur![48]

84
Make manifest the Hidden Ecstasy![49]
Disclose the Point that is concealed!

85
Dismiss from thy mind the disobedience thou hadst towards Us
And bring thy mind into a state of peace and reconciliation!

86
No cessation exists in the flow of the bounties of God! None!
Wherefore let there be no delay in responding to God's command! None!

87
Thou hast remained veiled by thine own veils,
shutting out thyself with a hundred gates by closing the one Gate![50]

88
It was thou thyself who didst contrive the notion of "otherness"
and thou who didst make thyself concealed from Us!

89
How long dost thou wish to remain imprisoned in flesh,
dwelling in the realm of limitations,

---

48. *Jalálíyyát,* the attributes of God's Grandeur: e.g., sublimity, loftiness, etc.
49. *Ja<u>dh</u>bih.* See glossary.
50. The Gate of God. By separating yourself from God, you have closed all doors for yourself.

90
Choosing to be moribund like Adam,
Whilst thy name hast the authority of "Báb"?[51]

91
Behold, My resistless Faith hath become established!
Behold the binding commandment, the subduing verses!

92
Cast off the garments of restraints and limitations!
Immerse thyself in the sea of My bounteousness!

93
Behold how all mysteries are disclosed!
how all veils are luminous and brilliant![52]

94
How long in this world—rabid with passion and decadence—
Wilt thou remain so far from your purpose, so pitifully far?

95
Establish thyself on the seat of Our throne of Authority
and display that vital power latent within thee.

96
From but two letters, *B* and *E,* Our command hath appeared!
The mystery of "We return unto to God" hath become revealed!

51. *Bábíyyat:* In the Shí'ih tradition, the role and station of those who were intermediary (or Gate) between the Hidden Imám and the believers. Here God is urging Adam (the Báb) to make manifest His exalted station.

52. A reference to the ḥadíth that for God there are seventy thousand veils of light.

97
Say: I am the *Ḥamd,* the One Who is adorned with the attributes of Beauty, He Who hath appeared from the station of Justice."[53]

53. *I'tidál',* meaning "justice," "moderation," or "equilibrium."

POEM 12

The Báb Proclaims His Station

(The original poem begins on p. 462)

The imagery in this poem makes clear that the narrative voice is that of the Báb. Similarly, in the Qayyúmu'l-Asmá', as the Báb interprets the Súrih of Joseph, on ten occasions the Báb alludes to Himself as a bird (*ṭayr*) singing on the Most Holy Tree (*s͟hajarih*) or else hovering in the celestial sphere beside the Throne (*'ars͟h*) or amidst the clouds of *'Amá*.

He is the Singer on the Branches of the Most Holy Tree

1
By the *Ḥamd* of the Lord on the throne of *'Amá*,
I will illumine all that is "other than Him!"[1]

2
With a rapturous melody, I will now release
All the wayfarers from their concealed abodes![2]

3
Verily, I am the eternal Bird of Paradise,
And I will manifest myself regally!

---

1. Material reality or the whole of creation that emanates from Him.
2. A reference to the asceticism of the mystics who secluded themselves.

4
With my melodies I will disclose the mystery of creation,
And I will manifest my splendor with the attributes of kings.

5
I will enlighten all the created things in existence
With sacred and incomparable songs![3]

3. This verse can also be read as "I will render all created things in existence, / with sacred and incomparable greenery."

POEM 13

Ṭáhirih's Prayer for Assistance

(The original poem begins on p. 461)

1
O Judge whose judgment is solace for the destitute,
From Thee doth descend comfort for the forlorn.

2
O Thou the Eternal, the universe hath become enkindled!
O Thou the Ancient, there is no comfort for me except from Thee!

3
No one in authority but Thee beareth witness to my plight!
Since my destiny is beyond my control, rescue me with Thy benevolence!

4
O Creator, O God, shouldst Thou abandon me to myself,
I would be utterly consumed by the flames from these fires!

5
O God! O beloved Friend! O Thou the Omnipotent, the Living!
Rescue me through Thy boundless benevolence and countless gifts

6
So that I might arise to serve Thy Cause
And reveal whatsoever Thou dost bestow upon me on this earth!

7
O God! Thou dost witness that no help for me exists except Thine,
And no other companion or helpmate on earth save Thee!

8
By Thine immaculate Essence, for Thou to abandon me
Would be contrary to both Thy concealed and Thy manifest manner,[1]

9
Because to those in need of mercy, Thou hast been the most merciful!
Mercy itself hath become realized through the potency of Thy command!

10
Through Thy compassion, rescue now this downtrodden speck!
Except for Thee, O Lord God Creator, there is no one else to aid me!

11
O My Beloved, to rescue this mote would accord with Thy tender mercy!
Since abandonment would be contrary to Thy ways, do not leave me forlorn!

12
God, rescue me through Thy boundless mercy and generosity
That I might become occupied with reflecting on Thy compassion!

13
O My Creator, because Thou art my helper,
I supplicate only Thee, O Lord, the Creator!

---

1. The eternal and unchanging tradition and practice (*sunnat*) of God.

14
O Thou my Friend, the world itself is meaningless, worthless
Until Thou dost bestow order on existence.

15
If the Countenance of Thy beauty doth become unveiled,
The entirety of existence would become ablaze from the sparks of Thy fire.

16
O God! Cast a glance of kindness[2] and bounty
In such a way that Earth itself might become completely refined!

---

2. *Laṭífát:* a reference to one of God's names, *laṭíf,* which means "kind." See Qur'án 42:19: "Kind is God towards His servants: for whom He will doth He provide."

POEM 14

Praised be God in this Day

(The original poem begins on p. 459)

A casual reading of this poem might lead to the inference that this is a prayer praising God and employing various poetic expressions to beseech God for assistance. Yet, if we regard carefully the terminology Ṭáhirih has used, we begin to recognize how the poem addresses philosophical and theological discourses similar to what we observe in the Báb's own writings. In this regard, the poem touches on concepts such as the relationship between transcendence and immanence, the arcs of ascent and descent, the three realms of God, the Command of God, the world of Creation, and the relationship between these abstract concepts and this singular turning point in human history in which the world as a whole will become transformed into a global commonwealth.

We can identify two major parts in this work: the ahistorical and the historical. The former (verses 1–9) deals with the metaphysical concept of "the Arc of Descent"—the descending levels of spiritual stations from the divine realm to creation.[1] In verses 1–3, Ṭáhirih explains that though all particles in the world of existence are expressive of some divine attribute—each in its own way—it is from the realm of Command, the realm of the Manifestations of God, that the physical reality is illumined. Otherwise, God Himself would remain transcendent beyond the access of all created things, even though the essence of God will ever remain transcendent and beyond any direct understanding by

1. See 'Abdu'l-Bahá, *Some Answered Questions*, p. 330 fn.

His creation. Verses 4–9 refer to the various stations of the Manifestations of God from the most transcendent to the most immanent, symbolized by four ways of worshiping God, which the Báb equates with the stages of the Arc of Descent. The second part of the poem (verses 10–23) relates to the Manifestation of the Primal Point and the effects of such a milestone Revelation on the world of being at this time in history. Verses 10–17 describe the magnitude of this process of Revelation in which God's Will, in His unquestioned authority to do whatsoever He pleases, from the station of the first stage of creation has descended to its fourth stage, as symbolized by the color red (*aḥmar*) in verse 17. In this verse Ṭáhirih's reference to the veiled world of plurality (*satríyyát*) has a particular significance in terms of the model of reality to which she is referring. "Veils" in this case refers to the various stages of descent from the realm of transcendent divine to the contingent realm.

Finally, in the closing verses (18–23), Ṭáhirih beseeches God to assist with her appropriate response to this astounding event, the long-awaited advent of the Day of Days as signaled by the advent of the Báb. (See endnotes for further information about this poem.)

1
The King of Kings is concealed in all that exists in the world of being,
Where not even a particle would appear except for Him!

2
By His Command the joyful countenance of creation becometh illumined,
From all that resides under heavens to the invisible realm above.

3
His incomparable existence is immaculate and transcendent,
Above all else besides Him and beyond the allusions of words.

4
The light radiating from the Garment of His shining beauty rendereth visible
The "glorification" of the Creator in each station[2] and for each era.

2. A reference to Qur'án 55:29: ". . . every day in (new) Splendour (*s̲h̲a'n*) doth He (shine)!"

5
The radiance from the beauty of His Face is naught but the *Ḥamd* of God
With such power and glory that the Garment becometh a proof of "Divine Unity."[3]

6
From His majestic verses doth *Grandeur* become manifest!
Alláh-u-Akbar[4] announces the joy of reunion with Him.

7
Anyone who doth discover but a drop from the cup of His love
Becometh cleansed from the dregs of imposters.

8
His countenance doth beam with the effulgence of His visage!
His breast expands with the brilliance of sparks of fire![5]

9
From the radiance of God, His heart doth become the source of Glory and Majesty!
From Him drops of light[6] descend into the world of creation.

10
O Lord, from Whom doth resound the reverberation of Majesty and Glory
So that the horizons of the world are brightened by His light?

---

3. Unity (*vaḥdat*), a variation of the word *tawḥíd,* meaning "believing in and praising the Unity of God." This is the third descending stage mentioned by the Báb. It is also an allusion to the Imáms and to the third stage of creation, which is Destiny (*qadar*).

4. "God is Great" represents the exaltation of God as the fourth station of worshiping God.

5. "Spark" is a translation for a<u>th</u>í<u>zh</u> (Steingass).

6. The phrase "a drop from this light" (*ra<u>sh</u>ḥun min <u>dh</u>álika'n-núr*) occurs in the Báb's writings (Shoghi Effendi, *Tawqí'át-i-Mubárakih,* p. 258).

11
O God, Who is this that hath caused all the people of *'Amá*
To swoon unconscious before the presence of His face?

12
O Friend, all the inhabitants of the Empyrean become humble
Before His presence, O Thou the Lord of the created realm.

13
O Lord, His glory is now made plain by the light from His face!
Through this radiance, the Bayán became the Seat of Ascendancy!

14
The exalted souls and so many cherubim, even the dwellers in the celestial realm,
Have prostrated themselves and become joyful as they behold Him.

15
O Lord, every created thing in existence is illumined by His light,
And the Army of *kun fa kán* is ready to assist Him!

16
Alláh is assisting again, and so the glory of God hath come,
As if it were Thine exalted Essence with majesty and grandeur!

17
With freedom to do whatsoever He willeth, He hath appeared from behind the veils!
Hath descended as the Crimson Point[7] with glory and exaltation.

18
Thy praise is "O My Beloved, *God is the Most Exalted!*"
From this point forward, my praise of Thee is *Alláh-u-Akbar!*

---

7. See glossary.

19
O Thou the Omnipotent God, with Thy benevolence,
Rescue this tiny spec that hath fallen under the shadow of tribulation!

20
If the merciful Lord be her helper and assister,
It will be none other than Thee, O Thou the Lord of the worlds!

21
By Thine infinite Grace, O Thou my Beloved, rescue me!
I have descended into humiliation among strangers!

22
O God, through Thy benevolence and boundless grace, rescue me,
For Thou art the Exalted, the Helper, the Assister!

23
I shall invoke no one save Thee, O Helper, O my Beloved!
Rescue me through Thy grace, for Thou art Lord of the worlds,

POEM 15

Proof of the Appearance of the Hidden Imám

(The original poem begins on p. 456)

As with other longer poems by Ṭáhirih, the reader of this poem needs to discern the narrative within the poem by identifying major points of transition, which are often associated with a change in narrator or with the person being addressed. In this poem, the narrators are Ṭáhirih herself, the Concourse on High, the Báb, and those who do not realize the magnitude of the new Revelation. The sequence of narrators would seem to be consisting of Ṭáhirih addressing the concourse of angels, who in turn observe the Báb and recount His utterances to God. At other times, Ṭáhirih seems to be directly addressing the Pen, God, and the reader.

The poem begins with the narrator/persona (most probably Ṭáhirih) urging the Pen to inscribe verses of God and disclose the once concealed mysteries. There follows a comparison of the conditions and circumstances in the divine and earthly realms that are taking place at this unique era in history (verses 1–24). For example, in the heavenly realm, the Sun of Unity of God has appeared, and the company of angels are in exultation. Yet, they witness the dire circumstances of God's Vicegerent on earth being held captive in the hands of the undiscerning ones, and they behold Him weeping and supplicating God for assistance.

After the angels rehearse His prayers and pleas (verses 25–39), God responds to His pleas, urging Him to reveal His station and disclose the mysteries of His Lord (verses 40–42). Ṭáhirih then urges all to respond to the new Revelation, and she explains how the prophecies of Shaykh Aḥmad and Siyyid Káẓim have been fulfilled with the appearance of the Twelfth Imám. She then prays to God that the new Revelation might issue forth from the Báb (verses 44–73).

In verse 53, Ṭáhirih employs a complex set of symbols alluding to the appearance of the hidden letter *váv* from God's command of "Be and it is" (*kun fa yakún*). Ṭáhirih's meaning here can be explained by some of the writings of Shaykh Aḥmad-i-Aḥsá'í and the Báb, though this symbolism can also be seen in Ibn-'Arabí's works. There is within these works a correspondence between the Book of Revelation (*kitáb-i-tadvín*) and the Book of Creation (*kitáb-i-takvín*), alluding to the process whereby the creation of the world takes place.

Next, the reaction of the people to this magnificent event is explained in verses 75–80. Instead of recognizing the Manifestation of God through His own Self—representing as He does the transcendent, living, and self-subsisting God (verse 74)—many demand proofs from the sacred scriptures of the past. Two categories of such people are identified in the poem: those who search in the verses of the past to discover the truth (verses 75 and 76) and those who are completely oblivious and categorically deny any signs of a new Revelation in the holy books of the past and thus demand clear verses as proof (verses 77–80). Ṭáhirih then describes how the hidden proofs and verses in the Qur'án have indeed become manifest (verse 81). Subsequently in verse 82, Ṭáhirih asks people what proof they will accept, if not the Word of God. In the verses that follow (83–91), Ṭáhirih emphasizes that the Báb Himself is sufficient proof of His truth and that God will punish and destroy those who do not respond to His message. She thus refers to the Báb with the word "sign" (*áyih*), an allusion to a verse in the Qur'án meaning "proof" or "miracle." In response to those who look for a verse (*áyih*) of the Qur'án as a proof, Ṭáhirih employs the word "verse" (*áyih*) in its alternative meanings, and thereby alludes to the Báb.

Finally, in verses 92–93 of the poem, Ṭáhirih reminds the reader of the Qur'ánic verse "Alláh will surely accomplish His purpose" (65:3), urging the reader to reflect on this verse in order to discover a clear understanding of the mystery of "Return." (See endnotes for further information about this poem.)

1
O Pen, from Rúmí's flute[1]
Bring into this world the fire from *Ṭúr!*[2]

2
From that which the essence of Thy reality beheld,
Subdue the garrulous ones with Thine own words.

3
From the verses of Him Who is hidden and inaccessible,
Share the mystery of an exalted and elegant utterance.

4
O Pen, from Thy station of ardor and glory,
Ascend to the station of discerning the mysteries of *at͟har!*[3]

5
No more willst Thou endure the diminishing of Thy light!
By the grace of God, such darkness will never again obscure Thy brilliance.[4]

6
The Sun of Unity hath appeared in the heavens
Reciting the hidden mysteries of God!

---

1. Qaṣabih Rúmiyyih. See glossary.

2. "Fire" (*qabas*) is a reference to Qur'án 27:7 and 20:10 in which Moses sees the fire atop Mt. Sinai, representing His access to the voice of God.

3. At͟har can be translated as "sign," which can be an allusion to revealed verses or to ḥadít͟h. It is also a term used for the astrological effect of stars on human life and fortunes.

4. Though the context is different, we find similar imagery in Bahá'u'lláh's assertion that "This is the Day that shall not be followed by night. . . ." (*The Summons of the Lord of Hosts*, ¶1.63).

7
Know that because of the warbling of this Nightingale,
The celestial Throne of the Creator is trembling in ecstasy!

8
All the sublime ones have become glorified!
The company of Cherubim have attained ascendancy!

9
The heavenly hosts are also in a state of elation and enchantment,
Impatiently waiting in bewilderment and suspense,

10
Exclaiming, "O Thou Just and Merciful God!
The Powerful and Self-Subsisting, the Living, the Chastiser!

11
A thirsting Particle from Thee hath plummeted,
Captive among those undiscerning ones!

12
Ordainest Thou, O Omnipotent God,
That in our wayfaring, we might attain His presence!

13
Perchance, with the bestowal of the Merciful One,
He might descend with the adornments of the Ancient of Days!"

14
Indeed, harken with care to this enchanting and glorious tale,
To the command which God hath portioned out.

15
Be entirely attentive, O thou expectant one!
This Master is none other than the Omnipotent King!

16
He hath appeared in the station of inscrutable providence!
The hosts of the Glorious King have hastened to this Báb.[5]

17
O all ye angelic hosts, assume thy places![6]
Situate yourselves on the thrones of glory,

18
For thy ability to attain firmness and power
Will not reside in regions of the earthly realm!

19
What He hath destined for those with discernment
Is not attained by clinging to the cords of arrogance.

20
Descend then from the heavens
Near His glorious dwelling as He prays.

21
Then shall ye clearly and palpably behold
That which His plan hath so plainly disclosed!

22
Then will ye respond, "O God, the Glorious, the Omnipotent!
We comprehend not the melodies of His nighttime vigils,

---

5. Literally, "to this Gate," though the double entendre (referring to the Báb) is obvious.

6. In the Báb's writings (e.g. Panj-Sha'n, p. 11), He refers to the believers in each Revelation as those who have taken their seats (sukkán) in (the paradise) of that Revelation. The image of believers seated on the thrones and positions of honor in paradise is found in numerous verses of the Qur'án, such as 52:20: "They will recline (with ease) on Thrones (of dignity) arranged in ranks; . . ." Figuratively, Ṭáhirih seems to be urging the angels to assume their appropriate stations in the heaven of the Báb's Revelation.

23
But in the Bayán, O Majestic Lord,
His tongue mentions naught else but Thee!

24
In this lowly realm of creation, He doth supplicate and weep
As He prostrateth Himself on the earth in prayer!

25
O Lord, His assistance cometh solely from Thee!
He possesseth naught else save Thy love!

26
O Lord, He speaketh with astonishing refrains!
He saith, 'O Thou Hearer, and O Thou Knower, and O Thou the Exalted One!

27
My lot is with Thee, but concealed from everyone!
It is not with Zayd or 'Amr nor with this one or that one!

28
Lord, by Thy wondrous magnanimity and bestowal,
O Thou Hearer! O Thou Knower! O Thou the Exalted One!

29
My lot is with Thee, concealed from everyone!
It is not with Zayd or 'Amr nor with this one or that one!

30
O Lord, by Thy wondrous magnanimity and bestowal,
Thou didst create every miraculous particle in existence!

31
Though working, struggling, and striving,
They gleaned but a fist full of straw for all their endeavors!

32
Thus, O Thou the Creator, it seemeth contrary to Thy generosity
That Thou didst designate Me as Thy Reality in the world?

33
O Thou Omnipotent One, My claim is exalted
Only because I am emptied of all but Thy verses!'"

ṬÁHIRIH BESEECHES THE BÁB FOR ASSISTANCE

34
How long must I be held imprisoned by calamities
Be held captive and in grievous afflictions?

35
O Thou, the Lord of the Bayán, bestow mercy on me!
Release me from the limitations of this mortal world!

36
Lift me up to the station of Thine exaltation,
Then manifest the signs of Thy glorious might!

37
O My Lord, rescue me through Thy benevolence!
Release me from the bonds of this life of mine!

38
O Thou inaccessible God, lift me up indeed
to the banquet hall of Thy glorious attributes,

39
For Thy grace is the leaven of my life!
The mystery of Thy justice is the foundation of my firmness!

40
O Thou Who art made manifest as Vicegerent!
O Thou Who art purified from the constraints of this world,

41
Unfold now the concealed signs
And thereby reverse the order of this day![7]

42
Speak of those once concealed signs and make them manifest!
Bring forth the mysteries of the Eternal Lord!

ṬÁHIRIH SPEAKS TO HER FOLLOWERS AND THE PEOPLES OF THE WORLD

43
Ye all must become detached from every temporal concern
That the mysteries of the heart might flow limpid and pure!

44
Worldly desires are vain, only a chimera!
They are illusions, nothingness, specious, and idle!

45
O ye who have longing and desire for the Unity of God,
Who yearn and aspire for glory,

46
Spread your wings and ascend to that station
That ye might savor the joy of an enduring reunion.[8]

47
Acquire from me the dazzling and majestic vista,
Then behold in it the traces of God's command.

---

7. Literally, "Turn the world upside down" by overthrowing the present-day conditions in which those in power are iniquitous, and the downtrodden are the most receptive to the Word of God.

8. Enduring reunion (*raj'-i-mudám*, literally "enduring return") is a reference to numerous verses in the Qur'án that indicate all people will return to God. For example, see 5:105: "Then shall ye all return unto me."

48
But for now, remain silent, O Thou venerable ones,
Until the time when the once Hidden One becometh manifest.[9]

ṬÁHIRIH COMMUNES WITH GOD

49
O Omnipotent God, O Thou Lord of the Bayán!
O Thou transcendent Hearer! O Thou the Truth of the Bayán.

50
As I behold the illumined fiery panorama,
All the signs of power come into view!

51
I behold Aḥmad[10] in all his glory and greatness
And then Káẓim[11] assuming his place on the throne of honor!

52
They are each assisting and encouraging everyone
With their comportment and utterances to become enamored with divine Unity!

53
O Lord, I behold so clearly revealed
How My once concealed *váv* hath appeared as *kun fa kán*!

9. Presumably an allusion to the Báb as the return of the "Hidden Imám" (the Twelfth Imám).

10. Shaykh Aḥmad-i-Aḥsá'í, who foretells of the advent of the Qá'im (the Báb) and the Qayyúm (Bahá'u'lláh).

11. Siyyid Káẓim-i-Rashtí, the student and successor of Shaykh Aḥmad-i-Aḥsá'í, and Ṭáhirih's teacher about the prophecies that are to be fulfilled by the advent of the Báb.

54
O God, He then became overcome with anger!
The fiery verse[12] in His hand bore witness to this!

55
O Lord! I behold before me how the Imám became slain
By fiery shards from the masses.[13]

56
O Lord, He did return and,
For the sake of mankind, opened all the gates of mystery.

57
O Lord, then this hapless rabble
Abiding in a drunken state of utter depravity

58
Assembled in a mountainous throng,
Rent asunder the garments of justice and order!

59
O God, then followed an ecstasy and a music!
From whence cometh this to mine ear, "O Thou Knower?

60
What could this haunting melody portend?
Who is this One with such a beauteous face and exalted station?

---

12. A ḥadíth mentioned by Shaykh Aḥmad Aḥsá'í (*Uṣúl-i-'Aqá'id*, p. 56) which interprets Qur'án 2:206 as meaning that Muḥammad will descend from the clouds with a weapon of fire in hand. Ṭáhirih is perhaps referring to this ḥadíth, interpreting "weapon of fire" as the divine verses with the character of fire, although the word she uses, *áyih*, can mean both "verse" and "sign."

13. Possibly an allusion to Imám 'Alí and his return in this Day, opening the gates in his battles as he did in the Day of Muḥammad.

61
It is as if from eternity He hath been entranced
Once He beheld the verse "Come thou back."[14]

62
O God, assist Him now
So that He might reverse the order of governance.

63
O Lord, distill the veils of dust
That the illumined Countenance might become revealed!

64
How long must He be confined in the snare of calamity?
How long must He be plunged into a desert of affliction.[15]

65
O God, in honor of this ravishing Countenance,
Bring the loftiest *Thaná'*[16] out from behind the veil!

66
Establish a world adorned entirely with light!
Let every soul ascend the heights of *Ṭúr.*

67
O Thou True God! O Thou Who answers every prayer!
O Thou, the Essence of every verity! O Thou Friend!

---

14. A reference to Qur'án 89:28.

15. Desert (*taih*), a desert in which one gets lost. In particular, this is an allusion to the desert in which Moses wandered for forty years with the twelve tribes of Israel.

16. See glossary.

68
People of fire[17] are fomenting rebellion and transgressions
Through their murky and dingy countenances![18]

69
But the people of light[19] are in a whirlwind of ecstasy from attraction
And are engaged in assisting, O Thou, the Lord of those who repent!

70
O God, O Thou the Creator, through Thy perfection,
Cause Thy mystery to become plainly visible!

71
Thy command was concealed within its own fire![20]
Its bearer was the Countenance of Him Who is Unconstrainted!

72
Aḥmad[21] had concealed it in His bosom!
From its ecstasy, Káẓim[22] dwelt in the heavens!

73
Then It suddenly appeared, O Creator!
It caused a new world to become manifest!

---

17. In this verse of the poem, "fire" (*nár*) has a negative meaning, in contrast to the light (*núr*) in the verse that follows. We observe this same contrast in the Báb's writing, as in His Commentary on the Súrih of Joseph, section 73 (Súratu'l-kahf) where He refers to Himself as the harbinger of the light and warner of the fire.

18. See glossary for "Darkened Faces."

19. "The people of light" (*núriyán*) refers to the Bábís in the sense that the Báb declares that He is the Light and was on the Sinai of Heart. (Súratu'l-'Aṣr, section 23). This concept is mentioned in the Báb's writings, either in the same or in similar analogies.

20. In this and many verses of Ṭáhirih, fire (*nár*) denotes the hidden and transcendent divine reality that manifested itself as light (*núr*) through the Burning Bush beheld by Moses on Mt. Sinai.

21. Shaykh Aḥmad-i-Aḥsá'í.

22. Siyyid Káẓim-i-Rashtí.

74
The Proof of His Manifestation is His own Sanctity!
The Qá'im, the Qayyúm, and the Living God![23]

ṬÁHIRIH SPEAKS ABOUT THE DIVINES WHO FAIL TO RECOGNIZE FULFILLMENT OF QUR'ÁNIC PROPHECIES

75
He, who like unto chilled charcoal from a lifeless ancient fire,
Doth dwell in the barren desert of outworn traditions,

76
He who studies the revealed verses
So that he might discover in them a spark of truth,

77
Whereas he who is veiled from the truth
Can be seen frozen in the depths of hell,

78
Complaining that he can discover no traces or signs[24]
That could cause such an effect to appear,

79
That he should be guided by the verses of God,
Those traces and verses revealed in the past!

80
He doth long to behold before him
Utterances revealing the power of the Creator,

---

23. "Qayyúm" refers to Bahá'u'lláh. Siyyid Káẓim-i-Rashtí, Shaykh Aḥmad's disciple and successor, had likewise written: "The Qá'im must needs be put to death. After He has been slain the world will have attained the age of eighteen." In his *Sharḥ-i-Qaṣídiy-i-Lámí'íyyih* he had even alluded to the name "Bahá." Furthermore, to his disciples, as his days drew to a close, he had significantly declared: "Verily, I say, after the Qá'im the Qayyúm will be made manifest" (Shoghi Effendi, *God Passes By*, p. 97).

24. See glossary for "traces."

81
But it doth exist in the verses in the heart of the wondrous Qur'án
That have emanated from a perfect Countenance![25]

82
O ye people espousing falsehoods!
What words will ye accept as true other than the Word of God?[26]

83
This single Sign[27] is sufficient proof of the Unity of God!
It refutes what the faithless believe and doth confirm the Unity of God!

84
This Sign hath also descended from the heavens
In order to conquer and eliminate the unbelievers!

85
This Sign is that mystery of mysteries
Which hath shone forth from the Mirrors[28] of the Omnipotent One.

86
His own person is sufficient proof of His Station!
It doth refute what the faithless believe and it doth confirm the Unity of God!

87
"Otherness" hath no place in the Bayán!
For the earnest seeker, all vain imaginings are vanquished!

---

25. The Báb.

26. Echoing the repeated rhetorical question of Muḥammad in Qur'án 55:13 as He cites the bounties of God: "Then which of the favors of your Lord will ye deny?"

27. Verse (*áyih*) also means "sign," and in particular, refers to the Báb as the Sign of God on earth.

28. See glossary.

88
All those not of Him are deterred and deluded!
Deaf and dumb,[29] they wander far away from Thy gift!

89
If you desire a verse from among the verses of God
Wherein ye might discover a proof of His cause in past revelations,

90
There is none in the realms of heaven or earth but He Himself alone
Who doth complete the *k͟hátam*[30] and reign in all the worlds!

91
In no wise is God required to vindicate Him! Never!
The abundance of His verses from God are among His mysterious proofs!

92
O Thou who hast floundered in the vast and limitless land,
God hath indeed brought forth a Cause which He shall bring to fruition!

93
Therefore, recite Thou these verses and cease thy prattling
That Thou mightiest discover the mystery of "Return" made manifest!

---

29. "Deaf and blind" is a reference to Qur'ánic verses describing the unbelievers, as in 2:171, 2:18, and 6:39.

30. "Seal" A reference to Qur'án 33:40: "Muḥammad is not the father of any of your men, but (he is) the Messenger of Alláh, and the Seal of the Prophets: and Alláh has full knowledge of all things." Ṭáhirih is referring to the Báb as the return of Muḥammad, the Seal of the Prophets. Bahá'u'lláh discusses this in full in the Book of Certitude, p.162 ff.

POEM 16

Free Will, Ezra, and the Ant

(The original poem begins on p. 451)

In this poem (verses 33 and 36), as in poem 15 (verses 28 and 29), Ṭáhirih employs a rhetorical device that we often see used in the Qur'án: the same phrase or sentence repeated in close proximity (e.g., in 56:27), or in various parts of the same Súrih (e.g., 55:16, repeated thirty-one times), or even in multiple Súrihs (e.g., 2:57 repeated in 7:160). While some might regard such repetition as aesthetically weak, Ṭáhirih utilizes this technique to her advantage by emulating and thereby alluding to this style as it is employed in the Qur'án. And because her principal audience at the time were Muslims, they would—if they were learned—immediately recognize her allusion to this technique, to the particular verses that are repeated, and most likely concern themselves with trying to discern her intent.

In terms of its content, the poem begins with praise of the divine reality of the Báb, urging humankind to recognize His station, even as the Hebrews were exhorted to recognize Moses. Drawing parallels between the revelation of the Bayán and certain Hebrew historical texts about being tested or doubting the omnipotence of God, Ṭáhirih focuses in particular on the Israelite prophet Ezra (verses 1–15). According to Qur'án 9:30, "The Jews call 'Uzair (Ezra) a son of Alláh." Yet, based on interpretations of the Qur'án,[1] there is another reference to Ezra in relation to his initial doubts concerning God's boundless authority:

> Or (take) the similitude of one who passed by a hamlet, all in ruins to its roofs. He said: "Oh! how shall Alláh bring it (ever) to life, after (this) its death?" but Alláh caused him to die for a hundred years, then raised him up (again). He said: "How long didst thou tarry (thus)?" He said: (Perhaps) a day or part of a day." He said: "Nay, thou hast tarried thus a hundred years; but look at thy food and thy drink; they show no signs of age; and look at thy donkey: And that We may make of thee a sign unto the people, Look further at the bones, how We bring them together and clothe them with flesh." When this was shown clearly to him, he said: "I know that Alláh hath power over all things" (Qur'án 2:259).

Ṭáhirih refers to this account of the enlightenment of Ezra in verses 5–11 of the poem. Verse 6 alludes to the exalted spiritual station of Ezra, that which had caused him to become a sign of the unity (*vaḥdat*) of God. Ezra is at first ignorant of the power of God (verse 6), or as we might understand from verses 7 and 8, was unaware of the power of God to bring about his spiritual rebirth and transformation. God thus demonstrates this power to Ezra and thereby shows him that he no longer has any excuse for depriving himself of the bounty of the fire of Sinai (verses 9–10).

In verses 12–15, Ṭáhirih portrays God's transcendence, and how perfectly He has created the world of existence and has endowed it with measured or prescribed capacities. In verses 16–25 she urges people to take advantage of their own nascent capacities and their free will in choosing to evolve spiritually, explaining in verse 25 that exercising this choice will demonstrate their belief in God's unity (*vaḥdat*), that same belief that was attained by Ezra (verse 6).

The delicate point Ṭáhirih is making in verses 6, 25, and 38 of this poem is that God's transcendence and singleness (unity) necessitates that He endow creation with free will. In this sense, the term "I am" (*inníyyat*) in verse 38—a term used in Islamic philosophy for "existence"[2]—alludes to the fact that the

1. See Riaz Ghadimi, Behnam Rahbin, and Ehsanollah Hemmat, *Riazu'l-Lugh̲át,* vol. 6, pp. 1163–64.

2. See Sachico Murata, W. C. Chittick, and Tu Weiming, *The Sage Learning of Liu Zhi: Islamic Thought in Confucian Terms,* p. 184.

purpose of human existence as designed by the Creator necessitates that everyone possess the power of free will.

Stated another way, if free will were not an inherent capacity of the human soul, then human ascent would necessarily be predetermined—a result of God's direct relationship with His creation and intervention in human history. But as Ṭáhirih notes in verse 13, because God is essentially unknowable, humankind is incapable of a direct knowledge of, or relationship with, God. Thus, according to God's plan for human enlightenment, human spiritual ascent depends upon the ability of seekers to penetrate the veils of material illusion and, by degrees of capacity (*qadar*) take advantage of the opportunity God provides, both through endowing all created things with the signs of His Beauty, and more obviously by designing human instruction through the progressive advent of successive guidance through the appearance of the Manifestations. (See endnotes for further information about this poem.)

1
O Judge, Thy Praise[3] is the ornament of all speech![4]
Nothing in the world exists except for Him!

2
All creation emanates from His light!
All humanity receives aid from His effulgence!

3
This drop of light is but a spark of His fire!
The Sinai of Revelation itself derives from His sparks.[5]

4
O Hebrew, thou who art being tested,
Abstract thyself from thyself! Indeed, become purified!

---

3. A reference to the Primal Will as manifest through the appearance of the Báb.

4. Bayán, translated here as "speech," can also refer to the entire corpus of the Báb's writings.

5. "Firebrand" (*qabasát*) is a reference to Qur'án 27:7 and 20:10.

5
Behold! Thy purpose is but to manifest the Causer of effects!
Behold disclosed the splendor of Ṭúr!

6
Know that Ezra is the sign of Divine Unity!
By His creative power, *Bá*[6] will commence once more!

7
Though lowly and unlearned,
He searched for what is distinct from what hath appeared.

8
Once again his Creator hath appeared!
Once again He hath demonstrated the sign of His power to create!

9
No hiding place exists where ye might take refuge
Or to be forgiven because of thy earthly pomp!

10
O ignorant ones, ye must purify your inmost heart
That ye might discover the ecstasy of the fire of *Ṭúr!*

11
From Ezra did the mystery of the All-Knowing One become illumined!
When He set out in search of it, the light of illumination shone forth!

12
No tie of direct intercourse existeth between the Creator and His creation!
All reality is constantly sustained by His *Qadar!*[7]

6. See glossary.
7. See glossary.

13
The essential reality of the Creator is devoid of causes.
They neither emanate from Him, nor does He beget them.

14
He doth make anew whatsoever He wisheth!
Whatsoever He doth make is complete, flawless, and exalted.

15
The measure of everything created by His command is without imperfection!
It is complete and exists in a predetermined[8] condition.

16
O Pen, through the attraction of the Beneficent Lord,
Unfold the mystery of existence.

17
Speak forth with a voice strident and exalted
So that the concept of "Return" is disclosed anew.

18
Declare with a voice resounding with palpable certitude:
"O Dissemblers! Let there be no compulsion in religion!"[9]

19
Because the "Hidden Mystery" is now disclosed,
Whosoever in the world desireth attraction to it

20
Shall become enlightened by the enchantment of the Exalted One
And shall discover the loftiest of inscrutable mysteries!

---

8. "Predetermined" (*thábitih*) or fixed, resembling "fixed archetypes" (*a'yán-i-thábitih*); the measure, character, and design of things in God's knowledge.
9. Qur'án 2:256.

21
While he who hath become shrouded by veils
Hath verily brought about all manner of calamity upon himself!

22
The condition of free will admits no form of oppression!
Why would God desire a love that is coerced?

23
None have any obligation other than fulfilling
The special gifts that God hath bestowed upon them.

24
One must become purged from all save God, from all other than Him
That the concealed Countenance mightest become revealed and illumined.

25
Free will is one's proof of the Unity of God,
Whereas constraint of free will would imply disdain and separation!

26
O Ye that attend to the verses of God, reflect carefully
That you might discover a mystery from God's concealed mysteries!

27
Regard the process of renewal in every particle of creation!
Is there a time when even a single atom is not in motion?

28
Thus, plainly even the most diminutive ant
Is the bearer of the enduring verity "*kun fa kán*"!

29
If from every direction the entire world
Should gather to set it in motion,

30
Without its own free will, not even the tiniest ant
Would be moved, nay, not even one iota.

31
Verily, behold! Once more examine with observant eyes
That thou mightest bear witness to the Countenance of the Venerable One!

32
The powerful ant humbly approached
Him who occupieth a station of power,[10]

33
Declaring, "The source of my life in this world is Power!
Except for me, '*Kun fa kán*' would not occur."

34
It is incapable of discerning any reality beyond itself.
For him, sovereignty seemeth to be a burden!

35
Even if a Solomon were to appear before it,
It would open its mouth to say:

36
"The source of my life in this world is Power!
Except for me, '*Kun fa kán*' would not occur!"

37
Indeed, observe, O Thou Bird of celestial vision:
The tiny ant is but a sign of God's *Qadar!*

---

10. Resembling Moses's humble approach to the Pharaoh, as in Qur'án 20:44: "But speak to him mildly; perchance he may take warning or fear (Alláh)."

38
When He saith "*I am,*" it is a proof of the Unity of God!
He doth demolish every notion of multiplicity and idol worship.

39
With His utterance and comportment He asserts,
"There is none among the kings manifest except me!"

40
Then behold and attend to the mystery of God;
Were it to contend otherwise, the ant would be consumed

41
by the fire of Command descending from the station of "*Kun fa kán,*"
For this is His long-established charge!

42
Were one to appear submissive before the king,
This same one would have assumed as his witness "other than God."

43
Indeed, behold how, through the attraction of *Ṭúr,*
All creation declareth the mystery of the Creator.

44
Then behold, and again behold how unconcealed truth
Shines forth from behind the veil in the symbol of the ant.

45
It enlightened the glorious Solomon
So that he could discover the countenance of beauty.[11]

---

11. The Queen of Sheba.

46
Read from the divine verses of the Súrih of the Ants[12]
From the untrammeled utterance of God.

47
After the ant awakened Solomon with its message,
He smiled in gratitude for the wisdom God had bestowed on him.[13]

48
He wished to acquire divine attraction!
He wished to reflect the attributes of the divine in his aspect!

49
Thus, he began to speak about the mystery of what he had witnessed,
Invoking God that He might bring into existence

50
The concealed signs of His countenance
And thereby remove the veil of concealment.

51
"O Lord, grant that I may perform righteousness![14]
Might recite with the sweet melodies of *Ṭá, Sín,* and *Há.*"[15]

52
Thus, behold how the mystery of answering the prayer hath become disclosed
By the command of the "Compensating One,"[16] the Beloved.

---

12. Súrih 27, containing the story of Solomon, which begins with the letters *Ṭá* and *Sín.*

13. Qur'án 27:19: "So he smiled, amused at her speech; and he said: 'O my Lord! so order me that I may be grateful for Thy favors, which Thou hast bestowed on me and on my parents, and that I may work the righteousness that will please Thee: and admit me, by Thy Grace, to the ranks of Thy righteous Servants.'"

14. Qur'án 27:19.

15. A reference to two Súrihs of the Qur'án: Súrih 27, which opens with the letters *Ṭá* and *Sín*, and Súrih 20, which opens with the letters *Ṭá* and *Há.*

16. *Shakúr.* A reference to Qur'án 42:23.

53
And Solomon reviewed the birds among his troops[17]
In order to bring to him the countenance of the Hidden Inaccessible One, the Queen.[18]

54
Clearly the bird represents the attraction of Solomon to the Queen of Sheba,
The attraction which was taught to him by a mere ant in the Era of the Bayán.

55
Indeed, recite the revealed verses of God,
Then drink deep from the goblets of that choice wine.

56
Then read the story of the city of Sheba,
And reveal again the attractions of "*Indeed!*"[19]

57
Understand what the future will bring by studying the past!
Say: Alláh is glorious in His Utterance.

58
O Lord, by the verity of Thy Truth, O God,
Bring about the fulfillment of the divine verses, O my God!

---

17. Qur'án 27:17: "And before Solomon were marshalled his hosts—of Jinns and men and birds, and they were all kept in order and ranks."

18. Solomon ordered Hoopoe to take a message to the Queen of Sheba. An exchange of messages between Solomon and the Queen eventually brought the Queen to Solomon.

19. Most probably a reference to the divine station of Muḥammad, referred to in Qur'án 27:89–92: "If any do good, good will (accrue) to them therefrom; and they will be secure from terror that Day. . . . [A]nd if any accept guidance, they do it for the good of their own souls, and if any stray, say: 'Indeed I am only a Warner.'"

POEM 17

Learning the Names of God

(The original poem begins on p. 447)

This short poem consists of two parts. The first part is comprised of praising God and thanking Him (*ḥamd*), but Ṭáhirih explains that the praise of God—which is effectively the praise of His names and attributes—is only possible thorough the sequential appearances of the Manifestations as we progressively learn more about the names and attributes of God through Their advent in each era or dispensation. Thus, while the essential reality of God is unknowable, the Manifestations of God constitute an eternal reality that is the first creation of the Creator, or "the Primal Point" from which the rest of creation emanates. According to the Bahá'í teachings, They provide us with the most complete knowledge we are capable of attaining, whether in this life or the next.[1] The second part of the poem is a prayer in which the supplicant requests to be deserving of illumination by the Manifestation, the ultimate source of all our enlightenment.

---

1. "We will have experience of God's spirit through His Prophets in the next world, but God is too great for us to know without this Intermediary. The Prophets know God, but how is more than our human minds can grasp" (From a letter written on behalf of Shoghi Effendi to an individual believer, November 14, 1947, quoted in *Lights of Guidance,* p. 209).

1
Praise be to God that from the ornament of Glory,
Praise be to Him that from the Exalted Countenance

2
His Vicegerent hath ever appeared in each era and dispensation,
That from eternity His Manifestation hath ever been radiant and luminous!

3
The pages of tablets became refreshed by Him!
The Spirit of all spirits became illumined by Him.

4
For He is the first created being in the universe!
Nothing hath existed in the universe before Him!

5
He is the Primal Point for the unfolding of creation![2]
He is also the last in the plan of God for creation![3]

6
He hath become visible and manifest,
Yet He is hidden, luminous, and splendid.

7
Verily, His perfections doth abound in the world!
Indeed, His bounty is momentous in the manifest reality![4]

---

2. See glossary for "Primal Point."

3. Bahá'u'lláh discusses this theological point—that each Manifestation is the First and the Last, the Beginning and the End—at length in the Kitáb-i-Íqán: "They are all the manifestation of the 'Beginning' and the 'End,' the 'First' and the 'Last,' the 'Seen' and 'Hidden'—all of which pertain to Him Who is the innermost Spirit of Spirits and eternal Essence of Essences" (¶178).

4. "Manifest reality" is our translation for *a'yán*, a mystical philosophical term meaning "God's effulgence in the world of existence" (*a'yán-i-khárijih*).

8
O Lord, by the truth of the One from Whom existence hath derived,
The Source of all joy and the knowledge of the mystery of existence,

9
By means of Those Who are the branches of this Tree!
Those through Whom are the roots bringing forth this fruit!

10
From Thine Own benevolence, cast but a glance my way
To release me from the oppressive tumult of idle chatter.

11
Close Thou our eyes to the vanities of this world!
Shut Thou our ears to the clamor of this world!

12
Render Thou our hearts to become sources of light!
Fashion our hearts into roots for the tree of *Ṭúr*.

13
Cause our faces to reap Thy bounty!
Cause the roots of that Tree to be our foundation, our bedrock!

14
Strengthen Thou our steadfastness with Thy safekeeping!
Likewise, do Thou safeguard the proven order of Thy design![5]

15
Inasmuch as Thou art the Creator of the entirety of existence,
All that proceeds from Thee is also excellent!

5. Ṭáhirih's repetition of the word "order" (*niẓám*), in conjunction with its derivative "orderly" (*munaẓẓam*), would seem to be a reference to social order and the spiritual order that the Báb designed, as prophesized in ḥadíths about the Qá'im.

16
O Lord, I have none but Thee! Therefore, provide me assistance!
When it is timely, reveal to me Thy firm command!

17
By Thy Truth, O God, O kind Lord,
Reject me not, waiting as I am at Thy gate.

POEM 18

How Wondrous!

(The original poem begins on p. 446)

In this ghazal, every verse ends with phrases containing similar exclamations that mean "How fortuitous!" or "How wonderful!" or, more literally, "How appropriate that it happened!" As is stated clearly in the first verse, this poem celebrates the revelation of that which is concealed or hidden in the personage of the Manifestation, the Primal Point.

In verses 2–5, through varied mystical imagery, the first half of each verse alludes to the divine and the second half to the effect of the revelation of the divine in the world of existence. Verse 6 completes the theme of the previous verse, denoting the effect of the glory of the Manifestation of God (the Throne of God) on the world, and the last two verses urge the reader to recognize and celebrate this union of the Hidden with the Manifest.

1
That concealed splendor became manifest. How wonderful indeed!
That Primal Point became explained. How wonderful indeed!

2
By means of a single amorous glance from the audacious One with sugar-shedding lips,
The Point appeared as a blazing flame. How wonderful indeed!

3
Through the intoxicating coquetry of that Attractive One of the Age,
That Point did appear, brazenly displaying His beauty! How wonderful indeed!

4
When this light shone forth from the captivating quarter,
The entirety of the world became as bright as Sinai! How wonderful indeed!

5
When that Monarch issued orders from the Throne of command,
That Throne of Glory began to tremble with joy! How wonderful indeed!

6
The Eternal Throne hath scattered sparkling gems!
By their light, the direction of the Qiblih[1] can be discerned! How wonderful indeed!

7
O thou hearer of the Divine Verses,
Remove this curtain that is also a veil! How wonderful indeed!

8
That thou mightest behold manifest the once hidden splendor from behind
This same curtain,[2] how He hath revealed His own countenance! How wonderful indeed!

---

1. When in the desert at night, Muslims can discern the direction of the Qiblih by studying the stars.

2. "From the veil of" (the same word as in verse 7). Philosophically, "veil" refers to various stages and degrees of the revelation of the divine, including the station of the Point. In this sense, each successive station both reveals and conceals.

POEM 19

The Awakening[1]

(The original poem begins on p. 445)

1
Lift Thou the pen— Rúmí's enchanted reed!
Drip the lights from Paran onto the verses!

2
Intone melodies from the mysteries of the Creator!
Cleanse Thou the dust from the mirror of existence,

3
Those same particles of dust that have become veiled
From the hidden splendor of that Master of the beauteous ones!

4
Behold how all are fallen, unconscious, forlorn!
For now, no single sign of them doth appear!

1. This is one of the terms designating the Day of Resurrection.

5
Pour choice wine from the crystal goblet
That thou mightest discover some lilting melody from the flask of the world!

6
O Thou Holy Nightingale, pour forth the wine and scatter the sweetness!
Behold the unveiled Countenance gleaming from behind the curtains!

7
Pour forth the wine and care not what did or did not appear—
Perhaps One like Thee, O Master of the beauteous ones.

8
O God, with perceptive eyes, I can clearly see
That in no station is there anyone comparable to Thee!

9
The beams of light from Thy face absorbed and abolished
Both the particles of rust and all extraneous religions and creeds!

10
By God, faith is not merely a subject for discourse!
Rather the magnificence of Thy Splendor is the root of Faith.

11
O Thou the Omnipotent Beloved, religion is naught but love for Thee!
By God, there is none but Thee in every recitation![2]

12
O Thou the Omnipotent Beloved, please make haste!
By God, there is none but Thee in every recitation!

13
O Thou the Omnipotent, Victorious One, please make haste
In abolishing now both the clamorous ones and the whisperers!

---

2. "Elucidation" (*tibyán*) is a title for the Qur'án.

POEM 20

The Primal Point

(The original poem begins on p. 443)

1
O Thou Who possesseth such stature, although beyond all considerations of stature!
O Thou Who art the origin of all utterance, yet without any utterance!

2
Through Thy hidden bestowals, bestow but a glance!
Pour but a sip from Thy ceaseless stream

3
That the Point of beginning might become manifest,
That His acclaim might become unveiled, without concealment or cover!

4
By the beauty of His countenance, He would bestow upon the entirety of the earth
That Master Who is the Creator of order and design.[1]

---

1. "Order" (*niẓám*).

5
By God, through His wisdom religion doth become established!
The world itself is sustained by Him, for He is the source of all sustenance.

6
The heart of religion is the love of that incomparable King!
By the attraction of His love, all acclaim the glory of His name!

7
If thou wouldst bear witness to His love, remove the curtain!
His healing verily attests to the truth of my avowal![2]

8
With the melody of the Creator, I declare plainly and patently
That religion is the love of striving to fulfill whatsoever He doth command.

9
Behold how all who have relied solely on their own wisdom and deeds
In so doing, they have been consumed by but a single word from Him.

10
Religion is our love for Aḥmad and the descendants of 'Alí![3]
This is the true meaning of religion, and verily His word sufficeth!

---

2. An allusion to the miracle of Christ's healing of the sick.

3. Aḥmad is Muḥammad, and the descendants of 'Alí are the eleven Imáms that succeed Him. Yet Ṭáhirih is not only referring to the holy figures of Islam. The return of these personages when the Qá'im appears has been prophesized in ḥadíths as recorded by Shaykh Aḥmad-i-Aḥsá'í in *Kitábu'r-Raj'at* (e.g., pp. 17, 143, 184). In the Persian Bayán, the Báb refers to Himself as the return of Muḥammad, and to the Letters of the Living as the return of holy figures in this Day of Resurrection (pp. 6–7).

POEM 21

The Countenance of the Beloved

(The original poem begins on p. 442)

In this poem, Ṭáhirih prays for assistance that she might be rendered capable of portraying that which is essentially ineffable and thus beyond the power of words, except by means of similitudes—symbols, metaphors, and other figurative devices. Within her supplication is her attempt to compass the astounding effects of the Revelation of the Báb. In line 13, she includes what would seem to be a reference to the martyrdom of the Báb, Who was executed on 9 July 1850. If so, that would date this poem as having been composed in the period of time between that event and Ṭáhirih's own execution in August of 1852.

1
O God, from Thy concealed benevolence, bestow but a glance
That I might make manifest the Primal Point,

2
That I might speak of His station, so pure and transcendent,
That through similitude and symbol, I might portray the flame of ecstasy!

3
There is no mention of aught but Him, the Beloved, the Beautiful!
By those monarchs of belief[1] seated in splendor atop their heavenly thrones!

4
By the beauty of His countenance, they were enabled to eliminate all their imperfections!
They possess no rank, no purpose except invoking the name of God!

5
O Alláh, how pure the world hath become once more!
Every horizon is replete with light from one fire after another!

6
O Alláh, it seems as though It hath at last appeared, the once concealed Countenance
Of Him Who hath now bereft us of all our security and composure.

7
For once we beheld the splendor of that Hidden Mystery,
We vanished into nothingness, without security or composure.

8
From the splendor of the beauteous Countenance of that Monarch,
The entirety of our being became consumed, like a spark from a blazing fire.

9
O Alláh, Thou dost behold our plight!
O God, I possess no real purpose except for Thee!

10
O Thou, my beneficent and generous Lord, I know for certain
That this spark hath not been emitted from any earthly thing!

---

1. The devoted followers of the Báb.

11
Rather it is the countenance of the Beloved that hath dawned from *'Amá,*
That hath entirely consumed with fire every place, even existence itself!

12
O Alláh! Thou art my beloved Witness in this world!
There is no source of aid except Thee, no security or composure.

13
Rescue me, for now hath disappeared from the world
That crimson Point[2] from Whom deriveth all security and composure!

14
O Alláh! Make manifest the splendor of the Beloved[3]
So that it might abolish and eliminate every burden!

2. Most likely an allusion to the martyrdom of the Báb.

3. Most probably an allusion to the advent of Bahá'u'lláh as the appearance of "Him Whom God will make manifest" as prophesied by the Báb.

POEM 22

The Way of God

(The original poem begins on p. 440)

In this poem Ṭáhirih discusses how, at this time in history, the events of the Islamic Dispensation have reappeared in the revelation of the Bayán. So, we read in verse 2 of the poem: "The mysteries of the religion of Aḥmad are now clear and disclosed! / The Ka'bih itself doth now disclose the direction of the Qiblih."

In His Commentary on the Súrih of Joseph, the Báb alludes to Himself as the *Ka'ba* (*baytu'l-ḥarám*), the Qiblih of the Islamic world (section 45). It is recorded that Muḥammad in the middle of the congregational obligatory prayer ordained that the Qiblih be changed from Jerusalem to Mecca, an alteration in spiritual law and practice that was a source of severe test of faith for some of His believers. In the same way, the Báb as the return of Muḥammad (Aḥmad) has also assumed the authority to change religious law, and thereby designated Himself as the Qiblih, even as Bahá'u'lláh would designate the Qiblih for Bahá'ís as His Shrine or burial place.

It is in this sense that the subtlety of God's methodology, manner, or mode of teaching humankind does not change: "God's method carried into effect of old, and no change can ye find in God's mode of dealing."[1] Through His

1. Qur'án 48:23.

Prophets, God attracts the hearts, and there then emerges a division between those who recognize the new Revelation and those who are veiled and refuse to abandon the laws and traditions of the previous Revelation, and thus fail to recognize the new Manifestation. Therefore, while some are ready to sacrifice their lives for the Cause of God, others reject and even disdain and persecute the Prophet.

This separation and distinction between these two groups, together with the degree of dedication and sacrifice of the believers, are the salient themes of this poem. As was the case with the history of Islam, those who were receptive to the Revelation of the Báb and were prepared for it, have become symbols of sacrifice in religious history. 'Alí, the first Imám, time and again demonstrated his dedication to Muḥammad, whether in risking his life in battle or in his constancy after the death of Muḥammad. Likewise, the sacrificial acts of supporters of the Imám Ḥusayn in Karbila represent for Shí'ih Muslims another example by which God tests the followers by separating the staunch believers from those who have failed to perceive the significance and accept the obvious proofs of the new Revelation.

This process whereby the faithful become distinguished from the faithless or the perfidious was occurring during the years Ṭáhirih was writing these poems. Indeed, this testing is precisely what Ṭáhirih is describing and experiencing. What is more, Ṭáhirih's deep admiration and affection for her sacrificial fellow Bábís (she refers to them as "kings" in some poems) is quite apparent in this ghazal.

1
Suddenly the world hath become the focus of God's regard!
Alienated ones have become mere flecks of dust in their remoteness.

2
The mysteries of the religion of Aḥmad are now clear and disclosed!
The Ka'bih itself doth now disclose the direction of the Qiblih.

3
By His magnetic glance, the Monarch of "*Kun fa kán*"
Hath severed all who have become alienated by rejecting the Beloved.

4
With but a glance from His eyes, any deserving soul
Hath become cleansed of malice and the taint of dust!

5
Such a one doth merit becoming a bearer of the Bayán!
Clearly by conveying it, such a one wilt turn toward the Qiblih.[2]

6
Remove the curtain and observe behind the cover!
Who is the One that lieth down to attain victory?[3]

7
By God, He did indeed enter Medina secretly[4]
That the world might become ecstatic by the light[5] from those flames!

8
If thou dost possess insight, discern the meaning of this account!
Whose attraction is this which now hath captivated the hearts?

9
O beholder, with cleansed eyes behold plainly
How God's ways in the past hath become the pattern for this day.

---

2. *Qibli-nimá*, literally "showing where the Qiblih is," and here signifying "functioning as a spiritual guide."

3. "Victory" (*ṭávalá*) seems to be a poetic rendering of the Arabic verb *ṭávala*, meaning "to overcome." A reference here to 'Alí, who slept in Muḥammad's bed pretending to be Muḥammad so that the Prophet could escape to Medina on the night that Arab tribes had plotted to kill Him.

4. An allusion to the Báb's 1845 travel to Medina.

5. A reference to the title for the city of Medina, "the illumined city" (*Madinih Munavvarih*).

10
Clearly the potent attraction of love is the *mizán*[6] for the truth of religion.
By the standard of attraction doth God distinguish the true believer from the foe.

11
The one who doth arise to confirm the truth
Until every joint in his body is wrenched apart

12
Fears not the chains of bondage, even to the extent of fleck of dust,
But in every condition, continues inviting all to the mention of God!

13
In every manner, such a one professeth, "I am patient in the Bayán!"
Until, through his steadfastness, the physical world is transformed.

14
Is this not this the changeless way of God?
Did not this practice of God become evident in the rows of *Ṭaf*,[7]

15
Did they not, with an air of happiness and joy, relinquish life and possessions,
And, though afflicted, proceed on the path of God with love and affection?

16
Some are slain and some detained in prison chains.
For them, the physical world hath become desolate, barren, and pointless.

---

6. "The standard" (*mizán*), as with a balance scale used to assay the weight and worth of precious metals.

7. A reference to the loyal followers of Imám Ḥusayn who, knowing they would be killed, fought beside him in Karbila where he was slain and beheaded.

17
No way remaineth on the path of love whereby they might flee!
Indeed, the constraint of prison hath caused their hearts to be separated from their bodies!

18
Is it not through this changeless method of God
That the station of the Bayán hath now become the source of guidance?

19
Row upon row, standing side by side with moonlike faces,
Their lives in the palms of their hands,[8] they are slain in the path of God.

20
Know of a certainty that now their inner selves have been disclosed,
For though all may seem the same, the soul of each is now made plain!

21
Some stand inaccessible, eternally renowned for glory and honor,
While others, glorying in the self, have degenerated into perishable flecks of dust.

8. They can avoid being slain—so they are told—if they but recant their belief in the Báb as the Qá'im.

POEM 23

In Praise of the Báb

(The original poem begins on p. 438)

In poems 23–30, Ṭáhirih uses a similar formula throughout what is a series of short, emotive lyric works that have several things in common. She begins these poems by portraying with exalted praise and delight some aspect of the new Revelation. In particular, she focuses on its long-prophesied impact in transforming the world and its peoples. In some instances, she cites the bounty and benevolence of God in caring for His creation. In others she concentrates on the Báb and how His revealed works unseal the mysteries of both abstruse traditions and sacred verses, especially from the Qur'án. And elsewhere, she praises the stalwart courage and personal sacrifices made by the Bábís as they bravely face persecution from the government and the clerics alike.

In these briefer pieces, we become more aware of the character of Ṭáhirih as speaker—the narratives seem less objective and philosophical. They are oriented more toward the emotions we expect from believers who are caught up in the devotion, dedication, and fervor of one Who is a recognized leader of a newly revealed religion. Likewise, we are struck with how the first part of these poems is optimistic and encouraging, even if alluding briefly to those who disbelieve or who are adversaries of the new Faith.

However, in these poems, even those who have not recognized the Báb as the return of the Hidden Imám are treated with deference. Ṭáhirih observes that it is their own loss and misfortune not to bask in the joy and delight of having found an answer to all the questions they may have had about their former beliefs.

In some of these poems, she refers to herself as an intermediary, as both a source of encouragement to the faithful and a purveyor of the announcement that a new age has dawned with the promise of unimagined enlightenment, an awakening of the human spirit, and a total transformation of the collective enterprise of the body politic. She is clearly aware of the important role she is playing in the unfolding of this new Revelation, and of her obligation to reach out to those who have yet to become receptive to the appearance of the Báb or to His teachings.

However, unexpectedly, immediately following this uplifting and ebullient tone in which she announces the "good news," Ṭáhirih expresses her desire to be rescued. And with most of these pieces, this notion of being assisted and rescued lends itself to multiple meanings. On the literal level, of course, she is most probably imprisoned at this time and knows that she will likely be executed. But the broader and more spiritual and poetic meaning is that this rescue involves her being removed from the earthly plane of existence, a notion reinforced by her subsequent plaint, "ferry me now to the mountains and valleys of *Ṭúr*!" Coming as these supplications do on the heels of a tone of power and resilience, the reader might find this shift somewhat startling. But anyone familiar with the story of Ṭáhirih's life, especially her stalwart acceptance of her fate at the moment of her execution, will readily understand the sincerity and authenticity of this pleading.

1
O Alláh, Thou dost witness our plight, whatever it might be!
Words are inadequate to impart the "how" or "why" of our story.

2
By Thy Praise, but an image of the essence of the Exalted, He is exalted!
By the light that shineth from His countenance, our nearness to God is attained!

3
His Bayán is on our tongues in every word we utter!
In our first and last utterance, naught except Him is mentioned.

4
Through Thy benevolence, redeem us that we might achieve our destiny,
That we might unfold a portrayal of the mystery of our spirituality.

5
Since Thou art powerful to bring about any creation in the world of being,
Render now in poetry and prose the mystery of our ecstatic belief.

6
O Creator God, as is befitting Thy nature,
Lift Thou the curtain to unfold this Day of Reunion!

7
O Alláh, I am a believer in Thy newly revealed verses
Because our Glory derives from the same mystery as the religion of Muḥammad!

8
That mystery, which was concealed in the veil of verses,
Hath now emerged from behind the veil, exalted in His Might!

9
Then, with palpable flashes of His glance, He ignited
That same brilliance that had veiled His Beauty from us!

10
Alláh! Thou dost witness that Thou art my helper, my assister!
We have nothing else to speak about except Thee!

11
Praised be Thou, the Beauteous, the Magnificent, the most exalted station of the arc![1]
No desire have we but attaining the limits of perfecting Thy Glory in ourselves!

---

1. Alluding to the concept of the arc of descent and ascent as discussed by 'Abdu'l-Bahá in *Some Answered Questions,* no. 81.9.

12
O Lord! Rescue me through Thy benevolence!
Purify me from whatsoever is contrary to piety!

13
Praised be He, the Beautiful, the Friend abiding in the ornament of grandeur!
Indeed, shed Thy rays upon us that we might strive towards attaining Glory!

POEM 24

The Bounty of the Beloved

(The original poem begins on p. 436)

Speak to me of Creation

1
O Bird of Paradise, whatsoever Thou beholdest
Doth become verses streaming down from the midst of "*Kun fa kán*"!

2
O Thou Who dost beget the eternal lights
To reveal the inner meanings of all mysteries concealed ere now,

3
Speak to us of what Thou didst discern in the verses of wisdom
So that the people of *há* might be filled with the joy of ecstasy!

4
Speak Thou of the signs of paradise evident[1] in this temporal realm!
Recount how the dew of twin lush gardens hath descended![2]

---

1. *Shuhúd* refers to witnessing God's attributes in all things.

2. The combination of the words *mud* and *hámatán* in this verse alludes to the appearance of spiritual bounties in the physical world, symbolically two lush and dark green gardens, one in paradise and the other appearing on earth on the Day

5
O Thou Who knowest the mysteries He hath created by shedding His light,
Hearken to that call, and by that melody, abstract thyself from thyself.[3]

6
A Splendor arrived in the comportment of manifest glory
Which had been concealed in a veil befitting the station of exaltation.

7
From eternity, portraying Him hath exceeded mere concerns of "how" and "why"!
He hath ever existed beyond the skill and ken of storytellers.[4]

8
Behold how everything that hath appeared from the mystery of the realm of creation
Hath been set aflame by the refulgence of the light from His face!

9
Behold the forms of beauty surrounding His dwelling,
the brilliance of their searing glances as they observe "this one" and "that one"!

10
And furthermore, O my Friend, behold with but a glance of thine eye
All that which hath been made manifest from the luminesce of those beauteous ones.

---

of the End. Based on Qur'án 55:64 as interpreted by Imám Ja'far Ṣádiq (in Shaykh Aḥmad-i-Aḥsá'í's *Kitábu'r-Raj'at*, p. 222). Ibn-'Arabí interprets the two gardens as two levels of witnessing God (*shuhúd*) by the wayfarer (*Tafsíru'l-Qur'ánu'l-Karím*, vol. 2, pp. 580–82).

3. Similar to 'Abdu'l-Bahá's description of the process of meditation or reflection: "Meditation is the key for opening the doors of mysteries. In that state man abstracts himself: in that state man withdraws himself from all outside objects; in that subjective mood he is immersed in the ocean of spiritual life and can unfold the secrets of things-in-themselves" (*Paris Talks*, no. 54.13).

4. *Mashshá'í*, which can also mean "peripatetic," thereby alluding to rational discourse.

11
From among the suns of glory, behold how the Báb of the Sanctuary
Doth stand in utmost detachment and, verily, with exultation!

12
O thou who art informed of mysteries, with but a single glance,
Observe how the Báb of beneficence is detached from "this and that."

13
Strive with vigor in supplication with glory and majesty!
Say: "Our Lord is the most holy and His word is infallible!"

14
O Thou who hast become illumined by the light of God,
Imbibe from thy goblet the crystal springs of Revelation!

15
Beseech thine Omnipotent Beloved Lord
To disclose for thee the mysteries of "*Kun fa kán*"!

16
O Alláh, the mighty, Thou Who art the eternal Beloved,
Rescue Ṭáhirih through Thy ceaseless bounty!

POEM 25

No God Save God

(The original poem begins on p. 434)

1
Behold unveiled the cherished face of *'Amá!*
How beams of light from that Countenance have attracted creation!

2
No longer is anything else visible or extant but Him!
Were there any other, its creator could not be God!

3
By Alláh, no creator exists but God!
He is the Creator, the Begetter of all that is not Himself!

4
Now withdraw the covering from the Builder's work!
Behold! For the near ones, He is closer than their life's vein.[1]

1. A reference to the ḥadí<u>th</u> in which God proclaims, "you assumed I am far from you, but in fact I am closer to you than your life-vein!" It is also similar to the Qur'ánic verse 50:16: "It was We who created man and We know what dark suggestions his soul makes to him: for We are nearer to him than (his) jugular vein."

5
See naught but Him in every particle of your existence!
Study how every created thing reflects His signs.

6
Without Him, nothing would be visible or existent!
From Him emanateth every particle in the whole of creation.

7
He, except for Whom all is non-existent, is my witness!
From Him doth appear the mystery of creation and destiny.

8
From the exalted realm of Truth, He hath informed
All "other than God" about the One Who occupieth the Throne of Benevolence.

9
Indeed, all things except God are but idols,
And every other good thing but mere evanescence.

POEM 26

This Longing

(The original poem begins on p. 433)

1
O Pen, pour forth for me fruit from the Palm-Tree of Paradise[1]
So that the hidden ecstasy might appear before me in this earthly realm.

2
Remove for me the veil from that Face, and hesitate not
That Thou mightest ferry me to the mountains and valleys of *Ṭúr!*

---

1. *Nakhl,* meaning "palm tree" and "tree" in general. The Palm Tree of Sinai (*nakhl-i-ṭúr*) is a reference to the tree of Sinai through which God talked to Moses. Furthermore, this verse is making a reference to Qur'án 55:68 about paradise: "In them will be fruits, and dates and pomegranates."

POEM 27

An Ode to Narcissus[1]

(The original poem begins on p. 432)

1
As thou dost open thine eyes, thou beholdest naught but the face of the Friend,
By which thou dost mean that as thou dost survey the world, only He exists!

2
Perhaps the hyacinth speaketh forth in poetic sounds,
But doth it derive any avail from the sparks of fire?

3
Thou hast appeared in the garden, recalling the Beloved's sinuous ringlets!
But what bounty is found for thee in the raven's nest?

4
True, all of thy flora hath blossomed majestically,
Hath brought forth blooms on your branches like jewels!

1. "Narcissus" in Persian poetry is an allusion to the beautiful eyes of the beloved.

5
But what doth this matter while the exalted Friend doth lie
Without ally or aid, fallen on the warring plains among infidels?

6
O Alláh, my Lord, O Thou the God of Veracity,
Show me how to become pure and appear with the ecstasy of Truth.

POEM 28

Upraise Me to the Realm of Glory

(The original poem begins on p. 431)

He is the Friend, the Most Excellent Friend

Come! O golden, precious Bird! Unfold Thy wings!

1
O Bird of *'Amá*, recite for us the verses descended from on high!
With enlightening and exquisite accents, attract the whole of creation!

2
How long hast Thou the firmness to ferry the weight of what hath been revealed,
O Thou Who hath descended from the loftiest branches of Grandeur?

3
Behold! The Throne hath become established by the light of the Unity of God!
Through Him the Throne of exaltation hath become manifest in the mirrors.

4
In the empyrean, the Sun of Glory revealeth its blazing Face,
Which, with its brilliance, will swiftly traverse the firmament

5
To reveal conspicuously the new splendor
Through the dazzling mirrors with majesty and grace!

6
O God! By Thy sanctified and unparalleled Essence!
O God! By Thy self-subsisting and exalted Self!

7
Reveal for me but a glimpse of Thine enshrouded lights!
O God! Do Thou release me from this realm of evanescent dust!

8
I am consumed by the hostile flames in this desert of sorrows!
Verily, I am bereft of patience and stamina to endure these afflictions!

9
O God! Purify me from this defilement,
O Thou Lord of life! Upraise me to the realm of glory!

POEM 29

I Set My Pen to Page

(The original poem begins on p. 430)

1
In the name of the Incomparable, the Mighty, the Benevolent,
Now do I set my pen to page to share the wondrous verities!

2
I will recount the glorious majesties of God!
I will disclose treasures concealed by the passing of ages.

3
I will divulge what was hidden in the radiant inmost heart!
I will infuse ecstasy and delight into all who are wearied with misery!

4
I will inscribe with my fingers what hath been concealed in the past!
I will elucidate what is intended by "the exalted" and "the obliterated!"[1]

---

1. A reference to Imám 'Alí in *Nahju'l-Balágha*, also referenced in the Bahá'í writings as meaning a reversal of stations and ranks in religion as a result of the advent and teachings of a new Manifestation of God.

5
I will explain the Cause concealed by veils,
To delight the heavenly concourse with joy and ecstasy at what they behold!

6
I will explain the evident verities of the Cause of the Omnipotent, the Most Great,
So that those who dwell in the city of doubt might become ecstatic and delirious!

7
I will no longer be occupied with bygone traditions!
I will enshroud the disbelievers with a thin, luminous veil.

8
So that they might behold that mystery that is before their very eyes
Without concealment, but disclosed in the robe of the Omnipotent, the Knower!

9
So that they might discover the mystery of God's might from God's manifest will—
This people that hath become constrained by the misery of their sins!

10
O God, the Omnipotent, the Most powerful, the King, the Helper,
With Thy benignity and bestowal, rescue this companion besieged with anguish and sorrow!

11
O my God, purify me by Thy truth from all those things
That are unworthy in Thy presence, Thou the Omnipotent One, the Knower!

12
O My Creator, enable me to comprehend Thy wondrous verses!
When I approach the end, upraise me to Thy paradisal exaltation!

POEM 30

But A Drop of Thy Musk-Scented Wine

(The original poem begins on p. 428)

1
O Thou with a heavenly presence, speak of the *ḥaram*[1] in these verses!
Once again pour into my goblet the pure musk-scented wine

2
That I might be delivered from the company of slanderers
And ascend with exaltation to the summit of the Sun.

3
Then will I enter the blessed domain of the forgiving Lord
And become entirely consumed by that sacred fire

4
Until I am totally purged of worldly affections
So that not even an iota of the most minute particle remains in me!

---

1. An Arabic term designating the sacred sanctuary at Mecca where no blood may be spilled. It refers to the Ka'bih, though the Báb explains that the true sanctuary to be worshiped is the Manifestation of God.

5
O Kind God, when Thou dost discover me in this condition,
Through Thy kindness, Thy attention, and Thine assistance,

6
Let descend a drop of truth from Thine exalted station
Fashioned by Thy command of *Qadar*.

7
Then, O Creating One, from attraction to Thee it will circumambulate,
As it recounts Thy station, O Thou Who dost confer Justice!

8
O God, He will reveal His face and become the Guide,
And by attraction to Him, O Thou the Omnipotent, He will incinerate all else.

9
Rescue me, O my Lord, for I have fallen, lost in the desert of sorrows,
Imprisoned, a captive of the wicked tribe of depravity.[2]

---

2. This allusion to imprisonment is both metaphorical and literal inasmuch as Ṭáhirih was imprisoned on more than one occasion.

POEM 31

The King of Kings Ascends His Throne

(The original poem begins on p. 427)

1
The Manifestation with the power of Bahá sits with the majesty of Bahá![1]
The King of kings sits with the elegance of praise on the Throne of exaltation!

2
With the beauty of His Countenance, He doth attract the gaze of the peoples of the world,
Even though those who possess power and regality still retain their rank![2]

---

1. Ṭáhirih knew Bahá'u'lláh. She helped in the planning of the pivotal events at Badasht with Bahá'u'lláh, and she indicates in other poems her awareness that He was to be the successor to the Báb. However, when Ṭáhirih uses the word "glory" (*Bahá*) to refer to a person, it might be a reference to the Báb because there are instances where the Báb refers to Himself as *Bahá*. Also, the poem describes a present situation as opposed to future events. Consequently, we include the word "Bahá" here without specifying to Whom she is referring, thereby allowing the readers to decide for themselves.

2. Religious and political leaders still retain their rank and power, their palaces and stations.

3
But on the throne of the summit of the Royal Court, naught is mentioned but His Cause!
Naught else is observed but Him, ensconced upon the throne of the Glory of His Grandeur!

POEM 32

Sparks of Fire

(The original poem begins on p. 427)

God! He is God! There is no God except Him, the Creator of wondrous new names!

1
The world of existence is broiling from sparks of fire!
The sea of light hath appeared with jubilation!

2
This is the Day of creation! The mystery of *Qaḍá* is manifest!
The Sun of *Qadar*[1] hath appeared anew throughout the world!

3
O Thou holy Bird dwelling[2] in Paradise, pour forth
The purest scintillas of fire into the flaming goblet!

---

1. See glossary.
2. "Dwelling" (*ma'vá*) is a reference to paradise, the dwelling place of the righteous, as noted in Qur'án 32:19, 79:41, and 53:15.

4
Behold now the Sun of Eternity, how it doth begin to rise
With the splendors of His countenance, visible, though inaccessible.

5
On the opposite side of the heavens, behold the moon of Divine Essence!
In the ecstasy of that light, it doth entrance the people of certitude!

POEM 33

The Bounty of *'Amá*

(The original poem begins on p. 426)

1
O Bird of Holiness, at this moment revealest Thou
What this tumult and ecstasy discharged throughout the world doth mean!

2
Hath it become embossed in green lines on the pages of the Book,
The Divine Splendor that hath been concealed in creation?

3
Drops of praise rain down from the clouds!
Glorious enchantments shine forth from the *'Amá* of *há!*

POEM 34

The Súrih of the Elephant

(The original poem begins on p. 425)

Based on the criteria established by the modernist movement in Western poetry, especially among the imagists, this could be considered one of Ṭáhirih's strongest poems. But understanding the power of this succinct representation of the elaborate concepts she presents requires an awareness of the two major conceits employed.

The first of these concerns the Súrih of the Elephant (Súrih 105 in the Qur'án). This Súrih tells the story of how an army employing elephants came from Yemen under the command of Abrahah Al-Ashram with the purpose of destroying the Ka'bih at Mecca. But to deter this incursion, God sent a flock of birds that had picked up with their beaks pieces of clay hardened like stones. Then, from on high, the birds dropped these stones with such force that the army was torn to pieces. Drawing on imagery from this story, Ṭáhirih compares the words of the Manifestation—responding to the attempts by the clerics and divines to repudiate His claims—to the clay stones.

The second allusion is to the Platonic allegory of the cave. In this narrative from Plato's *The Republic*, the physical world is portrayed as a realm of shadows and illusions. Humankind is confined to a cave as chained prisoners whose experience of reality is merely the perception of shadows on a wall emanating from the light of a fire directly behind them, which they are unable to turn around and see.

As the allegory proceeds, the Philosopher King dwelling among these prisoners extricates himself from the constraints of this world of shadows and ascends the cave to discover ever more lofty levels of the truth about reality until, at last, he espies the Sun itself, the One, the Good, the source of all reality. Having discovered the truth in its pure form, he then feels obliged to return to the cave to enlighten others, to help them unbind themselves from the world of illusion, and to lead them step by step into the world of reality and enlightenment.

1
The bird of Destiny is singing from the heart
And hath thereby caused commotion amongst those glorious specks,[1]

2
Besieged by clay-stones,[2] those people, hardened like stone,
Have fallen headlong into the fire and supplicate for help!

3
From the heaven of Command, a curse hath descended
From the tongue which itself is the source of supplication!

4
The Súrih of the Elephant beareth witness to this verity.
Indeed, God hath shown me what hath not been seen before.

5
Observe the failure of deceit of those casting shadows for proof,[3]
Contending with those who supplicate the fire instead.

---

1. "Particle" (*ḍarrih*) in Ṭáhirih's poems takes on various meanings, among them "particles of existence." Here the term refers to individual human beings.

2. "Hard stones" (*Sijjíl*). Refer to Qur'án 105:4, 15:74, 11:82. The story is told in Súrih 105, the Súrih of the Elephant.

3. The fire symbolizes the truth or reality, whereas the shadows are mere reflections or semblances of the truth. This analogy is reminiscent of Plato's allegory of the cave in *The Republic,* but it is employed similarly in the religious and philosophical writings of Middle Eastern scholars and poets.

6
Indeed, from the sky hath descended
The storied swarm of swallows[4] of *'Amá!*

7
O Thou who speakest the truth, beware!
For what reason hath the verses of separation been revealed?

8
Behold! The claystone is created by Thine utterance!
Now is it apparent that Thou art the Exalted One![5]

9
Pour them forth from the heavens and behold
all the melodious effectual stones of Thine utterance!

10
The sun hath descended from the sublime Empyrean!
Verily, the luminescence of its light hath banished the shadow!

4. The birds who dropped the clay stones on the elephants in Qur'án 105:4.

5. "Exalted;" Qur'án 15:75, 11:82: "We made the exalted one lowly by birds dropping stone on the contending army." In other words, the attacking army was exalted, but now it is clear that the clay stones symbolize the utterances of God conveyed by His Prophet—He who is truly exalted.

POEM 35

Behold!

(The original poem begins on p. 425)

This is a rhythmic poem filled with energy. Its tone is very musical, and it contains allusions to music and musicians. Each line ends with the word "behold," and, as is commonly the case with ghazals, the first hemistich in the first line of the poem also ends with "behold." Here we can observe an instance where "fire" is entirely positive, the force of a new Revelation, and the revitalization of the earth and its people.

1
The dawn-breakers are brimming with light! Behold!
The illuminated ones are displaying the aurora of morn! Behold!

2
With the melodic rhythm of drums, the light and the bright ones
Are becoming singed by a most holy burning. Behold!

3
O ye who are oblivious to the hidden divine mystery,
Observe what these beauteous hymns are now intoning. Behold!

4
From veils of glory, the Blessed Countenance
Is illumined and glistening with light. Behold!

5
With thy melodious tambourine, play thine own music!
How beauteous are the shimmering treasures! Behold!

6
The Luminous clouds brimming with water are covering the heavens!
The nurturing droplets descend one by one. Behold!

7
O thou yearning one, hasten to the divine banquet of the Lord!
The once Hidden Mystery hath become manifest![1] Behold!

8
O musicians, play a melody of praise!
The world is abounding with sparks of fire![2] Behold!

9
Abandon the veil of dust from verses of the Book!
Remove the veils and say, "The blazing fire! Behold!"

10
Swim in the ocean![3] Bring a brand from that roaring fire,[4]
Then perceive the reality concealed by the veils. Behold!

---

1. "Mystery" (*sirr*). See Qur'án 25:6.

2. In this and some similar passages, fire and sparks seem to refer to the Revelation of God to Moses through the Burning Bush.

3. A reference to Qur'án 52:6 and 81:6 about the sea of fire as the sign of the Day of Resurrection.

4. This refers to Moses telling His family when He beheld the fire atop the mountain, "Tarry ye; I perceive a fire; perhaps I can bring you some burning brand therefrom or find some guidance at the fire" (Qur'án 20:10).

11
Haste ye, for the Sun of wisdom is spinning with Glory!
The entirety of creation is engulfed by that fire! Behold!

POEM 36

Divinely Inspired Verses

(The original poem begins on p. 424)

This is one of the very best of Ṭáhirih's shorter lyrics. With a compression of thought into a handful of extremely powerful conceits, she manages to convey what she perceives to be the source and power of her poetry, though she may be employing the persona of the Báb as the narrator. In part, then, the effectiveness of this poem derives from her unabashed profession that her poetry is important and a valuable resource for the reader, whether or not they are a follower. At the same time, if Ṭáhirih is employing the persona of the Báb as speaker, then such an inference would be even more appropriate and understandable.

It is in this sense that her allusion to the source of her verse may be portraying the process of divine Revelation. If she is describing herself as poet and her art as divinely inspired, however, then she may be discussing a process very similar to the notion of inspiration described by some of the more notable poets of the English Romantic period, particularly the theories espoused by Wordsworth and Coleridge, or the theory (but not the practice) of Emerson.

She begins by describing succinctly how, by cleansing her mind and psyche of concerns about the self, she gains access to verities from the realm of the divine. Thence, by translating these abstruse truths into poetic tropes, especially those verities as articulated by the Manifestations of the past, she has become "endowed with power" to convey these same insights into poetically accessible terms.

She then boldly invites the reader to examine her words, especially if one is a seeker and wishes to become apprised of the truth she has discovered. And in the two closing lines, she concludes with an axiomatic observation that the essence of what the reader will discover is that everything she has observed about the course of history or the actions of God—His *Jalál* or grandeur—derives from the inspiration she received by simply meditating and reflecting on the ultimate *Jamál*—the beauty of God, the Beloved.

1
I discarded my jealousy, my possessiveness,
And disclosed all the hidden mysteries!

2
By assigning names to the signs of the heavens of grandeur,
I rolled up the past[1] and recreated its meaning in verse.

3
Through divine attraction to the dawning place of Eternity,
I became endowed with power to speak forth in every mode!

4
If thou art a wayfarer on the path of search, come!
All thou shalt discover in each of my verses is but the Truth.[2]

5
What thou shalt behold from the beginning to the end of *Jalál*
I have made manifest from the countenance of *Jamál*.[3]

6
Come! Consider not the mere shadows of things!
I abolished them all with but a single spark from my pen!

1. "Rolling up the skies" is a reference to what God will do on the Day of Resurrection as alluded to in Qur'án 21:104 and 39:67. It represents the renewal of old beliefs, religions, and traditions.

2. "Truth" (*ḥaqq*) is a term used by Ṣúfís as the object of wayfaring—the ultimate truth being that truth which unravels spiritual and philosophical mysteries.

3. See glossary.

POEM 37

The Ecstasy of Shiraz

(The original poem begins on p. 423)

With this poem, there follows a sequence of remarkably powerful but compressed tributes to the Báb and to the historical and world-embracing effects of His appearance, His Revelation, and His personal contribution to the transformation of human history on planet Earth.

Poems 37–41[1] focus on the full impact of the station of the Báb as the Primal Point, not only as the instigator of a new Cycle in human history—one that is destined, according to Bahá'í belief, to endure no less than five hundred thousand years—but as the end point, the objective for which all previous Revelations in the Abrahamic line of Prophets had been preparing their followers.

This particular poem begins this sequence by alluding to the Declaration of the Báb in the city of Shiraz, whereby the whole world became like a beauteous bride bestowing life upon the world of being. The term "breath-possessing" (*zi nafas*) in verse 2 of the poem—also appearing in verse 5 of poem 63—is an allusion to the well-known Ṣúfí term of Ibn-'Arabi, "the breath of the Merciful" (*nafasu'r-Raḥmán*), which appears abundantly in his *Fuṣuṣu'l-Ḥikam* (e.g., p. 119). This concept connotes God's bestowal of

1. A poem of one verse only has been placed at the end of the volume and a major part of poem 41 has not been translated since it is missing some verses.

existence on the universe, or stated more completely, the instigation of reality as a means of fulfilling His desire to be known by a being with free will. (See endnotes for further information about this poem.)

1
Now that creation hath been permeated with the ecstasy of Shiraz,
World upon world hath been transmuted into a bridal chamber of anticipation!

2
Naught else shall remain except the Essence of the Creator,
Manifest throughout the entirety of the universe in all who possess a soul!

3
Beholdest thou with acute and discerning eyes
How in every land the world hath been set ablaze!

POEM 38

Bring forth the Goblet

(The original poem begins on p. 423)

In this poem, Ṭáhirih urges the Báb to reveal His station and thereby revive the universe. Employing traditional Ṣúfí imagery, she asks the cupbearer to bestow wine to all, and by that action, create in them a new life.[1]

The "mystery of seven" in this poem refers to the seven levels of the Empyrean. In particular, it is an allusion to the seven stages of creation mentioned in several of the Báb's writings and in various Shaykhí texts. In the Persian section of the Panj-Sha'n (p. 27), the Báb mentions the seven stages of creation as the qualities that adorn the chosen believers in "Him Whom God Shall Make Manifest," the same attributes that these believers shall make manifest in their dedication and actions. We can also discern an allusion to the seven stages of creation in poem 64 (verses 3–8) of this volume in which Ṭáhirih urges the cupbearer to make manifest these stages, each of which she names sequentially.

---

1. The image of the cupbearer—a trope that occurs in several of Ṭáhirih's poems—is sometimes an allusion to the Báb, as occurs in the Báb's own Qayyúmu'l-Asmá' (Commentary on the Súrih of Joseph) (Section 92) where, alluding to Qur'án 76:5–6, the Báb refers to Himself as the Cupbearer (*sáqí*) of the fountain of camphor in paradise.

1
Bear forth the goblet of radiant crimson wine
Illuminating the cup to the brim,

2
Circling round the translucent crystal goblet!
Disclose "the mystery of seven" in the cycles of the spheres![2]

3
With heavenly ecstasy, with the melody of morning prayer,
Bring forth the goblet and discard what thou didst formerly know!

2. "Seven Spheres" (*sab'-i-ṭabáq*) is a reference to Qur'án 67:3 and 71:15.

POEM 39

The Four Pillars

(The original poem begins on p. 423)

This poem celebrates the advent of the Báb—God's mystery—and the establishment of the "throne of God" on "four pillars." The throne is thus a symbol for the Manifestation of God, which, as the "seat of God," represents God's authority. The four pillars of the throne can symbolize the four aspects of the Manifestation of God, thereby resembling Shaykh Aḥmad-i-Aḥsá'í's four pillars of the throne (*Sharḥu'l-Favá'id*, vol. 2, pp. 279–80). According to him, each pillar symbolizes one of the realms of existence: the most transcendent realm, the Universal Mind (*aqli-kullí*); the Universal Spirit (*rúḥ-i-kullí*); the Universal Soul (*nafs-i-kullí*); and the most immanent Universal Nature (*ṭabí't-i-kullí*). The trees of light in the last verse of the poem symbolize the Manifestations of God. The Tree is a frequently employed allusion to the Manifestations, sometimes expressed in terms of the tree on Mount Sinai, the "Tree of Life," and "the Divine Lote Tree."

1
O thou who doth seek divine grace, come!
Request whatsoever thou doth desire of mysteries!

2
Since the Eternal Gatekeeper hath opened all the gates,
His countenance hath appeared at each one![1]

3
The time hath transpired and eras elapsed!
Proofs and prophecies hath disclosed the mystery of God!

4
Eternal torrents of grace hath been bequeathed!
All the bestowals of Paradise are now at hand.

5
Behold how the exalted Throne hath become adorned,
Hath become illumined with divine lights!

6
The whole world bespeaks the first pillar of the throne!
From it hath dawned the Morn of Eternity!

7
From its second pillar hath the world become vitalized,
For the gates of praise have been opened!

8
From its third pillar hath the world become exhilarated,
Hath become illumined by the light of glory!

9
From its fourth pillar in that definitive mystery
From among the encompassing mystery and from the beams of light,

---

1. Clearly an allusion to the various religious prophecies being fulfilled with the appearance of the Báb.

10
The conflagration of trees hath been ignited!
The ocean of mysteries hath begun to be unfolded!

POEM 40

Cry Out!

(The original poem begins on p. 422)

1
Recount the story of love! Cry out and portray
How the roaring of His search hath provoked fear in the hearts!

2
How existence itself hath become overwhelmed and is quivering!
How all the verses of proof have been revealed!

POEM 41

The Primal Point

(The original poem begins on p. 422)

This poem is part of a larger poem in praise of the Báb. The original poem is missing some verses and thus is not translated in its complete form. In these selected verses, Ṭáhirih begins in the poetic style called "*mukhammas,*" meaning that each part of the poem has five hemistiches—two full stiches and a single hemistich. However, after two parts, the poem continues in the common style of consecutive series of verses, each consisting of two hemistiches.

The poem employs symbolism—used in Shaykhí literature and in the Báb's writings—that relates to the process of creation, employing references to verses from the Qur'án. In the first verse of the poem a reference is made to the Point, alluding to the Báb as the source of creation.[1] The Point, representing the image of a dot inscribed by the pen on a page, functions as the symbol for the origin of the process of creation, as the letters of the alphabet appear by the movement of the point on the page. As such, from the point, the letter *alif,* the first letter of the Arabic and Persian alphabet, appears. But *alif* itself appears in sequentially progressive stages, transforming its original transcendental quality into its manifestations in the world of existence. The first stage is the soft *alif* (*alif-i-layyinih*), which is still transcendent with no visible form

1. The Báb states, "I am the Primal Point from which have been generated all created things" (quoted in His Epistle to Muḥammad Sháh, *Selections from the Writings of the Báb*, no. 1.4.4).

and shape and is still embedded in the Point,[2] as if the soft *alif* represents the form and idea of *alif* before its materialization in any tangible shape and form.

After addressing the generative character of the Point, Ṭáhirih describes the historical process of the manifestation of the Point as it occurs with each successive Prophet. She begins with Adam, followed by Noah, and then alludes to Abraham as the builder of the Ka'bih, a task which, according to the Qur'án, He was commanded by God to undertake. References are then made to Moses and Christ, after which the poem concludes with an enigmatic allusion to Muḥammad. (See endnotes for further information about this poem.)

1

Thou art the embodiment of the Point of Beginning!
Thou art the Temple for the soft *alif!*

Thou art the power endowing concept with form![3]
Thou dost exemplify the essence of entification,[4]
For God hath endowed Thee with the station of Lordship

2

From Thee did Adam appear amongst men!
From Thy splendor was Noah brought forth!

The builder of the Ka'bih fulfilled the mystery of *hám!*
And Moses of Sinai conversed with God!
But it was by Thine aid that this utterance occurred!

---

2. See Nader Saiedi's article in *Pazhúhish Námih,* no. 6, 1999 (1377 Shamsi).

3. A reference to Qur'án 95:4: "We have indeed created man in the best of molds."

4. Similar to the sense of the previous line, the word *ta'yin* is a version of *ta'ayyun* or "entification," a Ṣúfí term meaning individuation of things in the world of existence or the determination of their essence. In Platonic terms, this capacity alludes to expressing the transcendent "idea" or "form" in physical terms. For example, the expression of beauty in a beautiful object. Though in this case, the transcendent concept is God's wish to be known, as expressed in the ḥadíth of the Hidden Treasure, whereby the creation of the human being fulfills this wish.

3
You are the Word that was the source of the Spirit[5]
Who assumed a human form because the Holy Spirit wafted from Paran.[6]

4
By the conjoining of the Divine Splendor with human form,
That Word recounted how Jesus became manifest!

5
Thy pristine Essence is transcendent and eternal![7]
By Him Who extendeth assistance, Thine attribute is "begetteth not!"[8]

6
Observe the limitations of whosoever hath been begotten!
Thy transcendent Essence is purified from such limitations!

---

5. Christ.
6. See glossary.
7. See Qur'án 112:2: "Alláh, the Eternal, Absolute."
8. Qur'án 112:3: "He begetteth not, nor is He begotten."

POEM 42

The Day of Resurrection Doth Tremble and Descend!

(The original poem begins on p. 421)

This poem is similar in structure and theme to Bahá'u'lláh's poem "Ras͟hḥ-i-'Amá" ("The Clouds of the Realms Above"). Ṭáhirih skillfully combines the gentle and melodious beauty of a Persian ghazal, normally a romantic lyric, with theological and mystical concepts, making references to the Qur'án, to ḥadít͟hs, and to various Ṣúfí concepts. The Beloved is the Point Himself, and much of the poem is a description of His attributes and His steadfastness in the face of calamities. It contains allusions to the tumultuous historical context of His appearance, which is, after all, nothing less than the Day of Resurrection.

Following the ghazal form, in the first hemistich of the first verse, and second hemistich of all verses, there is a rhyme, ending with a beautiful Persian poetic construction: *larzadu rízad*, meaning "trembles and rolls down (falls / pours)." The poet makes spiritual interpretations of the numerous verses in the Qur'án about the pouring of the water (*má*) from the sky (*samá*) on earth, and particularly the pouring of rain that causes revival of the earth after its dormancy (e.g.: Qur'án 2:164, 29:63, 16:65, 30:24).

We also note in the poem images of nature and natural phenomena: clouds, wind, lightning, fire, sparks, earthquake, flowers, dew, and bees, along with traditional mystical poetic images of wine, goblet, and references to the Qur'ánic verses and ḥadít͟hs related to the events and conditions surrounding the advent of the new Revelation. (See endnotes for further information about this poem.)

1
Tears shimmer and roll down the cheeks of that beauteous floral countenance
Like the morning dew on the petals of a flower glistening as it doth tremble and descend.

2
By reflections from His glorious robe, the commotion of Resurrection hath been raised!
By the brimming drops of His *badá*, the Empyrean doth tremble and descend.

3
When *Muṣṭafá*[1] the Chosen One, hears in paradise news of calamities He doth endure,
Tears from the face of that Worthy One tremble and descend.

4
When the melody of the buzzing bee[2] resonateth in lamentation,
The wine of utterance rusheth forth, doth tremble and descend.

5
When the holy lamentation of the trumpet is sounded,
With that sound earthquakes will tremble and descend.[3]

---

1. Muḥammad.

2. A reference to the ḥadíth that one of the indications that Muḥammad was about to receive a Revelation was that He would hear a buzzing like that of a bee. In the same manner, the wine rushing down in Ṭáhirih's verse alludes to the revelation of verses.

3. According to the Qur'án (39:68), there will be two trumpet blasts in the Day of Resurrection: "The Trumpet will (just) be sounded, when all that are in the heavens and on earth will swoon, except such as it will please Alláh (to exempt). Then will a second one be sounded, when, behold, they will be standing and looking on!"

6
Behold what commotion hath stricken the heavenly realm!
The pristine drops of divine holiness tremble and descend.

7
Know that from the enchantment of the Beloved's glance,
Wave by wave, East winds tremble and descend.

8
Behold how the rays from that same enchantment at the appearance of such beauty,
Like dew on the flowers in spring tremble and descend.

9
Behold the ornaments on His perfect stature
Which from the station of glory freely tremble and descend.

10
Behold how the crystal goblet doth reflect His face
Amidst the pure and flowing spring that doth tremble and descend.[4]

11
Behold how with but an attentive glance from His eyes, from the hand of Grandeur,
Crystal chalices of wine cannot help but tremble and descend.

12
If thou art among the people loyal to Bahá, Behold
How the verses from that powerful hand tremble and descend.

13
O Thou with the Beauteous face, bring Thy hidden attraction
So that, perforce, the orbits might tremble and descend.

---

4. Allusions to Qur'án 37:45 and 56:18 and similar verses referring to goblets of drink offered to those in paradise.

14
Be assured that with detachment, the same Point
Doth stand with redness, tremble and descend.

15
Behold on the earth's surface the illumined face of Zahrá,
How from the purity of her rays of light the Empyrean doth tremble and descend.[5]

16
Behold now the outpourings from the dawning-place,
How from the heavenly throne pure gold and jewels tremble and descend.

17
Then be not oblivious to the unravelling of these mysteries,
Which, like fire from the pen, tremble and descend.

18
Know Thou that the world[6] is like a bucket suspended in a well
Which, according to God's Will, doth dribble, tremble and descend!

19
And if thou dost experience wondrous ecstasy,
Know that from goblet's brim of this Illuminated One, it doth tremble and descend!

20
It is because of Him that everything in the heavens and beyond,
From the Empyrean to the earth, doth tremble and descend.

---

5. See glossary.

6. The indirect methodology by which God brings to fruition His plan for the spiritual and social evolution of humankind and the planet as a whole. The "Divine Plan" as mentioned in the rest of the line.

21
Behold His stature, the upright Qá'im and the self-subsisting Qayyúm,
The Points from which Glory and Fortitude tremble and descend.

22
Behold that whatsoever thou dost see manifest, issueth forth from this Point,
That water from Him which doth overflow, tremble, and descend.

23
Behold the dawning-lights from the summit of His mountain,
Glistening flawless gems tremble and descend.

24
Behold that whatsoever He desireth from that panoply of treasures,
From the source of blazing fire doth tremble and descend.

25
Behold that the water of mysteries[7] from the heart of Kawthar,
Like drops of rain, becometh manifest, doth tremble and descend.

26
Drink, thou, the water of love from the goblet of ecstasy
Which even now from the heavens doth flow, tremble, and descend!

---

7. "The water of mysteries" (*má'-i-buṭún*) is a term that also appears in verse 1 of poem 45. The term is observed in relation to the station of Imám 'Alí as noted in a letter of the Báb to Ṭáhirih (The Báb, "Letter to Ṭáhirih," p. 151).

POEM 43

The Tablet of Creation

(The original poem begins on p. 418)

This poem and those that follow are rhythmic ghazals or similar forms. They are ecstatic in their tone and resemble certain poems by Rúmí. This poem announces in a joyful and invigorating tone the appearance of the Manifestation of God and is sophisticated in language and concepts, employing enigmatic allusions to the Qur'án, to mystical perspectives, and to cosmological imagery.[1] It addresses the Revelation in terms of the process of creation and the appearance of the visible universe from the primordial transcendent divine.

As such, the main theme of the piece is the manner in which that which has been hidden becomes manifest. Therefore, in addition to a variety of allusions to this theme, we observe in the poem the use of the word *buṭún* ("concealment") seven times, the words for "manifest" (*'ayán* and *ẓáhir*) nine times, and several references to "veil," notably with the word "*hijab.*"

In verses 8–11 and 18–20, the poem alludes to the process of Revelation that takes place through an encounter with and subsequent conversation between the Temple of the *Qá'im* (the body or physical dimension of the Manifestation of God) and Gabriel (an allusion to an internal dialogue as the Holy Spirit communes with Muḥammad in the Qur'án), and, in the Bahá'í

1. The motion of planets has been used in certain Islamic literature to symbolize the religion as revealed by various prophets. (For example, see Seyyed Husssein Nasr, *Introduction to Islamic Cosmological Doctrines*, p. 65.)

context, what might be understood as the divine reality of the Manifestation. In this sense, the dialogue is similar to that which takes place between the Maid of Heaven and Bahá'u'lláh in the Súriy-i-Haykal, a conversation that can be interpreted as an internal dialogue, reflection, or meditation taking place between the rational mind of Bahá'u'lláh and the Holy Spirit operating through Him.

In verses 14–15, the words Throne (*'arsh*) and Seat (*kursí*), both mentioned in the Qur'án (5:20 and 255:2), also refer to Empyrion and celestial orbits, as they also do in Rúmí's poetry.[2] Ibn-'Arabí and other Ṣúfís have developed various interpretations of these terms.[3] References are also made in the poem to the Arabic alphabetic letter *nún* or its combination with the letter *káf* (even as the imperative "Be!" is represented in English by combining the letters "B" and "E") to represent God's command that the creation of the universe take place. These references can also be allusions to the Qur'ánic verses or symbols in Shaykhí and Ṣúfí literature. (See endnotes for further information about this poem.)

Assist Me, O Beloved

1
As soon as the mystery of concealment appeared from the station of God's command
Bestowing the dawn of illumination, it became established in the realm of *Nún.*

2
How often it orbited with magnetic attraction in the station of concealment
Until manifested as a distinct form, that splendor of the mystery of inscrutability,

---

2. See Siyyid Ṣádiq Gawharin, *Farhang-i-Lughát va Ta'bírát-i-Mathnaví.* vol. 6, pp. 295–96, vol. 7 pp. 268–69, for Rúmí's poems.

3. See Javád Noorbakhsh, *Farhang-i-Núr-Bakhsh Iṣṭiláḥát-i-Taṣavvuf,* vol. 2, pp. 306–11.

3
Until the countenance of Majesty appeared, adorned with Beauty
With attraction of the ecstasy of reunion, with coquetry, melodies, and artistry, saying:

4
"Harken, O people of the world! The divine mystery hath become manifest!
From the realm of *qaḍá*,[4] the *jamál*[5] of the Existing One hath become manifest!

5
This is that promised day, the day of reunion—He is manifest from the station of *innamá!*[6]
This is the splendor the Creator of the universe made manifest from the mystery of *káf* and *nún*.

6
Whosoever hath recognized His truth, is certainly of Him,
But whosoever remaineth veiled from Him, will be thrust into hell!

7
It is from this revitalizing call that fervor was incited in the world!
The totality of existence itself became invigorated and illumined by the Existing One!"

8
Unexpectedly, the Attraction rushed in from a remote and concealed abode,
And descended through the temple[7] of the Qá'im to fulfill the command of God.

9
In His hand was the Tablet of creation, inscribed with the ink of light, saying:
"O King of *kun fa-yakúnu*, O Thou Who art unconstrained in Thy command,

4. Decree.
5. Beauty.
6. See glossary.
7. Body or physical appearance of the Báb.

10
Behold with Thy divine glance what hath been inscribed in the revealed verses!
Today is the Promised Day! Verily, we receive from Thee

11
Whatsoever Thou hast in mind, O Thou the Omnipotent Creator,
Cause to appear in creation through Thy bounty those forms that mirror forth Thy wish.[8]

12
O God, with this fire[9] did the Sun begin its orbit!
The Sun of destiny dawned radiant, revolving in the shape of *nún*!

13
O God, through the attraction of Bahá, with brilliance and luster,
The once concealed light became visible, shone forth, and reverberated in glee!

14
With but an attentive glance at the veil torn asunder,
The Throne of the Omnipotent Lord pulsated by virtue of the Existing One.

15
Through the undulation of the Throne and the sacred verses,
The Seat of exaltation began to disclose the concealed mysteries

16
Until the light of the fire dawning from the Throne of Bahá
Illuminated the heavens with a light as bright as the sun itself!

---

8. Thy (God's) wish to be known, as set forth in the ḥadí<u>th</u> of the Hidden Treasure.

9. Alluding once more to the fire that appeared to Moses, through which God conversed with Him.

17
Praised be that Ancient Beloved Whose divinity became visible,
The Self-Subsisting Monarch, the Omnipotent, the Venerable, besides Whom all else is as naught.

18
By the light from the sun of utterance, the entirety of creation became entranced!
O Thou the Bearer of the mystery of 'station,' the Beloved of every mystic knower,

19
I beseech the Eternal Beloved, the Ancient Lord, the Everlasting,
That I be empowered to reveal what is concealed in the stages of fidelity,

20
That by the command of the Ancient Beloved, I might direct aright the Cause of God
So that the mystery of 'returning to God'[10] might become apparent to all!

21
O God, by this power which Thou hath invested in the Lord of Holiness,
He hath rescued creation from vain imagination, superstitions, and speculations.

22
O Nightingale descended from paradise, illumine creation with Thy light!
Declare what Thou hast beheld among the countless concealed mysteries!

23
O Thou who dost hear the verses of God, a fire hath descended from the heavens!
Because of what hath been uttered, the sun of *Qadar* hath now emerged from concealment!"

10. A reference to Qur'án 2:46: "Who bear in mind the certainty that they are to meet their Lord, and that they are to return to Him."

POEM 44

The Fire of Tests

(The original poem begins on p. 415)

Much of this poem focuses on the idea that the Manifestation represents God Himself, as clearly indicated in verses 1–4 and 8–10. However, the concepts of God's transcendence and remoteness, and God's tests, justice, power, and revenge, are also alluded to with images such as "veil," "fire," and "sparks."

At the heart of the piece, however, is the notion of the constancy of the Prophet in His mission in spite of His foreknowledge of the tests He will endure, and the fact that He persists in His constancy as He experiences the tests, knowing full well that it is His fate is to be executed—something the Báb refers to many times in His tablets.

One other significant point regarding the possible ontological implications of the first verse is the "condition of being appointed," possibly referring to the preparation of the young Siyyid 'Alí-Muḥammad prior to the first intimations of His Revelation, or perhaps it refers to a preparation taking place in the stage of pre-existence in the realm of the spirit. The Bahá'í writings assert that the Manifestations, "unlike us, are pre-existent."[1]

1. From a letter written on behalf of Shoghi Effendi, dated 5 January 1948, quoted in *Lights of Guidance*, No. 1699, p. 504.

1
While in the condition of being appointed, He arose to uphold fidelity to God!
The King of the realm of Eternity[2] lamented, creating thereby both joy and sorrow!

2
Gaze with unblemished eyes at the veil of fire—
The mystery of certitude that hath appeared from the verses of the amity of justice![3]

3
Recite inspired[4] melodies and attract the world of "all else,"[5]
For God Himself is engaged in lamenting the fate of His incomparable King.[6]

4
Indeed, hearken to the call of God if thou hast an ardent desire for the choice wine,
Whose certitude derives from verses about the chastisement of justice![7]

---

2. The Manifestation.

3. "Justice" is a translation of *'adl,* which also means "reward" and "punishment." The word is a title the Báb gave to His Commentary on the Súrih of Joseph and to the Kitábu'r-Rúḥ (the Book of the Soul). Furthermore, the "Book of Justice" can be a reference to a short book by the Báb. As such, in this verse and the verses that follow, Ṭáhirih might be urging all to read one or both of these texts, perhaps the first one, which is among the most important texts written by the Báb. This is the same text that she taught her students in Karbila, and which she herself translated into Persian—a translation which most regretfully has been lost.

4. *Fiṭriyyih.* See glossary.

5. All other than God.

6. The Manifestation.

7. In numerous places, Bahá'u'lláh states that the twin pillars of justice and of education are reward and punishment. For example, "The structure of world stability and order hath been reared upon, and will continue to be sustained by, the twin pillars of reward and punishment. . . ." (*Gleanings,* no. 112.1.)

5
God! O Thou the Ancient, the Living, the Beloved Who art the Exalted!
Thou didst cause the Day of Resurrection to appear before the eyes of the beholders.

6
This perfect Figure with illustrious majesty
Incinerated the delusions of the deceivers from all of creation.

7
O Lord, I now behold how the mystery of Eternity hath appeared
In enlightening forms, with glory and confirmation!

8
O God, O Beauteous Lord, the Beloved, the Living. O Majesty!
Thine own Essence hath appeared on the face of the earth in the West![8]

9
O God, the Ancient Beloved, the Living, O Beneficent Friend,
Thine own Essence hath become clearly manifest on illuminating pages!

10
O God! O Lord of the Bayán! O Attraction of the dawning place of the Bayán!
Thine own Essence hath appeared from the fiery enchantments!

11
O God! Solely through Thy command is this powerful One constant![9]
None except Thee occupy His every thought!

---

8. The "west," as Saiedi points out, can be referring to Shiraz: "In a number of places, including Seven Proofs, the Báb explains that His reference to the rising of the sun from the west refers to His own rise from Shiraz (*Fárs*), because His Revelation occurred at the end of the Islamic Dispensation, which is the sunset (the 'west') of Islam"(*Gate of the Heart*, p. 361).

9. In the Kitáb-i-Íqán, Bahá'u'lláh gives as one of the major proofs of the Manifestations, Their constancy in proclaiming the Word in spite of all They are made to endure: "Another proof and evidence of the truth of this Revelation, which amongst all other proofs shineth as the sun, is the constancy of the eternal Beauty in proclaiming the Faith of God" (¶257).

12
O God, by Thy rays of light, this world hath become replete with splendors of Revelation!
O My Living Lord, Thou Forgiver, revive all the souls who have fallen to the ground!

13
O God, O Thou the Avenger, the Just, the world is replete with fiery sparks!
The devouring flame of oppressors is obscuring the truth with images of Cimmerian shade.

14
O Thou Bird abiding in Paradise, devise melodies from our songs!
Uprear the dusty veils from the robes of those illuminated souls!

15
From the inspired verses, recite marvelous melodies
To absorb imaginations and inspirations from the countenance of the Sun of Certitude,

16
And say: "At your beckoning and amidst Thy tests,[10] I burn away the veils of vain imaginings!"
O Beloved, I approach Thee even as do the most humble among Thy creatures.

10. *Bidá'* here alludes to a change in God's plan and command that causes tests for the believers.

POEM 45

Now It Is as It Was

(The original poem begins on p. 413)

This enigmatic and elliptical poem is about the relationship of the Manifestation with God and Creation. It is extremely abstruse and is completely situated in the metaphysical realm of ideas and spiritual relationships and theological concepts. The difficulty derives from the fact that it is a discourse portraying, in mystical terms from a ḥadíth, the relationship between the divine and the human aspects of the Manifestation in His function as an intermediary or Vicegerent of God.

Verses 1–4 allude to the detachment of the Manifestations from the world of existence and how They are fully absorbed by the divine. This concept resembles the portrayal of the attraction of the Manifestation to the Maid of Heaven (a personification of the Holy Spirit) in the revealed works of both the Báb and Bahá'u'lláh.

In verse 3 of the poem, Ṭáhirih makes a reference to a ḥadíth that requires a rather detailed explanation. In this verse, when the reality of the Manifestation is attracted by God, the Manifestation enters the realm of veils—that which conceals the divine. But despite the veils, He sees that He (God) "*is as it was*" (*kamá kána yakún*). This phrase is an allusion to a ḥadíth that has been often recounted in similar terms, and is commonly articulated as, "There was God and nothing was with Him," followed by a Ṣúfí saint's response "now it is the same as it was."

This succinct but somewhat abstruse observation alludes to the absolute singleness (*aḥadíyyat*) of God. Stated more directly, it denotes the eternal transcendence of God and the fact that God is unknowable except as He chooses to manifest His names and attributes in the world of creation. Otherwise, God is alone and, relatively speaking, nothing else beside Him exists, and in that sense He is "the Existing One" (*má yakún*) as referred to in various verses of this poem. Even when He chooses to Manifest His attributes, His essence ever remains unknowable. (See endnotes for further information about this poem.)

1
When the intoxicated One of Eternity became cleansed of vain imaginings and infirmities,
He instantly imbibed the pure water of mysteries.

2
He beheld the holy divine verses from the illumination of the Countenance of God
Veiled within the verses of the "Existing One."[1]

3
With delight[2] He approached nearer to the glorious attraction of God
Until He pierced the veils and beheld "*is as it was*"!

4
Then He became devoid of self as He sensed the benevolence of God
And was utterly absorbed by a single glance of His Beloved!

5
O God, O Praiseworthy Lord! O True One with Thy veracious call!
O God, the Vicegerent, unconstrained in His order and plan,

---

1. *Má yakún*. See glossary.
2. *Ibtihá'* literally means "pride." But it seems that Ṭáhirih here uses the word in the sense of "glory" inasmuch as the word derives from the word *bahá*.

6
From the mysteries of *'Amá*, from the arc of return, He came,
The Knower of the mysteries of the realm of being, aware of the mystery of existence!

7
He completely rent asunder all the veils, descended from the realm of *'Amá!*
Engendering the dawn and illumination, He became established in the realm of *Nún*.

8
He beheld the mysteries of *Qadar* and the hidden verses.
The mystery then became plain, devoid of life's changes and chances.[3]

9
He discerned that whatever He might desire from God, the Lord had already made manifest for Him in creation,
That with but an amorous glance and a wink of the eye, all became realized throughout the earth.

10
Then, with the attraction of the forgiving God, He rotated the sphere of light,
And in accordance with their receptivity,[4] He revealed the verses of Sinai.

11
And because of His fidelity, He chose to be immersed in a sea of calamities,
And, with fiery dalliance, to become dissevered from all save God!

---

3. *Rayb-i-manún.* A term used in Qur'án 52:30. "Or do they say:—'A Poet! we await for him some calamity (hatched) by Time!'"

4. Qur'án 84:19: "that you shall certainly ascend from one state after another," a passage which some have interpreted as "making gradual progress." (Maulana Ali, pp. 1159–60)

12
He said, "O Thou Omnipotent God, the Helper, the One, the Victorious,
Because I am but one among the Chosen,[5] accept me, O Thou the most Merciful of the Merciful.

13
O Lord of the Ka'bih, through Thine infinite benevolence, rescue the people of peace[6] in their Return[7]
Who, in meeting their Lord proclaim, "*We verily shall return to Thee!*"

14
"O Rúmí's Reed! Verily, disperse the veils from their midst!
Within the tablets of the Bayán, proclaim, "We all arise in Thy presence!"[8]

5. *Idhn,* meaning "permission." The word is used in the Qur'án to refer to the special permission granted the Prophet by God to bring forth a Revelation (40:78, 14:11).

6. Muslims.

7. In their return to this world in the Day of Resurrection.

8. Arising from tombs in the Day of Resurrection and standing before God.

POEM 46

Unto God Shall We All Return!

(The original poem begins on p. 411)

This short poem seems to be continuing the theologically intense discourse of the previous poem. In this sense, we can imagine that it is a discourse that takes place after the Manifestation of God agrees to endure all the calamities and suffering He will experience on earth, and prays to be accepted by God for His mission of reviving the Muslims. The poem thus begins by describing the severe and unfortunate persecutions that follow this request by the Manifestation of God but ends with the glad tidings of the glorious outcome that will occur after these persecutions as a result of the constancy of the Manifestation and His followers in proclaiming the Faith of God.

1
Alláh, after this acceptance, there was a setting of the sun
amid the flames of rejection afflicting all the people of certitude,

2
Flames showered brightly from the rivers of those deceivers
Engulfing the enlightened ones—those adorned with glory, majesty, and faith!

3
From this spark, oppression such as no ear hath heard since the beginning of time
Hath taken place, as is apparent in the descent of this conflagration!

4
O God, O knowing Lord, O Thou the living and ancient Beloved,
Through Thine all-encompassing benevolence, rescue these unworthy followers.

5
O Bird of Paradise, O Thou Who doth resuscitate the dried bones,
Remove the veil from the verse "Unto God shall we all return."[1]

6
By the command of the Beloved of the Bayán, Glad tidings are descending to all wayfarers from the heavens, "*To all those who patiently persevere.*"[2]

1. Qur'án 2:155–56: "Be sure We shall test you with something of fear and hunger, some loss in goods or lives or the fruits (of your toil), but give glad tidings to those who patiently persevere. Who say, when afflicted with calamity: 'To Alláh we belong, and to Him is our return.'"
2. Ibid.

POEM 47

The Accounting

(The original poem begins on p. 410)

1
Cause the drops of Sinai[1] to be precisely ordered!
Indeed, discover in this book the elucidating verses.

2
Announce the renovation instigated throughout the earth
Now that the Day of God hath emerged from the realm of exaltation![2]

3
Depict the wondrous, refined handiwork wrought by the Most Great Creator
That hath been made to appear again through the Sinai of Command from the Transcendent God!

4
By the shadow of His creation, whatsoever is not of God hath ceased to exist.
Nothing pertaining to the sanctity of holiness remains except for Him.

---

1. See glossary for *Ṭúr*.
2. *Rafá'í* is a reference to Qur'án 19:57 and similar verses.

5
This power derived from the exalted edifice[3]
will most certainly discard whosoever doth oppose the luminescence of His Beauty.

6
Know now that descending from the heaven of command is a fire
That burns whosoever renounces divine guidance.

7
Indeed, the alluring Point appeared from behind the black veil,
And through attraction to the Countenance, doth absorb all that is ungodly.

8
And why? By virtue of the Cause of God having appeared in the past
With the light of exaltation and proofs from the Heavenly Realm.

9
Whosoever heard His call and chose the path of self-denial,
Through God's attraction became the splendor of the illumination of proofs!

10
Not so for him who hath chosen the path of remoteness![4]
For him a period of respite will be bestowed

11
So that in striving to attain a state of purity, he mighteth yet become reformed,
Perceive that which is manifest from the garment of transcendence,

12
And behold Him Who doth reside on the carpet of holiness with divine glorification,
And by His light, survey all horizons refulgent with His radiance.

---

3. *Ṣaráḥání* is perhaps a reference to Qur'án 27:44.

4. *Ghabar* also means "dust," as in Qur'án 80:40, describing the faces smeared with dust in the Day of Resurrection.

POEM 48

I Call on Thee, My God

(The original poem begins on p. 409)

Having assessed the impact of the Revelation on preparing the way for the transformation and unification of humankind, Ṭáhirih now returns to the very personal lyric form of self-examination. For stalwart and unshakeable as her faith may be, she unabashedly poses questions to herself and to God about her own readiness for the further torment that is to follow. She also assesses her life—a natural course of events as this life ends and the afterlife begins.

This and the next several poems are dramatic in their frank and honest supplication to God for assistance and mercy. Naturally, the reader is called upon to ponder whether these plaints represent Ṭáhirih's own concerns, or simply establish for us how we should emulate her humility and candor in assessing our own lives.

The climax of these three personal reflections is poem 50, in which Ṭáhirih becomes reconciled with her own status and rejoices in the recounting of this milestone in human history. In poem 51, she returns to her role as teacher, historian, and expounder as she beseeches all to take note of what has taken place.

1

O Thou Whose judgment rendereth justice for all who are without aid!
For those who have no help, all relief must derive from Thee!

2
O My God, no witness is there for me other than Thee,
For without Thee, I am bereft of all equity and justice.

3
I have rotated around in this elliptical orbit!
I have descended to the uttermost depths[1]

4
So that Thy proof might become evident in the physical realm,
And as an answer to supplications, might become apparent in the minutest particle!

5
By the truth of Thy veracity, which is omnipotent and assisting,
No more strength can be extracted from me that I might charge ahead!

6
Through Thy benevolence, make me emerge from the turmoil of adversity
That I might be exalted to the height of holiness, cleansed from the dust of affliction!

7
Thou doth witness what issueth forth from the dew drops of Divine decree,
How from the *há* it hath emerged to burn away all needless existence.

8
O God, Thou dost behold how in every concealed instance,
It cleanseth me with a fire that doth consume every worthless earthly treasure.

---

1. Literally "the depth of *samak*." *Samak* ("fish") is a symbol for the earthly realm; the ancients believed the earth to be placed on a fish. *Samak,* symbolizing the lowest point in the universe, is used by Rúmí several times.

9
Because Thou art the Omnipotent God, aid me through Thy benevolence
That I might become purified from every speck of dust.

10
Thou hast borne witness to the afflictions I have endured!
All these hath been encountered in the path of my love and affection for Thee!

11
O Thou the Knower, it is an easy task for Thee to rescue me now,
For Thy most great benevolence hath been revealed in the Bayán![2]

---

2. The sense here may be that inasmuch as the Revelation of the Báb is secured now that His revealed work has been completed and copied, her central task in explicating the teachings and accumulating followers has been accomplished.

POEM 49

Rescue Me!

(The original poem begins on p. 407)

1
O Thou the Omnipotent and Benevolent God,
O Thou the Powerful, the Self-subsisting, O Thou the Living and Testing One!

2
Because I am entirely shamefaced, rescue me with Thy grace!
Because I am overwhelmed, I cannot look into Thine eyes!

3
How long must I be a captive and imprisoned?
Protect me, O Thou the Powerful, the Living, the Omnipotent.

4
O God, because I am consumed with fire, rescue me through Thy benevolence!
O God, purify me from every concern about the things of this world.

5
My impatience hath caused me to become worthless,
Hath made the Sinaitic fire in my heart grow cold!

POEM 50

This Wondrous Panorama

(The original poem begins on p. 407)

1
Pour into my heart but a drop of the camphor of Paradise,
Or totally consume me with the light from the Sinaitic fire,

2
Recount for me the mystery concealed in the letter *Há!*[1]
Cause the friends to become completely ecstatic and transformed by the letter *nún!*[2]

3
Remove now the veil through the ecstasy of the Creator!
Thereby bestow the meaning of abstruse words in the scriptures of old!

4
With the frail sound of the feeble bee, by the melodious fluttering of its wings,
Cause those sacred texts to reveal completely the upheaval of the Day of Resurrection!

1. See glossary.
2. See glossary.

5
O Thou observer, behold with but a fleeting glance
Behind this splendid veil, the One Who appeareth in this panorama!

6
With a distinctive melody, portray the allure of the Point,
How It caused Thee to ascend from this crimson world![3]

7
O Thou Holy Bird, Thou Who doth possess a renewed vision,
This beauteous splendor hath totally absorbed me!

8
It is as if the entire world hath become but a reflection of His face!
Indeed, in the vast panorama, naught exists but that countenance!

9
In a dazzling manner, with a divine splendor,
It dawned with morning light in the abode of the heart.

10
O Thou observer, examine this with thy spiritual eyes!
Tell me truthfully, to whom doth this Countenance belong?

11
O Thou Celestial Bird and O Thou Divine Splendor,
How abstruse this subtle point is in the text!

12
I have become obliterated by what hath appeared at this moment in time!
Because of my knowledge of the Most Powerful, I have fallen from the heights!

---

3. Blood-smeared or contentious, because the earth has become stained with the blood of contending peoples.

13
That beauteous stature! That alluring countenance!
This region and this radiance in this vista and throughout creation!

14
It is as if I beheld Aḥmad, the King of Kings, with all His power,
But Who now hath appeared in another land, exalted in His comeliness and might!

15
Alláh, at this instant that splendor hath become entirely illustrious!
By means of the light from that face, the world hath become majestic and astounding!

16
This is her holiness Zahrá[4] on the throne of Beauty!
The world hath become glorious and majestic from the reflection of her face!

17
O Lord, through the sanctity of Zahrá, bestow on us a glance
That through Thy benevolent glimpse, I might tread Thy path with utmost splendor!

---

4. See glossary.

POEM 51

The Dawn of Thy Splendor

(The original poem begins on p. 405)

1
Lo! By the Grace of God, O thou who doth hear the divine verses,
Become completely attentive to that which hath been revealed by the spark at dawn!

2
Discern how the sun of knowledge hath emerged from the *'Amá* of holiness
That thou mayest become cleansed from whatsoever thou hast observed before!

3
Be vigilant now! Be acquainted with what hath been revealed from verses in the East!
From God hath now appeared that which is neither of the East nor the West.[1]

4
O Thou Beholder, discount now whatsoever thou hast observed before,
For glad tidings are now descending upon you from the vast realm of the Transcendent One!

---

1. See glossary for "East nor West."

5
Behold how God, the Most Great, hath become illumined with glory and majesty,
The Friend of God[2] Who manifests flawlessly all the divine attributes.

6
All the veils will be consumed by the blazing flash of His Countenance!
Creation itself hath become illumined by the dawning of this sign for all the peoples of the world!

7
Say: Praised be He, the Beloved, the Omnipotent, the Most Beauteous,
He who hath fashioned creation anew upon the expanse of the earth

8
Such that the entirety of existence hath been obliterated with but a single spark of effulgence
Which He hath made manifest by virtue of the Sun of His justice.

9
O God, by virtue of these detached souls with their beauteous faces,
Those who exist solely by virtue of Him Who truly exists,

10
Release me now from the station of earthly ascendancy!
Enable me to attain the exaltation and might of the station of true majesty!

11
No purpose exists for me besides Thee, and I have no beloved but Thee!
Thou dost bear witness to my condition! Indeed, Thou beholdest all that occurs.

---

2. A title for Muḥammad and an allusion to the Báb.

12
In this very poem, I am singing melodies that speak of Thee
In the hope that this terrestrial realm might become illumined by the dawn of Thy splendor!

13
God! O God! By Thine unconstrained grace, bestow upon me a glance
That I might become separated from all the separated ones!

POEM 52

Speak Thou, O Rúmí's Reed

(The original poem begins on p. 403)

Except for the concluding verses (verses 16–19), which are in the form of prayer to God—as is often the case with Ṭáhirih's poems—this poem is addressing Rúmí's reed (*qaṣabiyi-Rúmmíyyih*). The speaker reminds the reed that the Beloved has appeared in the clouds; that is, the station of the Manifestation of God has appeared (verses 1–2). Subsequently the poet explains to the reed the magnitude and nature of the events of the Day of Resurrection with the appearance of the Qá'im, (verses 3–14).

In verse 15, Ṭáhirih praises the reed for its melodies, tunes adored by the Beloved, and praises its reunion with the Beloved. Then in verses 16–18, Ṭáhirih prays to God to help her understand the various melodies of the reed that she might assist all the Bábís to understand them as well. Finally, in the last verse, she praises God for permitting such a Revelation to descend from the divine realm.

The term "Rúmí's reed" is seen in multiple poems by Ṭáhirih (poems 19 and 21 of the *Quickening* and poems 17 and 45 of this volume). It can be understood as the reality of the Manifestations of God, or alternatively, the divine reality of Ṭáhirih herself. We come across the word "*qaṣab*" ("reed" or "pen") in the Báb's writings as well. Considering the connotations of the term as it is employed in Ṭáhirih's poems, "Rúmí's reed" resembles other terms she utilizes repeatedly in other poems, such as her figurative use of the bird: "the Bird of Paradise" (*ṭeyr-i-ṭúbá'í*) in poems 5, 7, and 46; "the Bird of Holiness" (*ṭeyr-i-qudsí*) in poem 33; the "Bird of *'Amá*" in poem 9; and the "Bird of *Qadar*" in poem 34. (See endnotes for further information about this poem.)

1
O Rúmí's reed, enkindled with sparks, begin to speak forth about what you see!
Behold the face of thy Beloved made manifest among the people of *'Amá*!

2
By the grace of God, the tablets of the Bayán are raining down
From the bounteous cloud[1] to revive the souls of the dry bones!

3
Know that with certainty and without a doubt, the Day of Resurrection hath appeared!
Except for the Primal Point, nothing remaineth explained in the world.

4
Praised be God! Replete with sparks, how He doth stir up tumult in this world!
Such astounding power hath become manifest! Exalted be God for this clear proof!

5
From remoteness and hopelessness, the Standard of Victory hath become manifest,
But in the manner of the abasement, He hath fallen amongst those with darkened faces.[2]

6
Behold, O Most Great Beholder! How, by the allure of the Divine countenance,
The point hath been inscribed on the Tablet of wisdom among the fallen ones.

1. See glossary for *'Amá*.
2. See the term "Dust" in the glossary.

7
Exalted be Alláh, God the Hearer, the Powerful, the Omnipotent!
What magnificent and lucid verses have been revealed!

8
Indeed, O observer, harken attentively to His rapturous melodies,
How the world is in conflagration, set ablaze by the rays from the teeming fire!

9
Those who attend His banquet will instantly find refuge in its sparks,
But for the adversaries, these same flames will deny them refuge.[3]

10
Learn about His design—concealed ere now—according to the measure determined by the Exalted God,[4]
How the Qá'im is preparing to emerge from hiding by permission of the Powerful, the Victorious One.

11
Harken to His crying out "O Ye People!" to those who bore false witness against Him!
All of them collapsed, mortified once they beheld the fidelity of the Bábís!

12
Say: Praised be the Lord our God, the Avenger, the Almighty!
Now is that very same arduous Day, that most arduous of Days!

---

3. This is a good example of the dual and ostensibly contradictory symbolic uses of fire. It is a cleansing force, the power of renewal and regeneration, but also these same flames will consume antiquated beliefs and destroy those who cannot understand the fire's meaning.

4. Qur'án 20:15: "Verily the Hour is coming—My design is to keep it hidden—for every soul to receive its reward by the measure of its Endeavour."

13
Hearken again, O ye who have plunged into the Ocean of Transcendence!
Godliness hath appeared in the veil of *Há*[5] from the garment of *Bá*[6]

14
And what doth He say? If He doth appear that the concealed fire might become manifest,
Then must ye arise and heed not those who dissemble.

15
O Reed, thy joyful melody is heartily adored by the beloved!
Now is thy reunion also desired by Him who hath descended among the peoples!

16
Thou art familiar with the melody of the Adored One, the Powerful, the Omnipotent!
There is none except thee who can comprehend the mystery of His utterance!

17
It is because of your truth that He hath hoisted the veils!
He hath disclosed all the mysteries in His diverse voices.

18
O Beloved God, explain what He doth say, the One who hath now descended to renew the earth,
So that I might cause all Bábís to become witnesses to His utterance.

19
Praised be Thou, O God, the Powerful, the Omnipotent, the Most Powerful,
For the bounty that hath descended from the realm of *'Amá* in the presence of the people of *Há!*

5. See glossary.
6. See glossary.

POEM 53

Disclosing the Hidden Treasure

(The original poem begins on p. 401)

This poem is an elucidation of the three differing stations of the Manifestation of God—the station of Essential Unity, the station of Vicegerency (or Intermediary), and the station of Distinction (His human appearance). In referring to the Intermediary station, the poem alludes to "the Point" or the transcendent essence of God as made manifest in the realm of Creation. In this station, the Manifestation has the capacity to reveal divine mysteries, though incrementally at the appropriate times in the course of human history. As mentioned in so many previous poems in this collection, this particular time is a critical turning point in human advancement and is characterized as "the Day of Resurrection."

The poem is in the form of a conversation between the Holy Spirit and the Manifestation. Thus it focuses on the unique station and power of the Manifestation to bear the burden of perfectly manifesting the powers and attributes of God in the material world, the realm of creation or existence. As in Poem 43, this piece focuses on the process of the revelation of the divine or the Hidden Mystery. As such, the words "mystery" (*sirr*) and mysteries (*asrár*) appear abundantly in the poem. Likewise, "revealing" (*tibyán*)—referring to disclosure of the divine mysteries in the world of existence through divine verses—appears multiple times.

The poem begins with the divine aspect of the Manifestation (the Holy Spirit) proclaiming His Hidden Mystery and how He created Adam—a symbol for all Manifestations of God—and ends with the human aspect of the Manifestation praying for assistance to be able to perform the function of revealing the hidden divine mysteries.

1
I am that Bright Light that from eternity hath been concealed!
I am that Mystery of mysteries that from eternity hath been intended!

2
I am I, and no other creator hath existed except My Essence!
In the presence of the Crimson Point,[1] I assume the attribute of Unity.

3
O fiery Point bestowing ecstasy in this Day,
Know that nothing exists in Thy revelation[2] except My Essence!

4
As a testimony to My benevolence, I brought creation into existence!
I caused Adam to struggle in manifesting the mystery of my craftsmanship!

5
I enjoined him to exert every effort and endure every hardship to sanctify and praise Me,
that the mystery of creation might become unveiled among all created things!

6
As I searched with eyes of unalloyed love and mercy for those with capacities,[3]
I found none in existence among all those in the realm of creation,

1. See glossary.

2. *Tibyán.* In Qur'án 16:89, referring to the Qur'án itself: "and We have sent down to thee the Book explaining all things, a Guide, a Mercy, and Glad Tidings to Muslims."

3. *Qavábil,* a Ṣúfí term in Ibn-'Arabí's philosophy (*Fuṣúṣ'ul-Ḥikam,* vol. 1, pp. 3–4), mentioned by 'Abdu'l-Bahá in the Tablet of the Hidden Treasure.

7
Not one who might withstand the burden of manifesting the mystery of creation,
Not one whose stature[4] itself would bespeak the glory of creation.

8
Thus, I averted my glance, disregarded the world of existence,
And fashioned the foundation of all creation to praise and proclaim Me![5]

9
I then concealed My mystery in the essence of the yellow clot[6]
Until the time of its maturation arrived in fifty-thousand years.[7]

10
Then, with but a single verse, I elucidated the mystery of the Eternal One.
Exalted be God for this endowment! Glory be God for this revelation!

11
O hearer, I was the same One who appeared in the form of Aḥmad,[8]
But every aspect of my authority was entirely concealed within that clot!

12
At that point in time, I then created another realm, a transformed one!
In revealed verses I made clear and comprehensible all the mysteries!

---

4. Qur'án 95:4: "We have indeed created man in the best of moulds."

5. Qur'án 17:44: "The seven heavens and the earth, and all beings therein, declare His glory: there is not a thing but celebrates His praise (*Ḥamd*) . . ."

6. Qur'án 75:38: "Then did he become a leech-like clot; then did (Alláh) make and fashion (him) in due proportion." See also 23:14, 40:67, and 22:5 about the process of the creation of a human being that begins with a clot in the womb. Ṭáhirih interprets these verses, alluding to the process of progressive revelation.

7. A reference to the Day of Resurrection, as in Qur'án 70:4: "The angels and the spirit ascend unto him in a Day the measure whereof is (as) fifty thousand years."

8. A title for Muḥammad.

13
Exalted be God, the Potent, the Omnipotent, the Most Powerful!
The Glory of God is that Countenance that hath dawned in Cancer.[9]

14
I swear by Mine exalted Essence that none other than Myself
Was able to convey Mine utterance in the world of existence.

15
Harken to His entrancing singing that doth entirely quell perplexity:
"I am that hidden fire that was formerly veiled in concealment!

16
I am that conflagration of flames! I am that animating spark!
I am not merely a condition[10] of justice! I am justice itself, absolute justice!

17
I am sanctified beyond all comparisons in every revealed verse!
I subsist solely by the command of God made manifest in each Dispensation!

18
Whosoever hath chosen to desire Me, by My bidding
Shalt arise, awaiting My command, detached from both heart and soul!

19
Then shalt he whose nature deriveth from the flame of deceit
Become subdued so that the True Point might be revealed.

---

9. Cancer is a reference to the constellation in which the sun appears at the beginning of summer. An allusion to the intensity of the light of Revelation in this unique Day of God.

10. In this verse, the imagery relating to "fire," "spark," "just," and "justice" alludes to the transcendent aspect of God, the divine aspect of the Manifestation of God. "The Just" is among the names of God that point to His transcendence (Sachico Murata, *The Tao of Islam,* p. 690).

20
By my command He will ascend to His rightful station,
Will assert the truth that false ones have pilfered from the verses!

21
He will know that on this day, unconstrained by any limitations,
He shalt be established by command of the Lord on High!"

22
O God, the provider, the most powerful, behold my condition, O Thou my helper!
Provide me with assistance that I might espouse Thy mystery in the world of being

23
That I might become known for praising Thee in these sublime moments!
That I might render everyone unconscious and intoxicated by Thine attributes!

POEM 54

Or Nearer

(The original poem begins on p. 398)

This extremely well-constructed poem starts and ends with a reference to the Qur'ánic verses describing Muḥammad's Night Journey, or Miraj, as recounted in Súrih 17:1 and alluded to in Súrih 53:8–9: "Then he approached and came closer, / And was at a distance of but two bow-lengths or (even) nearer." This verse relates to the point in the narrative when Muḥammad approached God as near as was possible. Verses 1–4 of the poem are focused on praising Muḥammad—a reference to the Báb, Who appears as the return of Muḥammad and with this same station of attaining nearness to God ("or nearer"), and, Who, by means of His appearance has caused the entire world to become illumined and resurrected. The remaining verses of the poem are, in effect, rhetorical questions Ṭáhirih poses to God about these events, except for the last two verses in which she prays to God that she be deserving of witnessing the events.

1
The exalted *Thaná'* which is issued from the highest station of the exalted Source
Is deserving of ascent to the height of nearness to the Lord of "*or nearer.*"

2
He is the Friend,[1] the *Ḥamd* of God, the Beneficent, the One, the Powerful,
He without Whose Countenance, nothing in creation would exist.

3
His holy splendor doth shine forth from the Green Tablet!
The sign of His grandeur doth dawn from the garment of "*or nearer.*"

4
How wondrous this world hath become prostrate in ecstasy from praising Him!
This joyous ingathering[2] throughout the world, this spark of fire in the universe.

5
Hath the mystery of the Resurrection appeared in the world?
Hath the Countenance of the Beloved appeared from the *'Amá* of *há?*

6
Hath a new composition now appeared in the universe,[3]
So that from the exalted throne, the clamor of exaltation is heard?[4]

7
Perhaps Thou hast made manifest Thy once hidden splendor
With which the entire earth hath become ignited by a spark from His Beauteous Face!

8
Perhaps the station of glory that was enfolded in Thy decree
Hath now been spread abroad by Thy command from the exalted Throne!

---

1. The "Friend of God" (*Ḥabíbu'lláh*) is a title for the Prophet Muḥammad, here referring to the Báb as the embodiment of Muḥammad.
2. See glossary.
3. Composition; edifice (*baná*), as in Qur'án 40:64 and 2:22.
4. The joyful state of the believers in paradise: Qur'án 54:54–55.

9
Perhaps that unknowable Essence concealed from eternity hath appeared,
Made manifest by Thee through Thy beneficence in this realm of dust!

10
Perhaps the Hidden Mystery, concealed ere now by Thee,
Hath been made by Thee to appear through Thy Grace and Bestowal, O Beloved of *há!*

11
Perhaps, O Alláh, that Hidden Point which was concealed by Thee
Hath, through Thy glance, been made to ascend that it might behold Thee!

12
O my God, release me from all else through the truth of Thy Holy Essence!
O my Exalted Lord, guide me toward the House of Thine exaltation

13
So that I will not be negligent of the Beloved for even a moment
And might discover the joy of Thy nearness to the extent of "*or nearer*"!

POEM 55

The Timeliness of Disclosure

(The original poem begins on p. 396)

In the first six lines of this poem, Ṭáhirih expresses gratitude to God and indicates that His grace to her is so great at a time when all the people are as the dead in their graves. She also expresses gratitude that she can speak out, even though she is aware of her own limitations. With complete self-effacement, she beseeches God to release her from the contentiousness and disputes and to lead her to a condition of ecstasy and joy.

In verses 7–11 she reminds the seeker of truth—or perhaps herself as well—to be fully detached from self and base desires in order to recognize the glorious signs in the verses of the Báb and to comprehend their spiritual meaning. However, in the last two verses she reminds the seeker that it is not yet timely to disclose the full station of the Báb and all that can be discerned in His glorious verses, because God's mysteries are necessarily revealed by degrees and at the appointed time. This caution to others, and to herself, demonstrates the eagerness of Ṭáhirih to reveal the true station of the Báb, even though she is aware that for now she must restrain herself. (See endnotes for further information about this poem.)

1

Thou dost bear witness that for me there is no beloved but Thee!
Neither have I any goal in either world but Thee, the One True God!

2
It is through Thy most abundant grace that I am able to speak in such a Day
When the entire world is benumbed, all unconscious in this moribund place!

3
I see myself as being so ignorant in this plane of existence
That among the entirety of creation, none is more ignorant than I!

4
In all my conditions, Thou art the Powerful, the Helper, the one True God!
Thou the Beloved, the Desired One, dost behold my recognition of Thee!

5
Thus, O Very God, release me from the arguments of the contentious ones!
O God, enable me to attain the banquet of grandeur and ecstasy

6
That I might behold all the mysteries of truth,
That I might behold with joy the evidence of Thine appearances!

7
O thou seeker who dost embody the condition of purity,
Behold in the sacred realm the splendor of the hallowed One!

8
Observe what glorious verses are fashioned by His Bahá,
What praise doth dawn from His Praise!

9
Behold those with illumined faces and erect frames,
Standing row upon row, obedient to whatsoever the Beloved ordaineth!

10
Glance once more and examine clearly—what dost thou behold in this panorama?
But breathe not a word until He appeareth with Glory and Majesty!

11
Because the mystery of God must be manifest suddenly,
For now, there doth not exist another way to achieve it!

POEM 56

The Fire of Devotion

(The original poem begins on p. 395)

As a logical consequence of the principle of gradualness alluded to in the previous poem, the declaration of the appearance of the Manifestation must be withheld or concealed until it is appropriate or timely. As has been mentioned, the Báb declared Himself by stages or degrees, first as the Qá'im and ultimately as the author of an independent Revelation. In this poem, the speaker (most probably Ṭáhirih) beseeches the Bird of Paradise to reveal the full station of the Báb that the people of the world might be awakened from their spiritual slumber and lassitude.

1
O Thou the One True God, my True Friend, my Exalted Beloved!
O Solace of mine eyes, O joyous Spirit Who hath appeared in the Most Great Vista![1]

1. The Most Great Vista (*Manẓar-i-Akbar*) is a term similar to the Most Exalted Vista (*Manẓar-i-A'lá*), a Ṣúfí term referring to the place where God manifests Himself and invites all in paradise to witness Him. (Javád Nurbakhsh, *Farhang-i-Núr-Bakhsh Iṣṭiláḥát-i-Taṣavvuf*, vol. 2, p. 175).

2
I behold manifest in the world—which is the dawning place—the Mystery of Mysteries!
There is none other like Him—He Who is the Ancient, the Omnipotent, the Exalted!

3
O My God, Who is this Beloved Whose attraction begets such ecstasy,
He, O My God, Who hath aroused such desire that all have plummeted into the fire?

4
Indeed, though they boil and burn, it is a pleasure for them
To smolder in their devotion for Him in this wondrous conflagration of God!

5
O Bird of Paradise, if Thou dost peruse the tablet of the Bayán,
The mystery concealed since creation will now become evident!

6
O My Beloved, indeed I have perused all the tablets,
But did not discern such an attraction for the people amongst all the precious bestowals,

7
Unless it be from Thee, Who hath brought such a Cause into the world
And hath set aflame creation so that all else seems as naught!

8
O Thou One True God, through His Cause, make sober those entranced by His beauty
So that I might behold Thy face in an evident expression of Thy mystery, O Alláh!

POEM 57

"Ye Shall Hear and not Understand"[1]

(The original poem begins on p. 394)

In this poem, Ṭáhirih focuses on the notion of the oneness of God—an important area of discourse in Islamic theology and mysticism. "Oneness" (*tawḥíd*) is what separates the believer in the singleness of God from the idle worshiper (*mus͟hrik*) who believes that God is dispersed throughout creation and thus assumes "partners with God," the antithesis of what is perhaps the major theme of the Qur'án.

Islamic mystics have assigned great importance to oneness and have described it with phrases like "the pinnacle of all sciences," "the light of both worlds," "the divider between the friend and the enemy," and "the first sign of the existence of Reality."[2] But Muslim thinkers have also raised many questions in relation to this concept. Can God be said to be one, or is the

1. A prophecy by Isaiah cited by Christ regarding the Pharisees in Matthew 13:14.

2. *Kas͟hfu'l-Asrár,* quoted in Siyyid Ṣádiq Gawharin, *S͟harḥ-i-Iṣṭiláḥát-i-Taṣavvuf,* vol. 3, p. 293.

transcendent God sanctified from such attributions? They also raise questions regarding the relationship between the transcendent One and the multiplicities that exist in the world of creation, between the divine and the prophets, or the divine and human beings. For example, can human beings lose their earthly identity by being fully detached from the multiplicities of the world of creation, thereby becoming conjoined with the divine oneness? If so, can one willfully achieve this state through purity of heart, by praiseworthy actions, or through attaining a state of mystical ecstasy?

These are some of the questions—contemplated by Ṣúfís, mystics, and religious believers—that have prompted meditation on the ideas of the oneness of God or the unity of being (*vaḥdatu'l-vujúd*). In this poem Ṭáhirih addresses some of these questions, making references to certain speculations of the Islamic thinkers and mystics in addition to the writings of the Báb. In effect, she is advocating a unity of being, a concept that contradicts beliefs commonly held in Ṣúfí schools of thought.

Ṭáhirih uses two words in relation to the concept of the unity, singleness, or oneness of God. The first is *tawḥid*—meaning "monotheism" or "the declaration of God to be One"—which we have translated as "Oneness." The second word, *vaḥdat,* means "oneness," "singleness," and "unity," and we have translated it as "Unity." She also refers in various verses of the poem to several types of *tawḥid* as defined by mystics. For example, in the first verses, while addressing the Bird of Paradise—a symbol here of her own spiritual station—she alludes to the philosophical question of the relationship between transcendence and immanence, that is, the oneness of God *(tawḥíd)* and the multiplicity of reality and names in the world of existence. In verse 4, she equates oneness *(tawḥíd)* with unity (*vaḥdat*) and uses these two terms interchangeably throughout the rest of the poem.

Subsequently, in verses 5–16 she reminds the Bird of Paradise—again, her own spiritual consciousness—to acquire the qualities of true belief in the oneness of God. In these verses she refers to several definitions of *tawḥid* by the Ṣúfís. In verses 17–28, she describes her observations about the many who claim to believe in the oneness of God but who are superficial in the confession of their beliefs. Finally, in verses 29–31, she asks the bird to witness how the emblems of belief in the oneness of God *(tawḥíd)* are reflecting glorious divine realities in the holy mirrors of their own selves. (See endnotes for further information about this poem.)

1
O Bird of Paradise, with melodious utterances,
Recount the stories of the Holy Ones!

2
First speak about the divine transcendence of the Incomparable Essence!
Render joyful those attuned to Thy words!

3
Because creation hath become realized through the Divine Unity,
The entire world hath been generated by Its grace!

4
For inasmuch as this Divine Unity implies Oneness,
It is the annihilator of any basis for infidelity[3] or belief in duality!

5
Thou must be truthful in Thy pronouncements
Through light emanating from the Glorious Mirrors,

6
Your deeds should be the proof of Oneness,
Not disputation, whispering, slander, or clamor.

7
Since Thy banquet of Oneness is so exalted,
The condition of separation is powerless to refute it!

8
Because it is pure light, it is undefiled by shadow!
Verily, it is the Banquet of God, and undiluted by "otherness"!

9
If thou hast the zeal and longing for Oneness—
That desire for flight like the eagle of Glory—

---

3. See glossary for *S̲hirk*.

10
Then release thyself from earth and dust!
Purify thyself with the sparks of fire!

11
Cast thy gaze away from those moribund ones!
Ascend on high to the dwellers of Paradise!

12
Regard all other than God as mere nothingness!
Behold the actions of those who deviate from this truth!

13
Then, through thy glorious verses, after beholding God,
Rend asunder the most grievous of veils

14
That thou mightest behold manifest the face of the Desired One
In a hundred glorious conditions and stations!

15
Then wilt thou be loosed from all that is other than God,
And thou wilt collapse unconscious in the Banquet of *Innamá!*[4]

16
Indeed! Thou wilt become consumed by beholding the Creator!
Then wilt thou comprehend the mysteries of thy calling:

17
That the Unity of the Lord of the Bayán
Is not merely calling out with thy tongue alone!

---

4. See glossary.

18
There are instead multitudes upon multitudes,
Indeed, countless millions of souls,

19
Those who think only the sounds of ordinary words are being uttered,
Those attracted solely to the outward garment of verses!

20
Little do they comprehend the mystery of Unity!
Indeed, however covertly, they echo epithets of "infidelity" and "polytheism,"

21
Sharpen thine eyes and discern the false claims
Of those mirrors[5] among the leaders!

22
Behold how all are immersed in their own doings![6]
Behold how all are lost in a desert of distraction!

23
Behold how the point of idolatry[7] is inflamed
By so many whose visages are perverted by hate!

---

5. *Qavábil* means "those facing something." It would seem to be a reference to the clergy who claim they are facing God, but their mirror of heart lacks the capacity to reflect God's attributes. In the Persian Bayán (3:8) the Báb explains how, facing the sun, each thing reflects its own reality, whether positive or negative.

6. "Doings" is our translation for *af'álí,* which can be a reference to the term *tawḥíd-i-af'álí,* the "Unity of Actions," the Ash'aríyyih's deterministic belief that human actions are predestined by God—a notion that Shaykh Aḥmad and the Báb explicitly rejected.

7. See glossary for *Shirk.*

24
Indeed, thou canst behold every ray from that point
Reflected on the faces of the haughty leaders![8]

25
Some have become captivated by specious words!
Others are entrenched in their own arrogance!

26
One sect is benumbed by sloth and idleness![9]
Another is disgraced and consumed by fire!

27
The world is replete with embers, infidelity, and depravity!
Thou dost behold them burning, but without sparks!

28
They recite, "There is no God but God!"[10]
Yet inwardly they are faithless and comprehend not!

29
Thou who dost behold the rays of light made manifest
And thou who hast cast aside all that is separate from God by treading the straight path,[11]

30
After casting into the fire all otherness, behold the splendor
From those holy mirrors shining so gloriously!

---

8. A reference to Qur'án 4:47: ". . . before We change the face and fame of some (of you) beyond all recognition, and turn them hindwards, . . ." The "face" (*vajh*) also means "leader" or "authority."

9. A reference to dervishes who do not care about having an occupation.

10. The *Shahada,* an Islamic oath that is part of the call to prayer, and, as the declaration of faith, one of the Five Pillars of Islam.

11. Qur'án 67:22: "Is then one who walks headlong, with his face groveling, better guided,—or one who walks evenly on a Straight Way?"

31
Behold the letters of Oneness so magnificent,
Each disclosing sublime realities![12]

12. Most probably an allusion to the Letters of the Living, as mentioned in the introduction to the poem.

POEM 58

Praise of the Creator

(The original poem begins on p. 390)

1
With praise of the Creator Who is manifest in the world of being,
I will adorn these illuminating tablets with my verses.

2
I will disclose that mystery which, from the beginning, hath been concealed!
In the realm of creation, I will illumine the world with His countenance!

3
Praised be God, He Who hath ever been extant and evident in creation,
Whose exquisite method is more evident than aught else in the world!

4
Exalted be God, Who with the power of His glances,
Burns to ashes the lies of deceivers[1] with their blackened faces!

1. "Deceivers" in Qur'án 3:24: ". . . For their forgeries deceive them as to their own religion."

5
Nothing remains in the world except His glorious *Thaná'*!
The eyes of all the noble ones are observing the heavenly paradise!

6
O beholder of the Countenance of God, view the verdant panorama!
Note the Hidden Mystery manifest in the realm of the brilliant Sun!

7
How He stands so jubilant with such magnificence and heavenly majesty!
How His Cause hath descended from the midst of the dawning place of Paradise!

8
O beholder, observe the panorama on the other side of the world!
Regard those faces illumined by seeing the countenance of the Exalted One!

9
Then discover another splendor by peering into the realm of Mystery,
As though it were the Greatest Name amongst the dawning place of names.

10
He doth stand, wielding in His hand the same tempered sword![2]
Say: "God is great, our venerated Lord! Indeed, it is a new creation!"[3]

11
Now beseech the Beneficent Lord, "O Glorious Mystery!
that Thou hast opened all the gates of *'Amá*"!

2. An allusion to the sword of Muḥammad, though here Ṭáhirih may be alluding to the words of the Báb inasmuch as the sword is sometimes employed as a metaphor for the tongue.

3. He wields the same power as Muḥammad, but manifests it in a new Revelation.

12
God, O God, O God, Thou the Mighty, the Most Mighty!
Through Thy benevolence, cast but a glance to sever us from all else save Thee!

13
Do Thou cause all my supplications to be but a single prayer
That I might find myself abiding eternally in Thy presence, O God!

14
So that, intoxicated with ecstasy, I might behold this luminous vista!
I can observe naught save Thy beauteous face, gleaming from the station of divinity!

15
So that I might declare what Thou hast disclosed to us in the world of being!
That exalted praise of Thee should be glorious, beauteous, and complete!

16
O My Beloved, Thou art independent of all save Thyself,
And Thou art the Manifest, the Fashioner Who fulfillest all Thou dost desire!

POEM 59

The Manifest Mystery

(The original poem begins on p. 388)

The setting of this poem implies that the station of the Báb and the totality of His names and attributes remain hidden. As the last verse of the poem says, the full exposure of the Báb's Revelation will occur suddenly, but at this time, it is discerned only among early believers like Ṭáhirih and the other Letters of the Living, who grasp the impact of the Báb's appearance as both the Qá'im and a Manifestation of God.

1
O Thou seeker of God's aid, behold the Exalted Realm made manifest!
Behold all the hidden names behind an opaque veil!

2
Then behold with the eyes of mystery the inscrutability of manifestation,
Which is beholding the Face of the Unconstrained One concealed by the veil!

3
Behold once more the verdant vista with a refreshed glance!
See how that mystery of utterance is rising amidst the dawn!

4
What else cometh into view when thou dost behold the entire world?
It is naught but the manifest mystery residing within God's bounteous creation!

5
But by thy truth, breathe not a word in this time of quiescence!
For this mystery must become unfolded suddenly and with utterance alone![1]

1. As opposed to spreading the religion by the sword.

POEM 60

All Things Made New

(The original poem begins on p. 387)

1
O Beloved, Thou art so adored as to be the desire of every beloved one!
Would that I might sacrifice myself for Thee, whether in times of joy or sorrow!

2
O Beloved, I have nothing to offer Thee but the sacrifice of myself!
O Thou Who knoweth every lowly one, allow me to become beloved by Thee,[1] sacrificed for Thee!

3
So many souls I behold, entirely unsullied by the things of the world!
Indeed, this is the fulfillment of that very Promise[2] inscribed in the Holy scriptures!

---

1. Qur'án 89:28: "O (thou) soul, in (complete) rest and satisfaction! Come back thou to thy Lord, well pleased (thyself), and well-pleasing unto Him!"
2. "Promise" (*va'd*), a reference to the Day of Resurrection in Qur'án 45:32.

4
Praised be Thou, O God, the Able, the most Able Who alone art the Most Great Helper!
This is that very same mystery of Testimony[3] revealed amongst the whole of creation!

5
Bring into being He Who desireth to appear with the beauty of the Face of the Beloved
That He might stream forth an abundance of ceaselessly flowing verses.

6
O Beloved, this is that same Return[4] Thou hast made to appear,
That same cyclical return,[5] O my Desire, which Thou brought forth through Adam!

7
O Thou Fashioner of all sublime signs of the Beloved in the world of existence,
I behold before me all things Thou hast begotten anew![6]

8
Where are the utterances from the past and those meant to succeed them?
Where is the dawning of the Countenance of God? Where are the majestic tablets?

9
All have become decimated, completely decimated—burnt to ashes, mere ashes!
A single glance hath abolished them, a glance surveying Paran!

---

3. "Testimony" or "Gathering" (*mas͟hhúd*): a title for the Day of Resurrection in Qur'án 11:103.

4. "Return" (*raj'*) is the reappearance at the time of the advent of the Qá'im of the holy figure along with evil doers as recorded in detail based on ḥadít͟hs in S͟hayk͟h Aḥmad-i-Aḥsá'í's *Kitábu'r-Raj'at.*

5. "Cyclical Return" is a translation of *karr,* meaning "return."

6. Most probably an allusion to Revelations 21:5: "Then He who sat on the throne said, 'Behold, I make all things new.'"

10
O ye hearer of the verses, know that the verses are fashioned in familiar terms,
But with this new Revelation, all their meanings have become transformed!

POEM 61

He is the Exalted, the Absolute!

(The original poem begins on p. 386)

1
Now that comfort hath come to me, let me extoll the Great Omnipotent One
that in gratitude I might unfold the mystery of mysteries.

2
Within the *'Amá* of holiness, my Beloved is unrivaled, the Exalted One,[1] the Absolute!
By the radiance of His Countenance, He is regarded as the Primal Point![2]

3
From this Point hath emanated the entirety of creation!
Every new conception in every era bespeaks the subtlety of His power!

4
Blessed be God, the Glorious, the Omnipotent, the Beloved, the most Exalted,
For verily He is indeed the source of every created thing.

1. Literally "the Praised" (*ḥamd*). See glossary for "*Ḥamd*."
2. See glossary for "Primal Point."

5
Within the exalted veils, none doth exist save Him!
Within every Tablet inscribed with ink, I behold none save Him!

6
The mystery of this Point is extraordinary, so amazing, so entirely amazing
That the whole world hath been inflamed by nearness to His presence.

7
From the reflection of the splendor emanating from His ecstasy
Derives the structure and craft of fashioning inspired by the Creator.

POEM 62

Behold Once More!

(The original poem begins on p. 385)

This is an extremely abstruse piece that requires many readings, a great deal of imagination, and a study of the various levels of symbolism being employed. Ṭáhirih incorporates various images and allusions that the Báb Himself (as the Primal Point) has utilized in reference to various aspects of His own reality: "water," "fire," "snow," the "inmost heart" (*fu'ád*), "Mention," (*dhikr*), "the Lote Tree," the "Burning Bush" in Paran, and "the Mystery of Mystery." Whether or not the reader can recover all the allusions, the poem has a mystical beauty demonstrative of the depth of Ṭáhirih's intellect and poetic prowess. We venture to provide an interpretation of this poem that can be enhanced or complemented by alternative interpretations.

The poem consists of three parts: In the first ten verses Ṭáhirih urges the Bird of Paradise to behold the magnificent impact of the new Revelation on the universe. This is followed by Ṭáhirih's contemplations on these events in verses 11–17, and the poem ends with again addressing the bird, summarizing her explications.

1
O Bird of Paradise, behold now the most sublime vista!
From attraction to the White[1] Point, behold revealed the mystery of Water![2]

2
Behold how, by Its subtlety, the orbits of exaltation are revolving!
Behold how the Countenance of the Point assists the morning star[3] to blossom like the full moon!

3
Look again! Behold the tabernacles erected by Its mystery in the universe,
Shining and completely illumined by the ascendancy of the crimson veil!

4
Look! Behold once more how the face of *'Amá* hath appeared,
As if the disclosure of the mystery of mysteries hath occurred!

5
Look! Behold again how He hath fashioned the heavenly Throne
And is seated at the divine banquet with great glory and exaltation!

6
Look! Behold once more the vastness of the banquet of the Point
As He Reclines upon His throne, the Exalted, the Sacred, the "even nearer!"[4]

---

1. "White" (*bayḍa*) is a symbol for the transcendence of the Point.

2. Qur'án 21:30: "We made from water every living thing." In the Báb's writings, even fire, a symbol for the spiritual reality of the Báb Himself (the Point of Fire), is rooted in the water (as in the first Súrih of the Qayyúmu'l-Asmá'). The fountain of water in paradise denotes the station of the Primal Will, the first stage and the source of creation (see Nader Saiedi, *Gate of the Heart*, pp. 68–75).

3. A reference to Qur'án 86:1–2.

4. See glossary for "even nearer."

7
Look! Behold yet again how the wine of Power is aflame!
Exactly the same as that fire that descended from the Divine Tree.[5]

8
Look! Behold once more how the delighted Heart[6] hath become joyous!
Look! Behold again how the breeze of the spirit is wafting fragrantly!

9
Look! Behold once again how the mystery of stillness hath been disclosed!
Verily, it is He seated on the carpet of honor and acclaim!

10
Behold how the stature of Our utterance hath transpired,
That very same speech that is the glory of words emanating from Him!

11
O Omnipotent God, at this moment endow me with new eyes,
Cleansed from the dross of estrangement!

12
The reason the path to guidance hath now become barred from the world
Is that all must needs behold the Exalted Countenance with their own eyes![7]

13
Then wilt one exclaim, "Exalted is He, the Beautiful, our Beloved Lord, the new Revealer,
Seated on the green carpet with glory and exaltation!"

---

5. The Burning Bush, which is also a symbol of the Divine Lote Tree, or the Abrahamic lineage from which the Prophets descended.

6. The "delighted heart" is a translation of *thalj,* which also means "snow" in contrast to "fire" in the previous verse.

7. Cf. Bahá'u'lláh, The Hidden Words, Arabic, no. 2: "The best beloved of all things in My sight is Justice; turn not away therefrom if thou desirest Me, and neglect it not that I may confide in thee. By its aid thou shalt see with thine own eyes and not through the eyes of others, and shalt know of thine own knowledge and not through the knowledge of thy neighbor."

14
Praised art Thou, the Omnipotent God, the Most Powerful, the Lord,
The Beautiful, the Most Beauteous Beloved endowed with renewed Beneficence.

15
O Thou One True God, thanks be to Thee, the Friend, the Omnipotent, the Most Powerful!
Release me from tribulations and assist me to attain the station of *Há.*

16
God brought the world into existence from the reflection of this very Point,
From Whom derived guidance to the Eternal Countenance, the splendor of beholding God

17
So that when suddenly His mystery issued forth from the station of Glory,
He once again created a new world in the realm of being!

18
But because the dwellers in this world were not attentive to the mystery,
All have descended into the depths of debasement, non-existence, and annihilation!

19
O Bird, chant a verse for those who delight in hearing again the name of God
That Thou mightest behold the veil removed from the Desired One!

20
Sing about that Hidden Mystery with a melody about God the Creator,
Disclosing how God hath indeed created a new creation to praise the Hidden Mystery.[8]

---

8. This is yet another allusion to the ḥadíth of the Hidden Treasure.

21
The ḥadíth of Ṣádiq, a descendant of God,[9] appeared in the world in this Day,
The very time when the Point doth recite all that hath been mentioned before!

9. Considering Ṭáhirih's reference to the process of new creation in the previous verse, the ḥadíth mentioned in this verse should be Imám Ṣádiq's ḥadíth about the six stages of creation, which has been explained by the Báb in many of His writings and addressed by Ṭáhirih in detail in poem 64. In His Interpretation of Bismillláh (INBA 60, p. 4), the Báb ascribes this ḥadíth to Ṣádiq who was the sixth Imám and thus ordained by Muḥammad with authority and the capacity to interpret sacred utterances.

POEM 63

The Tumult and Tests of this Day

(The original poem begins on p. 382)

1
In praise of God, the Glorious,
I loosen my tongue to let forth sparks of fire!

2
I shall recount the mysteries of God's retribution!
I will recount the mystery of His avenging wrath!

3
I shall disclose why He hath unloosed such a tumult in the world on this Day of the Ingathering
So that none may find solace or safety save in His Countenance!

4
The sparks and flames from every side
Have encircled the world and the totality of existence!

5
At this time, I fail to behold a single living soul secure!
All are suffering with their souls afire, pleading for mercy.

6
The inferno of this fire is so intense
That all have fallen onto the desert of annihilation!

7
O Thou Creator, I know not what Day this is
In which the world is consumed in a convulsion of flame!

8
O Thou God of grandeur, Thou the Glorious, the Powerful,
Thou the Visible, the Hearer, the Knower, the Seeing!

9
For the sake of the witnesses who are stalwart in steadfastness,
Who remain standing, graciously awaiting in the station of honor,

10
Those who have not been polluted by slander,
Who remain purified from the traces of all material things,

11
Their faces aglow in their exalted station,
Their countenances radiant with steadfastness,

12
Fearing not whatsoever is not of God,
Those with sturdy frames and evident pride!

13
O My God, it is for the sake of the truth of the leaders such as these
That Thou hast purified me from the dust of this Day,

14
That Thou wouldst conduct me into this glorious state,
And cause me to be established in the most exalted heights

15
Because of these detached souls adorned with noble character,
Those who, by Thy command, now stand erect row upon row!

16
They seek no aid except from God!
They speak naught but the truth and are content with Thy Word!

POEM 64

The Eve of History

(The original poem begins on p. 381)

In this poem,[1] Ṭáhirih urges herself, and implicitly the entire body of believers, to realize the magnitude of the new Revelation and to make manifest the spiritual light bestowed on all (verses 1–4). She continues referring to the seven stages of creation (as alluded to in poem 62), originally discussed by Imám Ja'far Ṣádiq (the sixth Imám) but subsequently mentioned by the Báb. An allusion to the spiritual regeneration of humanity is indicated by the word *badá* in verse 4. Then in verses 5–8, Ṭáhirih mentions these seven stages sequentially: Will (*mas͟híyyat*), Determination (*irádih*), Destiny (*qadar*), Decree (*qaḍá*), Permission (*id͟hn*), Span of Time (*ajal*), and the Book (*kitáb*).

In verses 9–12, Ṭáhirih refers to the symbolism of "shadow" (*ẓill*), an allusion she has also employed in other poems. This concept is discussed in the Qur'án (25:45) in terms of how God spreads the shadow, a metaphor interpreted by Islamic mystical philosophers as the realization in the world of existence (physical reality) of the archetypes (*a'yán t͟hábitih*) inherent in God's knowledge. Or stated more simply, this image alludes to God's plan for having creation gradually emulate ever more precisely the attributes of

1. A clear copy of the manuscript shows horizontal line notations after verses, 8, 11, and 21, which might mean the piece consists of four smaller poems. These divisions match our thematic division of the piece.

the spiritual dimension of reality, especially as regards the enlightenment and spiritualization of human beings.

There is another analogy that Ṭáhirih uses in relation to the conceit of "shadow" that relates to the concept in Islamic philosophy of the spheres and heavenly bodies symbolizing the intermediary station between the divine and the earthly world of dust.[2] In contemporary cosmology, planets are the central point for the moons that orbit around them, and the planets themselves orbit the sun. Of course, we now know that the solar systems are themselves in orbit around a central point in each galaxy.

But the point is that in Islamic astronomy, which still employed the Ptolemaic view of the cosmos, it was believed that some planets moved in their own orbit (an epicycle), even though that epicycle itself orbited the center of the cosmos. This was believed to be the Earth in the Ptolemaic view. As such, in verse 9 there is a reference to "epicycle" (*falak-i-tadvír*) that would seem to be an analogy for progressive revelation inasmuch as each religion has its own dispensation or era—its own organic duration with specific laws and purpose—and yet each dispensation operates within the overarching context of the eternal plan of God for each planet as a whole.

Finally, in verses 22–28, Ṭáhirih portrays her feeling of helplessness in her own desperate situation, as if she has fallen alone in a remote expanse of the earth, like a person being punished by God for not answering His call, a reference to Qur'án 46:32. (See endnotes for further information about this poem.)

1
O thou Who art adorned with the ornament of light,
Appear now from behind the veils of brilliance!

2
Hoist all the veils!
Reveal the mystery underlying wisdom itself!

2. Seyyed Husssein Nasr, *An Introduction to Islamic Cosmological Doctrine*, p. 159.

3
Bring forth intelligence from thy musk-laden goblet!
Blot out all current strength and knowledge!

4
Bring it forth and be not concerned with aught else,
For the Mystery of God hath appeared anew!

5
According to the dictates of Will, transcend thy station!
With the flash of Determination, seize thou the reins!

6
Cast away the twists and turns of Destiny!
Behold instead the unveiled Decree of God!

7
By the approval of God Who doth embody majesty,
Fashion the garment of Permission and Dispensation!

8
Revealed and manifest is the Book of Utterance
At the noontide preceding the eve of history!

9
Know thou that the shadow of reflection that was formed
Was assisted by the rotation of the spheres![3]

10
Now, as the light becomes completely dispersed,
Countenances have dawned from these newly revealed rays of light!

3. Larger expression of God's plan assisting the specific plans of individual planets.

11
Now they are reciting glorious utterances!
They have become united by the wonder of praising God!

12
No longer is there a mere shadow among the shadows!
Now the entirety of the universe is aglow with unsullied light!

13
If thou hast any heavenly desires,
Render exalted this robe of Glory.

14
Behold the Moon-Face One, distinct from every other zealous one,
Standing erect[4] with grandeur.

15
He pays heed to naught save the utterances of God!
Now doth He declare the mysteries of *'Amá!*

16
The angels in their assorted forms stand waiting
Until the command issues forth from one drop of utterance.

17
With the ecstasy and ardor of glory they sing!
They disclose the mysteries with flute and drums!

18
From the heaven of *'Amá* they descend!
Instantly they defeat the entire army of elephants.

4. An allusion to the Qá'im, "He who will arise from the family of Muḥammad," even as the Báb was a Siyyid or lineal descendant of Muḥammad. See Madelung, W. (2022a). "Ká'im Ál Muḥammad" in Bearman, P. (ed.), *Encyclopaedia of Islam* (Second ed.). Brill Reference Online.

19
Even the tiny gnat who doth struggle to survive
Hath been dissevered from this mortal life!

20
None remains who might assist the regions of the world
Except the Essence of the Creator Himself.

21
In fulfillment of His word, He doth bring forth Bahá!
As a proof of His Truth, He doth embody *Thaná'!*

22
Jehovah, Lord, Alláh, God,[5]
Thou who dost behold even a useless particle,

23
Other than Thee, it hath no helper!
There remains no other recourse for it!

24
My God, rescue it from the machinations of this world!
Uplift it to the banquet of your benevolence and justice!

25
It hath not been bestowed any strength, like one unloved,
He who hath fallen remote on the surface of Thine earth.

26
O Thou Creator, make manifest Thy dawning
That the mystery of Thy plan might now become discernible.

5. In the original, repetitions of the word *iláh,* meaning "God."

27
O God, where lieth one iota more of patience or endurance
That mightest beget its ascent? O Where is it?

28
With Thy splendor, O My God, deliver it!
Convey it to Thy banquet of justice and joy!

POEM 65

He is God

(The original poem begins on p. 380)

In this poem, Ṭáhirih follows the structure and pattern we observe in many of her other poems in which she begins by praising God, then follows as narrator/persona by addressing other characters—the Bird of Paradise, for example—and urging them to join in the praise of God.

This brief introduction is often followed by the narrator/persona (presumptively Ṭáhirih herself) sharing observations about what is taking place in this special Day—the Day of Resurrection—and affirming that the prophecies of the past have now been fulfilled, that all the mysteries have been disclosed, and that the Manifestation of God is in the process of renewing the world of being.

These poems often end with verses containing Ṭáhirih's humble supplication to God to assist her with overcoming her shortcomings and helping her accomplish whatever God wills her to do. In this poem, however, a number of the verses (16–45) consist of a prayer praising those steadfast followers of the Báb who inspired her and who serve as a model for her. She thus prays that she might be empowered to follow in their footsteps.

Traditionally with Islamic prayers, believers invoke certain holy figures to intercede for them in obtaining assistance from God, with phrases like "By the truth of Muḥammad," "By the truth of 'Alí," or "By the truth of Fáṭimih Zahrá" (Muḥammad's daughter). In this same context, we observe in verses 34–38 what appears to be a hierarchy of the stations of figures that Ṭáhirih invokes for aid. She beseeches God to grant her assistance for their sake, and by their truth.

Yet, we can say that Ṭáhirih is in fact invoking certain aspects of the reality of the Báb Himself. In verse 33, "the ensigns in the banquet of Bayán" can be a reference to the Báb as He, in the Commentary on the Súrih of Joseph, refers to Himself as the Ensign (Súrih 78). In that sense, the first station (verse 34) is the first thing that was created, a reference to the station of the Primal Will. As we read in the Persian Bayán, the Primal Will is the first entity God created, and all other things in existence were created or caused by that primal force (p. 3).

Then in verse 35, she refers to the station of the Lordship of the Báb (*Rabb-i-A'lá*), a station that alludes to the essence and attributes of God. In verses 36 and 37, she alludes to the station of the Manifestation of God, Who manifests perfectly all the attributes and powers of God in the world of creation. Still another station can be discerned in verse 38, which alludes to the capacity of the Manifestation (the Báb in this case) to reveal new laws. This is followed in verse 39 by an invocation to "the lofty luminous branches," and we observe that in the Commentary on the Súrih of Joseph (Súrih 24) the Báb makes a reference to the leaves and branches of the Burning Bush in Sinai. He calls on the inhabitants of the heavens[1] to hearken to His call raised from the precincts of the fire amidst the leaves of these branches.

In most cases we have generally translated "Bahá" as "glory." Yet, there are instances where, because of the grammatical structure of the verse, it would be problematic to assume that she is employing "Bahá" as an attribute of God rather than as an allusion to the Báb or Bahá'u'lláh. One clear example of this usage can be found in Poem 41 of our volume *The Quickening:* "With grandeur, with the majesty of the Lord, the King of kings / Bahá, is seated formidable in the court of power." In such cases we have not translated the word "Bahá" as "Glory" nor have we deigned to translate "Bahá" as "Bahá'u'lláh." We have instead simply retained the original word "Bahá," thereby allowing the reader to infer the meaning.

---

1. It can also be read as "O people of Throne"—"Throne" (*'arsh*) being a symbol for the Manifestation of God.

HE IS GOD

1
By reciting the name of God, the creator of all life,
I will with certitude reveal the meaning of the Hidden Mystery.

2
Now will I bear forth the goblet of love!
I will cleanse the mirror of all vain imaginings and superstitions.

3
O Thou Who art bedecked with the adornment of light,
Hearken to the verses concealed within the Creator's melody

4
Declaring that this Day is the day of recompense for loyalty,
That the reins of all matters are held by the hands of God.

5
None is there who abides in any exalted station
Save the immaculate essence of the Exalted One, the Knower.

6
Recognize that all the verses from every prophecy have been fulfilled,
That the enigma of all the copious mysteries have been disclosed.

7
Not a single thought that can be understood remains veiled any longer!
Thou canst not discover a single spark concealed among the exalted realities!

8
The turbulence from the ceaseless fire[2] is now evident!
Every land hath become brimming with the rays from this Sinaitic light!

---

2. A reference to the fire encountered by Moses in the Burning Bush through which God showed His splendor to Him.

9
Realm upon realm hath become engulfed with this flame,
As age after age this message hath been proclaimed.

10
No trace remains of any cycle of time,
For the Empyrean itself hath now appeared by God's command "*kun fa kán*!"

11
From eternity, the mystery of the appointed time for every dispensation hath been established,
Nor can there be any extension of that time, nor any delay in its commencement![3]

12
It is patently clear that the Lord of Eternity is ever creating!
Indeed, even today He yet abideth in the station of fashioning![4]

13
Thus doth He bestow divine majesty on whomsoever He wisheth,
And He bestoweth glory and lofty exaltation,

14
Will fashion him hearty, but with a moderate disposition,[5]
Will cause him to declare the mysteries of the Return!

15
Except for Him, no purpose for creation would exist,
A creation mighty, enduring, and praiseworthy!

---

3. The verse refers to the concept in the Qur'án (10:49, 7:34, 15:5) that the period of time assigned for the life of a religion will not be extended or changed. See Qur'án 10:49: "To every people is a term appointed: when their term is reached, not an hour can they cause delay, nor (an hour) can they advance (it in anticipation)."

4. A reference to the Qur'ánic verse 55:29: "every day in (new) Splendor doth He (shine)!"

5. A reference to Qur'án 82:7: "Him Who created thee. Fashioned thee in due proportion, and gave thee a just bias."

16
O God, the Powerful, the Great, the Exalted,
The Giver, the Noble, the Ancient, the Beautiful,

17
Relieve me from the calumny of this earthly condition!
Hoist me to the heights of sublimity

18
So that I might imbibe heartily from the goblet of love
That all traces of my separation might be abolished,

19
So that whatever is distinct from Thee might be annihilated in my sight
And by means of divine sobriety I might generate fire![6]

20
Through my attraction to Thee, I would unfold the mysteries!
Through Thy justice, I would strengthen every just endeavor!

21
Through Thine Order, I would bring about order in the world!
I would defend the ascendancy of Thy Covenant!

22
I desire naught to see in creation except Thy Face!
I seek naught but that which pleaseth Thee!

23
By demonstrating the proof, I would cause steadfastness!
By recitation of the verses, I would instigate life!

---

6. Annihilation and sobriety (*maḥv* and *ṣaḥv*) are a pair of Ṣúfí terms referring to being completely intoxicated by the love of God and thereby becoming spiritually conscious again.

24
Heartily would I imbibe the choice wine from the goblet!
I would disclose that mystery of the station of Bayán!

25
I would cause the entirety of creation and existence to become illumined!
I would make it verdant and, aided by God, dynamic and vibrant!

26
O my God, by those who bear witness to justice,
Those incomparable souls who abide in Thy presence,

27
Those erect with ecstasy and glory at the Day of the Ingathering,[7]
Prepared, readied, that from them the mystery of Return will be manifest,[8]

28
As if they have assembled in response to the Call,
All of them arrayed with majesty and splendor,

29
Rescue this insignificant particle
That Thy power might become evident in this solitary soul.

30
She hath no helper save Thee!
Thou art the sole witness to her solitude!

---

7. See glossary.

8. See Qur'án 61:4: "Verily God loveth those who, as though they were a solid wall, do battle for his cause in serried lines!" (Rodwell).

31
O my God, purify her from the defilement of strangers!
Release her from the ignominy of infidels!

32
Thou art the Creator of everything other than Thyself!
Thou art the Sin-covering, the Forgiver, the Sovereign over every victory!

33
By the sanctity of Thine Ensign in the banquet of Bayán,
By *Thaná'* which is now made manifest,

34
By the truth of the First of the new creation,
He before Whose face, all are humble,

35
By the truth of the Second, O Thou encompassing Creator,
From Whom the attributes of God became manifest!

36
By the Truth of the Third, O Creator of the Manifestation,
He Who is speaking forth about the mystery of creation,

37
He to Whom the ensign of the Eternal became revealed,
He from whom emanated the gifts of the One True God!

38
By the truth of the Fourth, O Thou Beneficent Creator,
From whom restraint and benevolence have emerged!

39
By the lofty luminous branches!
By the newly dawned ensign,

40
By Thy benevolence and graciousness, O Creator,
Rescue me from whatsoever in this world Thou dost deem abhorrent

41
That Thou mightiest behold me clearly in love with Thee,
Mightest behold me proclaiming the mystery of Thy Glory!

42
O God, the Majestic, the Powerful, the Seeing,
Thou art creator of every majestic and powerful one!

43
Nothing else exists except Thy transcendent Essence!
Thou art the Existing One, and all else is mere non-existence!

44
Bless my tongue with mention of Thee
That Thou mightest plainly unveil the divine mystery!

45
Praise be to Thee, O God of *Thaná'!*
Benevolence is Thine, O my true Lord, Bahá!

POEM 66

Awakening the Reed

(The original poem begins on p. 377)

In this poem, as well as in poem 71, the two figurative images of the Bird of Paradise (or *'Amá*) and the reed (Rúmí's reed) appear together in the same poem. In both poems, a relationship of hierarchal dependency is established between the two. The bird needs to sing its ecstatic melodies in order to awaken the reed so that it might resume playing divine melodies.[1]

The implicit context is that the bird represents the voice of the heavenly or divine realm, while the reed, having grown in a marsh, represents the earthly realm of water and clay. But when the reed resumes playing its enchanting melodies, it is manifesting the "Hidden Treasure," the spiritual attributes of God as revealed in the verses or utterances of the Manifestation. Stated simply, prior to revealing His station, the Manifestation, like the reed, has potential to inscribe the Revelation, but only after revealing His station does the "ink" (like the Holy Spirit) flow through the Pen and become manifest in words. In this sense the bird signifies the divine aspect of the Manifestation of God, and its singing awakens and refreshes His earthly reality, which in turn manifests the concealed divine mysteries latent in creation. The poem demonstrates how ardently Ṭáhirih wished that the Báb would reveal His full station—symbolically, that the Bird of Paradise would awaken the unconscious reed to begin revealing its melodies.

1. A reference to Qur'án: 52:20 "They will recline (with ease) on Thrones (of dignity) arranged in ranks . . ." and similar verses.

Finally, the bird and the reed can also refer to the same twin aspects of Ṭáhirih herself, both her divine nature and her earthly reality. Additionally, the reciprocity between these twin symbols also alludes to the metaphysical (spiritual) and earthly (physical) aspects of the world of being, inasmuch as she employs these images in various parts of the poem. This latter allusion is much clearer in the last two verses of poem 71 in which the reed desires to remove those veils obscuring the jewels and essences in the world of existence and to bestow life on the dead.

1
Through the praise of the Omnipotent Beloved will I purge all rust from existence!
I will swallow every slander and thereby bring forth the mysteries of the essence of all things.

2
In this world, I shall behold no creator except my Beloved!
By the light of His Cause, I will illumine the appearance of existence!

3
O Bird of Paradise, from among those ecstatic melodies, sing
That Thou mightest impart sheer joy to those who dwell in the exalted paradise.[1]

4
Behold how the world hath been rendered benumbed, intoxicated by thy call!
Behold once again! Rescue this unconscious and inebriated one

5
But know this, O Bird of Paradise, that Rúmí's reed
Shall never become conscious until it doth discover the mystery of Paran.[2]

---

2. Until, like Moses on Mt. Sinai, the Báb reveals His full station, which at the time of Ṭáhirih's writing, the Báb has done by degrees.

6
If Thou dost possess any ecstasies from discerning the signs of God in creation,
Reveal them that the reed might disclose to thee those ecstatic countenances.

7
O thou attentive one, cast from thy hands whatsoever is not of God
That thou mightest find a mystery whose meaning thou canst grasp.

8
Know thou that from this very same reed hath the Hidden Treasure become manifest,
Though the ignorant world doth fail to discover the ecstasy of Him Who is "even nearer."

9
O Thou One True God, possessor of glory, power, and majesty,
It is plain to Thee that the reed doth possess the long-promised mystery!

10
Yet because Thy people are heedless of the truth of these verses,
They have descended into remoteness, have cast aside the very foundation.

11
O my God, cause my tongue to be blessed with Thy mention
That Thou mightest make manifest the meaning of the hidden mysteries!

12
O God, I beseech Thee by Thine exalted and sanctified Essence, Thou One True God,
That the immaculate station of the reed might serve to sanctify all conditions.

13
In any era in which Thou art in grandeur, Thou dost display yet another splendor!
Through Thy attraction, Thou dost illumine the entirety of creation.

14
O my Creator, would that Thou mightest rescue me by Thy benevolence
That I might awaken the unconscious reed and cause it to intone its melodies.

POEM 67

The Mention of Thee

(The original poem begins on p. 375)

In terms of style, this poem is marked by a device Ṭáhirih often employs—using various words for praising God and for referring to the Primal Point (the Báb). We encounter this same praise in Bahá'í and Bábí literature: Using the word "*dhikr*" or "mention" (of God) as an allusion to the Báb in various forms; "Mention," "The Most Great Mention of God," (*Dhikr'ulláhu'l-A'zam*) and "The Mention of the Name of the Lord" (*Dhikr-i-Ism-i-Rabb*).[1] Therefore, in this poem where the reference to the Báb is obvious, we have capitalized the terms used for praising God, each with a particular meaning in the Báb's system of symbolism: "Magnification" (*takbír*), "Sanctification" (*taqdís*), "Mention" (*dhikr*), and "Praise" (*ḥamd*).

1

By the Magnifying praise of Thee, all mysteries will be fully disclosed!
By Sanctifying Thee, Thine immaculate countenance can be discerned!

1. See Riáz Ghadímí, *Sulṭán-i-Rusul Ḥaḍrat-i-Rabb-i-A'lá* (King of the Messengers the Báb, the Lord, the Most Exalted), p. 16 for a list of the Báb's titles.

2
O My Precious Lord, bestow certitude on me through my Mention of Thee
So that Thou mightest reveal whatsoever is concealed neath the shelter of Covenant!

3
This is true because Thy Mention is cause for the restoration of light in both worlds!
None occupieth the throne of splendor save Him.

4
All except God come into being because of Him, the Primal Point.
O Thou the Powerful, the Forgiver, all revival is caused by attraction to His countenance.[2]

5
O God, by this bestowal is praise of the Praised One fit for Thee,
Because from Him assistance doth appear in the form of utterance.

6
O God, through the purity of His incomparable essence,
Bestow but a glance by Thy concealed benevolence, O Thou, the Omnipotent, the Most Powerful!

7
That Thou mightest behold Thy Point of attraction become manifest,
Release Thou every atom from consternation in this delusive realm!

8
O God, Thou wouldst then cause every mouth to utter Thy Mention
Until, O Helper, O Just One, Thou wouldst behold rectitude in every soul.

---

2. This verse is an allusion to the arc of descent (the appearance of the universe from the Primal Point), and ascent (its return to that divine origin).

9
I now conclude this verse of adoration with Praise of Thee!
O Helper, through Thy Mention will I now consume all the Holy Verses!

POEM 68

Through the Mentioned One

(The original poem begins on p. 374)

In this poem, Ṭáhirih urges "the Mentioned One" (the Báb) to reveal His station and to create the world anew.

1
Make the world illumined through the Mention of the Omnipotent Beloved
So that the justice of Paran[1] might become manifest in the created realm!

2
Cause holiness to become glorified in this world,
Then make the world radiant through words of exaltation!

3
Recount Praise of the Beloved, Who is irresistible and omnipotent!
Through Him, the whole world lieth outstretched on the ground from the ingathering.

1. A reference to Qur'án 7:159: "Of the people of Moses there is a section who guide and do justice in the light of truth."

4
May His *Thaná'* be proclaimed with the glory of paradisal holiness!
Bring His glory to every soul and make all His gifts appear!

5
Arouse the murmuring of the bee![2] Pour out the choice wine!
This would be a ransom for me, a remedy for all the maladies of my soul!

6
Play the flute and sound the tambourine, all that which is exceptional in this world!
Recreate the world with calamity and with the loyalty of sacrificing souls!

7
O God, the Omnipotent, the Most Powerful, the Helper, the Beneficent, the Most Beneficent,
Overshadow the flame of this fire with Thy brilliant light!

2. Another reference to the ḥadíth that asserts that Muḥammad used to hear a sound like unto the buzzing of a bee before He would begin revealing those verses that were conveyed to Him from God through the Angel Gabriel.

POEM 69

His Promised Day Hath Now Appeared!

(The original poem begins on p. 373)

1
O Thou the One True God, I behold all those set apart from Thee in a stupor!
Is it that the true verses issuing forth from the splendor of Thy light are being uttered?

2
O Thou God of Grandeur, it is as if the tumult of Ingathering hath appeared in the world,
As if the attraction of the Absolute is reassembling all that hath become divided.

3
O God, the O Powerful, the Most Knowledgeable, the Living, the Life-Giver, the Assisting,
It is as if that new Revelation hath appeared with astounding ecstasy!

4
Indeed, O beloved beholder, at this time in Our sight,
The attribute of perfection hath appeared in the utterance of Him Who had been silent

5
So that He might reveal this wondrous new mystery from among the mysteries,
That He might utter that which hath suddenly become manifest in the world!

6
Say: Thanks be to God, the Glorious, the Powerful, the Most Powerful,
That His Promised Day hath at last appeared like drops descending over parched land.

POEM 70

Rescue Me! Rescue Me!

(The original poem begins on p. 372)

This ecstatic poem may well be the most fervent and direct expression of all the poems penned by Ṭáhirih. Devoid of much imagery or indirection, she cries out to God with her whole heart in a language that is potent and unabashedly humble and pleading. The focus is only minimally on her own function and station, but instead she proclaims outright that she is solitary and bereft. She calls out to God for relief, assistance, and fulfillment of the prophesied Day of Days when the world will finally be recreated by the advent of the Manifestation and the enactment of His laws and guidance.

Her impatience for the spiritual renewal of the world and the establishment of divine justice and order is patently clear in her emphatic and passionate pleas in verses 18 and 19 of the poem. The image of the appearance of the Qá'im and His efficacious ordering of the world by the aid of His army of the devoted believers—a common belief among the Shí'ih—is obvious in these verses.

For Ṭáhirih, however, this image is merely symbolic, not literal. Poetically, verse 18 of this poem refers to God's beauty (*jamál*)—a term commonly contrasted with God's might (*jalál*). This same verse can also simply be understood as the Beloved lifting her veil, then slaying the lovers with the blade (*tígh*) of her eyelashes—a commonplace image in Persian poetry.

The terms "justice" and "order" in the next verse justify interpreting these verses as alluding to the act of jihad undertaken by the Qá'im, though most likely Ṭáhirih is proclaiming that the order for jihad that was expected to be established by the power of the sword will, instead, be established through the power of adoration of the Beloved's beauty, a concept that also appears in Bahá'u'lláh's writings. (See endnotes for further information about this poem.)

1
In the form of Bayán and the evident mystery,
I will unfold the mysteries of "*kun fa yakán*"!

2
Now I will explain the hidden mysteries!
I will render the entirety of existence inverted!

3
I thus supplicate to God, He Who is Most Glorious,
He from Whom emanates the divine mystery, to give me discernment

4
So that I may behold in the world naught but His countenance,
And that I might eliminate all the dust obscuring the Bayán.

5
I would discard altogether every single veil,
For the sparks of Bayán are eminently more consuming!

6
O my God, assist me to make this intention become fulfilled
That all I pray for might be achieved.

7
By the truth of the Prophet, hear my plea!
By the majesty of Thy Vicegerent, behold my sorrow!

8
O my God, Thou art the Powerful, the Omnipotent!
Thou art the Helper, the Victorious, the enforcer of Justice!

9
If not for Thy transcendent Essence, nothing would exist!
All that is separated from Thee will cease to exist!

10
It is from Thee that all glory and praise have descended!
It is from Thee that both the prayer and its answer have appeared!

11
By Thy light, "*kun fa kán*"[1] hath become enlightened!
He Who was foretold hath dawned from the bosom of Bayán!

12
What amazing names become visible in that light!
What verses in accordance with prophecies!

13
They behold naught except Thy pure countenance!
They behold naught but Thine exalted face!

14
They all are illumined by Thy holy light!
They all are venerated by the honor of Thy Glory!

15
They have naught to say except their praise of Thee!
They possess no language except words extolling Thee!

16
O God, by Thy majesty and glory,
Which is so plainly discerned in the station of Bayán,

---

1. The world of existence.

17
Ordain that from the bountiful gifts of light,
The heaven of the Manifestation might appear!

18
He would remove the veil from the divine countenance!
He would unsheathe the sword of vengeance and slay the world[2]

19
So that nothing would be seen except for Thy ceaseless action,[3]
And no action would take place but the exactness of Thy justice and order!

20
Because I possess no other desire except Thee,
No dwelling have I in any other abode.

21
O God, the Beloved One! O God, my God!
There exists no witness nor shelter save Thee!

22
O Lord of the universe, Thou art my haven!
O exalted and avenging King, Thou are my refuge!

23
Rescue me! Rescue me! Rescue me! Rescue!
Cause me to attain that divine purity, that verdant abode!

---

2. Being slain is a poetic expression denoting being overcome by love. Likewise, the sword often symbolizes the tongue. In effect, the Manifestation would appear and subdue the world with His utterance. The vengeance is the recompense for the distortions, lies, and tribulations wrought by the followers of the previous Manifestation.

3. "*Fa"ál*" as in Qur'án 11:107 and 85:16: "Doer (without let) of all that He intends."

POEM 71

O Bird of Paradise!

(The original poem begins on p. 371)

1
O Bird of Paradise, recite the name of God, the Most Glorious,
Then spread thy feathers and stretch thy wings!

2
Intone the songs with the melody of Ḥijáz[1]
that the reed of Rúmí might engage in prayer!

3
From the tone of the heart it arouses a roar
From creative melodies and artful dalliance.

4
It doth bring forth a goblet brimming with musky wine
And obliterates the consciousness and strength of all!

1. A mode of Arabic and Persian music. Ḥijáz also refers to Arabia. In Section 41 of His Commentary on the Súrih of Joseph, a book revealed in Arabic, the Báb refers to Himself as being of the people of Ḥijáz and also as the Arabian Youth.

5
Recount how the divine stations are made manifest!
Disclose the concealed modes of utterance!

6
Portray the beauteous forms with their effulgent virtues
That the mystery of *nún*[2] might become manifest!

7
Declare whatsoever Thou hast beheld with God's permission!
Indeed, guide us to the Path with proofs of "the Eighth,"[3]

8
But disclose not the hidden mysteries
That this reed might commence its quest,

9
And by its essence, make manifest the mysteries,[4]
That by attraction to Thee, the dead might emerge from their graves,

---

2. See glossary for *Nún.*

3. "The Eighth" (*thámin*) is a title for the eighth Imám of Shí'ih Islam, Imám Riḍá. The proofs of the Eighth can perhaps be a reference to the ḥadíths attributed to this Imám about the Qá'im. Among them is the fact that the Qá'im will be young.

4. "Mysteries" (*satr há*); literally means "veils." Manifesting veils from essence (*jawhar*) is an allusion to the Primal Point manifesting various aspects of His station. "Essence" is the Primal Point; it is the Realm of Essence: (*Kawn-i-Jawharí*) in Shaykh Aḥmad's hierarchy of the realms, also called the "White Veil" (*hijáb abyaḍ*) (*Sharḥu'l Favá'id,* vol. 2, p. 278). This white color manifests its various stations through other lower stations (sequentially getting darker and closer to the contingent world): the yellow, green, and red veils. In that sense the poem means that the Primal Point, through its Essence, makes manifest the veils of different colors or different stations. As the Báb, in relation to the similar hierarchy of the first four stages of creation, alludes to these stages with various levels of mystery (*sirr*) (Nader Saiedi, *Gate of the Heart,* p. 136), we have translated "veils" as "mysteries."

10
All those who become enlightened by the holy brilliance,
All who begin praising Thee and considering the Hidden![5]

5. A reference to Qur'án 57:3: "He is Manifest and Hidden."

POEM 72

See with His Eyes![1]

(The original poem begins on p. 370)

This poem begins with a reference to an abstruse term (*fárat tannúru*), which appears in the Qur'án (11:40, 23:27) in relation to the story of Noah. While some translators and interpreters of these verses have employed interpretations such as "the oven boiled" (Palmer) or "the earth's surface boiled up" (Rodwell), many have translated the term as "the water gushed"—an interpretation that makes sense in the context of the story of Noah, as the gushing of water was the result of God's anger, which brought about the flood.

Yet the term can also be read as "the raging of fire." The use of this term—in both this poem by Ṭáhirih and in the Báb's Commentary on the Súrih of Joseph—connotes an outburst or an eruption of positive spiritual forces. The eruption of the abode of fire (*tannúr*) is used by the Báb in reference to the events related to the Day of Resurrection (Suratu'-s-Saṭr, section 11) and as the condition of the hearts in response to His Cause (Suratu'n-Núr, section 20). Likewise, Ṭáhirih uses the term in conjunction with "light" as alluding to an auspicious event. (See endnotes for further information about this poem.)

1. This phrasing brings to mind Bahá'u'lláh's exhortation that the believers should aspire to understand His Revelation by assuming His perspective and objectives: ". . . behold My Revelation through Mine eyes" (*Tablets of Bahá'u'lláh,* p. 242).

1
Behold! A new Day hath dawned, and God is made manifest!
The abode of fire and light hath appeared in blazes!

2
Behold thou clearly with the eye of truth!
Behold thou the One, the likes of Whom none hath ever seen!

3
But O thou learned one, see with His eyes![2]
Behold what thou dost see made manifest!

4
If thou dost see with the eyes of others, He will be entirely concealed![3]
He would be concealed in a stunning fashion in a garment of glory!

5
O thou learned one, He is refined, the Most refined!
Among all the mysteries of the universe, He is astonishing, the most astonishing!

6
Thou dost not possess eyes to perceive Him and shed tears!
But then, thou dost possess a diminutive mind!

7
Behold what tumult is occurring amongst the dwellers in both realms!
He hath descended amidst the sparks from heaven and earth!

---

2. See Bahá'u'lláh, The Hidden Words, Arabic, no. 44.

3. Compare Bahá'u'lláh, The Hidden Words, Arabic, no. 2: "The best beloved of all things in My sight is Justice; turn not away therefrom if thou desirest Me and neglect it not that I may confide in thee. By its aid thou shalt see with thine own eyes and not through the eyes of others, and shalt know of thine own knowledge and not through the knowledge of thy neighbor."

8
Behold how a company of believers became detached from the world!
They stand in rank, ready for sacrifice with their lives in hand!

9
They have no objective except the Friend!
Through them hath the world been set aflame!

10
No goal have they except their Lord!
They have abandoned family and kindred alike!

11
O thou ignorant ones, what wonderment they beheld
Who choose to dwell in such flames for so long?

12
Were thou but to open thine eyes to all this,
Thou wouldst behold the mystery of Return made plain!

13
Thou wouldst also behold how all the mysteries
Have now become disclosed from behind the veils!

14
No longer doth there remain a single mystery concealed!
Except for God Himself, the whole world is aflame with this fire.

15
Shouldst thine own detachment show thee the way,
Thou couldst even now discern the mystery of the God of the universe.

16
Thou willest become illumined with divine lights!
Thou willest become rectified through the power of the Exalted One.

17
The path of steadfastness will attract thee!
It will deter thee from standing still!

18
Yet I fail to behold thee attaining such a state
That thou wouldst detach thyself from base worldly things!

19
O intelligent one, make thy manner of supplication sincere!
Seek assistance from Aḥmad and His descendants[4]

20
So that the world itself might behold disclosed
The advent of bearing witness according to the Bayán!

4. Aḥmad is another name for Muḥammad, and "His descendants" here alludes to the Imáms. The Báb in the Commentary on the Súrih of Joseph (Súratu'l-Ḥaqq, section 85) refers to Himself as one of the descendants of Muḥammad.

POEM 73

Awaken to the Day of Reckoning!

(The original poem begins on p. 368)

He is God, the Beloved King

1
From the east with hallowed light now appeareth
The Sun of Glory with majesty and rank!

2
By mentioning the glorious God,
It hath spoken with a tongue of fire.

3
It hath brought the world into tumult and confusion,
As if this were the Resurrection, the Day of Reckoning!

4
O Thou Holy Bird with Thy blissful tidings,
Hear from the song of the flute the mystery of "*There is no doubt*"[1]

1. Qur'án 2:2: "This the Book; in it is guidance sure, without doubt, to those who fear Alláh."

5
With ecstatic tunes attract the people of spirit,
For the Ocean of Power is now roaring!

6
From that melody, attend the hidden mysteries,
And forge them into a form of Bayán,[2]

7
Because the Sun of Eternity hath become inflamed!
It hath become illumined with the mystery of *Qadar*.

8
One side of Venus hath become visibly bright
From being ignited by transformative sparks of fire!

9
The torch is bright with rays from the light!
The veil of the Countenance of Glory[3] hath been lifted!

10
The world hath been set ablaze with tumult and embers
From the flames of the Sinai of the Sun of Qadar.

11
Pour forth now the coals of fire!
Ignite now that luminous torch

12
That the people of light might see
How the divine mysteries have appeared!

---

2. Fashion the ephemeral music into the revealed Word.

3. "Glory" (*Bahá*) here should be a reference to the Báb, as in the Commentary on the Súrih of Joseph He calls Himself Bahá (Súratu'z-Zikr, section 108).

13
The veils have been consumed by its sparks!
The letters[4] speak of its verses!

14
No mystery remaineth veiled!
The mystery of the mysteries hath become divulged!

15
All who abandoned whatsoever is not of God
Have instantly beheld the majestic countenance of Glory![5]

16
Behold how God hath become manifest according to the law of *Qadar!*
All worldly things have become entirely annihilated,

17
While whosoever hath become deprived of beholding Him
Hath also become entrapped in mere shadows![6]

18
O thou who art ignorant of our condition and plight,
Come now and behold the glory of our majesty,

19
How we have entirely abandoned whatsoever is not of God,
How with but a glance we have become absorbed by the Countenance of Eternity.

20
Behold the tumult of resurrection in our court!
Behold the Day of Resurrection in our world!

---

4. This might be a reference to the Letters of the Living
5. "Bahá," as in verse 9a, is a reference to the Báb.
6. Here again, a metaphor reminiscent of Plato's Allegory of the Cave.

21
We are all aligned with the Order of Bahá![7]
Through His Mystery, the Grace of God is manifest to all!

22
Come! Reside within the expanse of this majesty!
Arise with the elegance and honor of reunion

23
So that the majesty, beauty, glory, and light
Might all become apparent to thee!

24
Indeed, O thou who hast become accustomed to the path of ignorance,
Awaken from the slumber of thine interminable anticipation.

25
With the honor of glory, purity, and light,
Erect the tabernacle of exaltation

26
That thou mightest behold how the Countenance of Bayán
Hath at last appeared manifest before thee!

---

7. This reference is reminiscent of a passage from the Báb cited by Shoghi Effendi regarding the World Order of Bahá'u'lláh: "To this World Order the Báb Himself had, whilst a prisoner in the mountain fastnesses of A<u>dh</u>irbayjan, explicitly referred in His Persian Bayán, the Mother-Book of the Bábí Dispensation, had announced its advent, and associated it with the name of Bahá'u'lláh, Whose Mission He Himself had heralded. 'Well is it with Him,' is His remarkable statement in the sixteenth chapter of the third Vahid, 'who fixeth his gaze upon the Order of Bahá'u'lláh, and rendereth thanks unto his Lord! For He will assuredly be made manifest. . . .'" (Shoghi Effendi, *God Passes By*, pp. 324–25).

POEM 74

Waiting! Waiting!

(The original poem begins on p. 367)

This short poem is most probably a response to the Báb's advice to Ṭáhirih that she should have "patience, patience,"[1] as He urges her to withhold herself from disclosing to others all the truth she alone understands.

1
"Patience! Patience!" So long! So terribly long!
Thine absence! Thine absence! Come, O Thou Wise One!

2
The face of God hath been manifest from robes of light!
Behold the Day of Advent, of ascending from the graves!

3
By Command hath the advent of the Resurrection become guided!
By Primal Cause hath the ordering of order become accomplished!

1. *Ṣabran ṣabran.* The Báb's letter can be found in Muhammad Afnán, *Majmú'ihyi-Maghálát-i-Doctor Muḥammad Afnán*, p. 235.

POEM 75

A Poem to Bihjat in "This Day"

(The original poem begins on p. 366)

In one respect, this poem has a special historical significance. As in poem 70, Ṭáhirih makes a reference to the common expectations of the S͟hí‘ih that when the Qá’im appears, He will establish justice and destroy His enemies with the sword. In contrast, the verses of this poem focus on this Dispensation or Day of God, a time when the law of jihad and spreading religion by the sword has been abolished. Bahá’u’lláh in several places utilizes the sword as a symbol of the tongue, and considering the totality of the Báb's writings, this prophecy or expectation should also be understood in this metaphorical or symbolic sense—the religion of God will be spread by the word (Bayán).

Nevertheless, because this claim would constitute a radical change in Islamic thought and the S͟hí‘ih culture of the time, Ṭáhirih could not publicly declare or explain this change. On two occasions, she may have even held a sword in her hand[1] as a symbol of defiance, determination, and the fulfillment of S͟hí‘ih expectations. Yet, like the Báb Himself, she rejected expansion of the cause of the Báb through force and riches when she was offered an army of thousands and urged to embrace such an approach.[2] But in this poem written to Bih-jat—an enlightened friend of hers with whom she communicated frequently

1. Asadu’lláh Mázandarání, Kitáb-i-Ẕuhúru’l-Ḥaqq. vol. 3, p. 258.
2. Ibid., p. 253; Nabíl-i-A‘ẓam, The Dawn-Breakers, p. 212.

by means of exchanging poems—she makes clear the distinction between this particular Day (*imrúz*) and the prior Dispensation of Muḥammad insofar as the law of jihad is concerned.

Since the Báb identified Himself with all the major Prophets of the past, in Ṭáhirih's poetry we see that the qualities attributed to these Prophets are mentioned in relation to the Báb and His actions. Among these is her reference—included in our previous volume *Adam's Wish* (poem 7, verses 51–69)—to Noah's anger when He cried out to God "O my Lord! Leave not of the Unbelievers, a single one on earth!" (Qur'án 71:26).

Yet in the present poem, Ṭáhirih focuses on Jesus Christ, the epitome of love, tolerance, and forgiveness. In this same vein, she admonishes the Bábís to respond to their cruel enemies with a similar forbearance. Clearly this allusion to Christ importantly reflects the expectation of Muslims, as well as Christians, that Christ would return at the Day of Judgment.

In other words, spurious claims by some that Ṭáhirih was a revolutionary fighter and at odds with Bahá'u'lláh's peaceful teachings are the result of shallow assessments of her own written testimonies and thus lack any historical accuracy. In fact, as later historical events demonstrate, in addition to the symbolic allusions to this concept in her poetry, Ṭáhirih's thoughts and actions were completely aligned with the laws and teachings of Bahá'u'lláh. This of course includes His exhortations that believers maintain obedience to the rulers and governments of the lands in which they live, and that they follow the path of spiritual enlightenment, employing education and personal example to instigate change, rather than rebellion and violence.

This guidance is in stark contrast to the combative actions and tactics employed by Ṣubḥ-i-Azal (Mírzá Yaḥyá) and the so-called "Azalís" (his followers), who pursued political means in attempting to subvert the government of Iran and to alter the Iranian political systems—a common reaction of the Islamic world to Western imperialism.

Finally, because of problematic copying of the text, a part of this poem was not readable in the manuscript originally available to us, but we were able to obtain a copy of this poem that exists in the Princeton University Archives[3]

3. William McElwee Miller Collection of Bábí Writings and Other Iranian Texts, 1846–1923, Microfilm images, pp. 70–71.

and compare it with our own copy. Though the Princeton University copy also has some mistakes, it helped us to construct a complete version of the poem. After receiving Dr. Egea's copy in which all lines of the poem were readable, we used it as a source. However, in three instances we have adopted the words used in the Princeton University copy, as they made more sense. These are footnoted in the original Persian version at the end of this volume.

1
Be aware that in the center of *Qáf*[4] there is in this Day a Manifestation!
In this Day, all the ecstatic divine verses are being revealed!

2
The command of God hath descended from the direction of the court of *Qadar*[5]
That there should also exist today verses that are not from *'Amá!*[6]

3
But despite this, the Letters[7] should arise with delight,
Should surmount such antipathy, for today there is Light!

4
They should, with unsullied sight, consider everyone as pure,
For today through them is the mystery of the Forgiving One[8] made plain!

---

4. A mountain on which the mythical phoenix lives. The Báb alludes to Himself as the *Qáf* and states that His call can be heard from the bird which is flying in the atmosphere of the mountain in the land of this Qáf (Súrah of the Bird or Súratu'ṭ-Ṭayr, section 86) In Rúmí's poetry, Qáf refers to the realm of grandeur and self-subsistence (Siyyid Ṣádiq Gawharin, *Farhang-i-Lug̱hát va Ta'bírát-i-Mat̲hnaví*, vol. 7, p. 134).

5. *Qadar:* the "measure" of things in existence as allotted by God.

6. See glossary.

7. The Báb uses the term "letters" at times to refer to the followers of a religion. That is, He alludes to religion as a book and its followers as the letters in that book. For example, He refers to the letters of the Gospel, the letters of *Furqán* (Qur'án), the letters of the Bayán, and the letters of the Book of Him Whom God Shall Make Manifest. (Panj-Sha'n, p. 86).

8. "The Forgiving" is a name of God in many verses of the Qur'án.

5
They should refrain from discussing the wickedness of the stranger,
Because in this Day, the lights of divinity are divulged!

6
They should expunge from their sight every trace of debasement,
But rather proffer forgiveness, the mandate of the Rewarding One[9] in this Day!

7
Thus, forgiveness is appropriate for the nature of their exalted station!
Neither should there be mention of the contentious ones, for today is the Day of joy!

8
O Bihjat, try to grasp the cause of Fáṭimih's[10] plaint!
Now doth she long for the splendor of forgiveness from the Forgiving One!

9
Certainly all of them were unjust to everyone among them!
All have bowed their heads in shame in this, the Day of Resurrection![11]

10
O ye illumined Letters, ye should become the light-givers!
In this Day it is incumbent that forgiveness be available to all!

11
Jesus, Son of Mary, Who embodied the Holy Spirit, abideth in the world![12]
In this Day, when thou hast surpassed the darkness, thy heart will become illumined!

---

9. *Shakúr* is a name of God as He freely rewards even seemingly insignificant actions (Dehkhoda).

10. *Fá*, which stands for "Fáṭimih," Ṭáhirih's given name.

11. The Day of Judgment when all shall be called to account for their deeds.

12. A major theme in the teachings of Christ is that forgiveness is available to all.

12
O ye company of Letters, each one of you must needs appear
Like unto Jesus, Son of Mary, Who hath returned in this Day!

13
Ye should not publicly disdain the deeds of the unbeliever,
Rather show to him the light that shineth within thee!

14
Indeed, O Bihjat, thou who art aglow with excitement and sparks of fire,
I believe thou art endued with the deportment of a child!

15
No more shouldst thou pen verses about the unbelievers!
Efface the shadow of their darkness that hath appeared in this Day!

16
Whatsoever hath been created throughout the entirety of existence in the universe,
Hath descended from the heavens, and the Omnipotent One is patient in this Day.

17
Indeed Behold! O thou who doth stand in the panorama of wonderment,
Patiently awaiting permission to realize thy nature and powers in this Day!

18
O, our Bihjat! thou shouldst commence singing,
For gaining such approbation is needed in this Day!

19
Thence will wondrous verses descend from you to Ṭáhirih,
For thy verses will render the heart joyful in this Day!

20
And admonish the illumined Letters also to sing,
For God doth appear in the station of exalted splendor in this Day!

21
O Bird of Paradise, fill Thou my cup
That I might cry out that it is God the Creator revealed this Day!

22
The Holy Bird that hath spread its wings with golden feathers
Is waiting to sound the trumpet this Day![13]

23
And another standeth waiting for permission to be issued forth,
That he, too, might blow[14] forth the breath of life this Day!

24
Indeed, behold the other realm and observe the self-subsisting Qá'im
Seated on the throne of authority, issuing forth commands this Day!

25
Say: Alláh! God! He Who is the Beloved, the Beautiful!
This is the Day of fulfillment of the Covenant, and He is forgiving in this Day!

26
From the Throne of God,[15] verses issue forth,
Moment by moment, exaltation of the light of Revelation appeareth this Day!

27
He desireth to draw forth His sword to slay the world and its people,
But Ṭáhirih is beseeching Him that God is forgiving in this Day!

---

13. A reference to Qur'án 74:8–10: "Finally, when the Trumpet is sounded, That will be—that Day—a Day of Distress,—Far from easy for those without Faith."

14. Qur'án 36:51: "The trumpet shall be sounded, when behold! from the sepulchers (men) will rush forth to their Lord!"

15. Literally "throne of the throne of God." It can be a reference to the Báb as the Gate to (the throne of) "Him Whom God Shall Make Manifest," Who Himself is the Throne of God, or a reference to Mullá Ḥusayn, the Báb being the Throne of God and Mullá Ḥusayn His throne. The extreme reverence of Ṭáhirih for Mullá Ḥusayn is evident in her letter addressed to him.

28
Thus should the mystery of Thy forgiveness become disclosed,
For the mystery of Thy name—the Bestower, the Protector—is divulged this Day!

29
Thou shouldst show forth forgiveness in the forgiving manner of the Forgiver Himself!
The Greatest Name for thee is the Beneficent and the Thankful this Day.

30
O Bihjat, behold in us a glimpse of the light of Bahá![16]
Pour forth into the cup of enlightenment all that is attainable this Day!

31
Make conspicuous these wondrous conditions!
Pour forth from thy pen without delay since the banquet is this Day!

32
Know with certainty that the eyes of all are brightened
By Thy elucidations that doth dilate the hearts in this Day!

33
Pour the purest honey into thy cup to exalt the Exalted One,
For the universe emanates the purity of brightest crystal in this Day!

34
Thou shouldst demonstrate with wondrous new strains
Elucidations of the divine verses, which are like unto light this Day!

---

16. "Glory" (Bahá) might be an allusion to Bahá'u'lláh, though as we have noted, the same term was sometimes employed to allude to the Báb.

35
Since from the Eternal Helper an increase in assistance hath descended for thee,
Pour! Pour forth again! For these verses herald the Rewarding One this Day

36
So that the splendor of the Creator might descend to thee,
And attract thee![17] Such is the command "*g͟hayúr*"[18] in this Day!

17. An allusion to the enlightenment of Abraham.

18. *G͟hayúr* means "jealous," "intolerant of rivalry," and "zealous." It is a name of God employed in the Old Testament of the Bible: "For you shall worship no other god, for the Lord, whose name is Jealous, is a jealous God" (Exod. 34:14).

Endnotes

POEM 2

In verses 4–7, Ṭáhirih seems to be referring to the appearance of the specific qualities and conditions of Adam, Noah, and Abraham in the personage of the Báb and in relation to His particular situation. Adam is alluded to by the quality of fire (verses 4 and 5); Noah by the quality of water (verse 6); and Abraham, the one absorbed by the stars and the sun, by the quality of air (verse 7). The word *spirited* or *animated* in verse 7, *taravvuḥ,* implies wind (*reyḥ*)—a reference to the third element, air. The Báb is alluded to by the quality of earth, the most important of the four elements (fire, water, air, and earth,), that which causes the combination of all of these constituent ingredients to become realized in a perfect manner to serve the purpose for which they were created. Referring to the symbolism of the four elements, the Báb writes: ". . . nor canst thou perceive in the station of my body aught but the station of dust for the realization of the three stations of fire, air, and water. . . ."[1] He continues to describe how all four spiritual stations symbolized by the four elements are present in Himself. Likewise, verse 8 of the poem refers to the dormant state of the first three elements, all of which will become manifested and realized by means of the fourth quality, the earth (verse 9). Verses 10 and 11 describe the propitious outcome of this process.

In verses 12–19, Ṭáhirih addresses the eternal and unchanging tradition and practice (*sunnat*) of God, which is the cyclic appearance of the reality of the Manifestation of God. She refers (in verse 12) to a sentence appearing in

1. The Báb, quoted in Nader Saiedi, *Gate of the Heart,* p. 103.

two verses of the Qur'án (33:62 and 48:23): "no change wilt thou find in the practice (approved) of Alláh." Verses 13–19 of the poem are about the process of cyclic revelation as an unchanging tradition of God, the ruling and ordering of His Cause (*amr*), and the return of that Cause to the celestial realm (*raj'*), as indicated in the Qur'ánic verse 32:5: "He rules (all) affairs from the heavens to the earth: in the end will (all affairs) go up to Him, on a Day, the space whereof will be (as) a thousand years of your reckoning." The notion of God's Cause (*amr*) and His regulation of its affairs is mentioned in verse 13 of the poem, and the return of the Cause to God in verse 17. A certain interpretation of this Qur'ánic verse has been that the Islamic religion will return to God a thousand years after its revelation to Muḥammad and the completion of its regulation and ordering by the eleven Shí'ih Imáms, the process that was concluded in the year 260 of the Islamic lunar calendar when the eleventh Imám passed away. Accordingly, a thousand years after that, when the Cause of Islam returns to God, would be 1260, the year of the Báb's declaration in Shiraz. The cyclic process of the manifestation of God's Cause (*amr*) and its return to God is symbolized by the story of Adam, in this order: Adam's creation in a perfect form (verse 13), His fall on earth for the purpose of advancing humankind (verse 14), His trials and calamities and His seeking return (*raj'*) to the spiritual realm (verse 15), and His eventual redemption and return (*raj'*) to paradise (verse 17).

In verses 20–30, Ṭáhirih points out the wisdom of calamities endured by the Prophets as allusions to the purpose and wisdom of the sufferings of the Báb and how the perfections and attributes of the previous Prophets of God have appeared at this time in the personage of the Báb. Direct and implied references to Adam, Noah, Abraham, Moses, Jesus, and Muḥammad are clearly in relation to the appearance of the attributes of these figures in the personage of the Báb. It is implied that the calamities They have faced were for the preparation of humanity for the advent of the Báb.

The earth symbolizes the embodiment of the reality of the Point in the material world, necessarily a limiting and taxing state of existence. This carrying of the Load of Trust is something that only man, the Perfect Man, accepted to do.[2] In His writings, the Báb calls Himself Adam, the Prophet

2. "We did indeed offer the Trust to the Heavens and the Earth and the Mountains; but they refused to undertake it, being afraid thereof: but man undertook it . . ." (Qur'án 33:72).

Whose descent on earth in Ṭáhirih's poetry is a symbol of the sufferings of the Prophets for the purpose of advancing the world of humanity (see *Adam's Wish,* poem 7). Noah's sorrow and grief due to the tragedy of the rejection of His call by the people brings to mind the Báb's disappointment with the deniers. Abraham's building of the Ka'bih and sacrificing of His son allude to the Báb's pilgrimage and declaration of His station at the Ka'bih, and to the death of His son. In a prayer on the occasion of the loss of His son, the Báb expresses the wish that this Abraham (Himself) had a thousand Ishmaels[3] to sacrifice on the path of the love of God.[4]

In verse 25, the words "square/cubic" (*murabba'*) and those related to visiting "'Arafát" (*ta'ríf and mu'arrif*) and the word "mystery" (*sirr*) are references to the words the Báb has employed in the Commentary on the Súrih of Joseph (Súrih 108). After making references to circumambulation of the Ka'bih (Ka'bih being a symbol for His own station), and mentioning the process of pilgrimage, the Báb emphasizes how difficult it is to understand the mystery of His station. "Pilgrimage" and "pilgrim" are translations for *ta'ríf* and *mu'arrif.* The first word refers to the halt of the pilgrims of Mecca in Arafát, a place on the east of Mecca where pilgrims stop on the ninth day of the month of Dhil-ḥajjih and go over a mountain of the same name to listen to the pilgrimage sermon. The second word means the one who stops at Arafát.[5]

In these closing verses of the poem, Ṭáhirih consoles herself and Bihjat, a follower with whom she has been corresponding, reminding them both that God's eternal tradition has been that only through sufferings of the material world, will human perfections be materialized as exemplified by the lives of the Prophets of the past. The poem ends with the glad tidings that the results of the process of progressive revelation are now manifest, and with the urging of Bihjat to understand this hidden reality.

POEM 8

If these symbols and conceits are interpreted in their traditional sense, they would not seem to recount a coherent narrative. However, in light of the

---

3. In the Qur'án and Islamic texts, Ismael was the son of Abraham intended to be sacrificed, as opposed to Isaac indicated in the Bible.

4. Nabíl-i-A'ẓam, *The Dawn-Breakers* (Persian translation), p. 61.

5. Siyyid Ṣádiq Gawharín. *Farhang-i-Lughát va Ta'bírát-i-Mathnaví,* vol. 2, p. 726.

symbolism employed by the Báb, the poem can be understood as alluding to the various stations and qualities of the Manifestations of God, as well as to Ṭáhirih's historical and spiritual connection to the Báb Himself. The warbling nightingale, the cupbearer, the immaculate personage, Moses, and the Beloved can thereby be understood as merging into one single reality as each of these tropes symbolizes a certain aspect of the station and function of the Manifestation of God. Likewise, the interaction between them can be read as allusions to the dynamics of what transpires in the heart of the Manifestation.

A review of the imagery used by the Báb in His Commentary on the Súrih of Joseph (Qayyúmu'l-Asmá') makes this point clear. Mullá Ḥusayn had decided that, were he to encounter one who seemed to fulfill the requirements of the Qá'im as set forth in various prophecies and ḥadíths, especially as these were elucidated for him by his teacher Siyyid Káẓim-i-Rashtí, such a one would, unasked, provide him with a satisfactory explication of the Súrih of Joseph in the Qur'án. And the first portion of such a work is precisely what the Báb revealed to him that evening of May 22, 1844, in the residence of the Báb in Shiraz.

That commentary by the Báb is so unusual in its style and content that it was rejected by traditional scholars, theologians, and literary experts. Their rejection was similar to the rejection of the Prophet Muḥammad by the generality of the public: "'Nay,' they say, '(these are) medleys of dream!—Nay, He forged it!—Nay, He is (but) a poet! Let him then bring us a Sign like the ones that were sent to (Prophets) of old!'" (Qur'án 21:5), and the particular rejection of Muḥammad and the Qur'án: "What! shall we give up our gods for the sake of a Poet possessed?" (37:36).

Certain examples of the Báb's symbolism in the Commentary on the Súrih of Joseph that relate to the imagery in this poem by Ṭáhirih should suffice to demonstrate this point. For example, regarding the symbols that relate to the conversation of God with Moses through the tree on Mount Sinai (*Ṭúr*), the Báb refers to His own self as the fire (*nár*)[1] that appeared in the tree and talked to Moses, the light (*núr*) of that fire,[2] the tree (*shajar*) itself[3] on which

1. The Báb, Qayyúmu'l-Asmá', Súrih of Ẓuhúr, section 78.
2. Ibid., Súrih of Inshá', section 67.
3. Ibid., Súrih of Anvár, section 27.

birds are moving,[4] the voice of God that talked to Moses,[5] God who talked to Moses[6] and revealed the book (the Ten Commandments) to Moses,[7] and the Prophet Moses Himself Who received the Revelation from the tree.[8] The Báb also refers to Himself as a bird[9] and as a cupbearer that bestows the water of Revelation on Mount Sinai (*Ṭúr*).[10]

In relation to the central theme of this poem, the reader would do well to consider the authoritative explanation by ʻAbdu'l-Bahá about how the first intimations of the Revelation of the Manifestation—often signalized by some dramatic dream—does not represent some change in the station of the Manifestation, but rather a divine signal that the time has arrived for Him to reveal Himself and actively convey to others whatever God inspires Him to reveal.[11]

POEM 11

In the first six verses of the poem, through a conversation with the Bird of *ʻAmá,* Ṭáhirih appeals to the Báb to reveal His true station. But these introductory verses also provide a preview of the contents of verses she is about to inscribe: It is the time for the hidden divine mystery to become manifest in the world of existence, and Adam (the human aspects of the Manifestation of God) to return to His paradisiacal state (His divine reality) and to reveal Himself. Then, following this opening, the central body of the poem describes how, if it observes and listens carefully, the bird can discover all that is occurring. In this respect, the dialog with the bird is Ṭáhirih's conversation with herself.

A particularly important concept alluded to in this poem is the dual nature of the Manifestations of God—Their human and Their divine natures, or what Bahá'u'lláh in the Kitáb-i-Íqán describes as Their station of distinction

4. Ibid., Súrih of Iksír, section 57.
5. Ibid., Súrih of Kitáb, section 41.
6. Ibid., Súrih of Ṣabr, section 53.
7. Ibid., Súrih of Bá', section 83.
8. Ibid., Súrih of Aḥkám, section 50; and Súrih of Aʻẓam, section 82.
9. Ibid., Súrih of Ṭair, section 8.
10. Ibid., Súrih of Qadr, section 24.
11. See ʻAbdu'l-Bahá, *Some Answered Questions,* no. 16.8–10.

and Their station of essential unity.[1] Another central concept is the idea that the Manifestations of God consciously and strategically withhold revealing fully Their divine station, first because it is beyond the comprehension of human understanding, and, most importantly, because the enlightenment of humankind must take place by degrees. Therefore, each Revelation is tailored to the exigencies and capacities of a particular period in history.

It is in this context that the fall of Adam is not an indication of the failure or sin of Adam, but rather an allusion to His wish or desire to reveal the fullness of His station at a time when the people are incapable of grasping such knowledge. Therefore, He becomes aware that, like all the Manifestations, He must teach only what is appropriate for the dispensation in which He appears. This realization is—in a poetic sense—a source of Adam's sorrow and suffering, analogous in many ways to Bahá'u'lláh's poetic expression of His ardent desire for reunion with the Maiden of Heaven (the Holy Spirit) and His lament for not being able to attain it, a theme expressed with poetic power in His "Ode of the Dove."

Because the purpose of creation is the appearance of the divine perfections in physical expression, Ṭáhirih explains how the divine light of knowledge becomes visible or understandable as it "enlightens" the physical realm in general, and as it becomes expressed most completely and perfectly in human terms through the incremental evolution of human society. More particularly, Ṭáhirih alludes to the theological/philosophical notion that all of creation is "enfolded" in the human reality—the concept of the relationship between the macrocosm and the microcosm—as expressed by the Imám 'Alí in a verse cited by Bahá'u'lláh in the Seven Valleys: "Dost thou deem thyself a small and puny form, When thou foldest within thyself the greater world?"[2]

Another noteworthy theme explored in this poem concerns allusions to mystical philosophical concepts expressed symbolically in natural phenomena, such as astronomical entities (the sun, the moon, the stars, their orbits, the constellations) and the metaphoric use of light and shadow. In verse 8 of the poem, fire (*nár*) is a symbol for the transcendent divine—the divine aspect of the reality of the Manifestations of God, which manifests itself through its light. This is the fire that shed its splendor on Moses atop Sinai (verse 9), the

1. See Bahá'u'lláh, The Kitáb-i-Íqán, ¶191.
2. Bahá'u'lláh, The Seven Valleys, ¶70.

intensity of which Moses could not bear. The transcendent and essentially hidden fire would thus represent the source of the divine light in the world of existence. It is manifest in the "sun" of prophethood, which, in terms of Shí'ih theology, is reflected in the moon of vicegerency or 'Alí (*shams-i-nubuvvat va qamar-i-viláyat*). In verse 11, Ṭáhirih uses the term "The sun of prophethood" (*shams-i-ḥikmat*), as the word "*ḥikmat*," commonly meaning "wisdom" also means prophethood (*nubuvvat*).[3] Thus, in one respect, the sun and the moon in verse 11 refer to the return of Muḥammad and 'Alí in the personage of the Báb—hence His name 'Alí-Muḥammad, though the symbolic usage of the sun and the moon also occurs later in the poem.

In contrast to the light, which symbolizes the splendor of the divine in the world of existence, Ṭáhirih employs shadows (*ẓill*) to represent the absence of light. Shadow in one sense symbolizes the corporal world that is dependent on, and in need of, the divine light. Yet, in verse 12, Ṭáhirih points out that in this, the Day of God, the intensity of the light of Revelation is so great that the lights and shadows have merged so that no shadows remain.

The divine is also alluded to as an ocean and the corporal world as the land. The shore of that ocean is thus the place where the corporal and divine realities meet and comingle. A similar analogy can be found in Persian mystical literature, such as the Mathnaví of Rúmí in which the ocean alludes to "the Ocean of Unity" (*baḥr-i-tawḥíd*), the hidden divine reality, while the shore (*sáḥil*) alludes to "the manifest and contingent world."[4]

In verses 13–33, Ṭáhirih portrays the uniqueness of this "Day of God," the symbolic return of Muḥammad and 'Alí, and the fulfillment of the prophecies from the Qur'án and various ḥadíths. In this Day, the Beloved is urging all to be reassured and confirmed in the Cause, to hasten to Him in ecstasy. Then, following her description of the greatness and special bounties of this Day, Ṭáhirih, in verses 34–40, urges the Bird of Paradise to attend to a particularly relevant verse from the Qur'án, the "Verse of Light" in the Súrih of Light (24:36).

---

3. See Riaz K. Ghadimi, Behnam Rahbin, Ehsanollah Hemmat, *Riázu'l-Lughát* under "ḥikmat."

4. Siyyid Ṣádiq Gawharín, *Farhang-i-Lughát va Ta'bírát-i-Mathnaví*, vol. 5, p. 220, vol. 8, p. 140.

She cites certain key words and concepts from this Qur'ánic verse—almost exactly in the order in which they appear in the Qur'án. The Qur'ánic verses are (with words Ṭáhirih uses in italics):

> Alláh is the Light of the heavens and the earth. The Parable of His Light is as if there were a "Niche" (*mis͟hkát*) and within it a "Lamp" (*miṣbáḥ*) enclosed in a glass globe so that the glass shines as if it were a brilliant "star" (*kawkab*) lit from a blessed "Tree" (*s͟hajar*), an Olive tree that is neither of the east nor of the west, whose oil is "well-nigh" (*yakádu*) luminous, though the fire has scarcely touched it. The result is "Light" (*núr*) upon Light! Alláh doth guide whom "He will" (*yas͟há'u*) to His Light: Alláh doth set forth Parables for men: and Alláh doth know all things.

In lines 41–59, Ṭáhirih resumes employing cosmological analogies to describe the process of physical and spiritual creation, the latter being the process of manifestation and revelation. She alludes to the fact that the divine light (an analogy for the Primal Point—the source and origin of the world of existence) had existed under the shadow of the transcendence of God and was thus sanctified from the limitations of the world of being. But because of the boundless grace of God, the world was created when it emanated from the Point (*nuqṭih*), but it comes into being by degrees according to the appropriate or preordained measure, and according to timeliness, thereby gradually ordering the universe as a whole.

After manifesting His own beauty in the world He has created, the Creator hides Himself behind the veil of transcendence. The image alluding to this station resembles a similar station depicted in the ḥadít͟h of "the Hidden Treasure" as explained by 'Abdu'l-Bahá in His erudite and elucidating commentary on the abstruse axiom contained in that ḥadít͟h. At this stage the Manifestation of God has not yet revealed His station in the realm of creation, but the sun of glory attempts to discover that hidden transcendent mystery of the universe—the "Mystery of Há." After searching the heavens and traversing constellations, the sun finds the most perfect manifestations of that divine mystery, hidden not in the heavens, but on earth and in Adam, the one expelled from paradise and suffering from His separation from God.

In verse 58, using the analogy of the shadow (*ẓill*), Ṭáhirih seems to be altering and thereby correcting the Ṣúfí discourse that has implicitly led to a superficial interpretation of the concept of the Unity of Being. This discourse assumes that by direct connection to God, the mystic can bypass or disregard any indirect path, even the guidance and laws and person of the Manifestation of God. The symbolism of the "shadow" derives from the Qur'ánic verse 25:47: "Hast thou not seen how thy Lord lengtheneth out the shadow? Had He pleased He had made it motionless. But We made the sun to be its guide" (Rodwell, 228). And in the verse that follows this, we read about the shadow: "Then We draw it in towards Ourselves—a contraction by easy stages." (Yusuf Ali tr., Súrih 25:46).

Renowned philosopher, poet, and mystic Ibn-'Arabí states that the relationship between God and the world of existence is like the relationship between a person and his shadow. In one sense, the shadow is not the person, and clearly there is a vast difference between the essential reality of the human being and the image cast by their corporeal reality—even as this same distinction is portrayed in the famed allegory of the cave in Plato's *Republic*. The shadow is dark, as opposed to the light that illuminates reality. Nevertheless, the existence of the shadow derives from its relationship to that which is real—the person, in the case of Plato's analogy, and God in the discourse of Ibn-'Arabí.[5]

Therefore, the verse "But We made the sun to be its guide" signifies that without the light, the shadow has no existence. Also, Ibn-'Arabí observes that in the verse "Then We draw it in towards Ourselves—a contraction by easy stages," Muḥammad reveals that God draws shadows to Himself because, in reality, everything else in creation is actually only a shadow of His essential reality. Consequently, the axiom that the shadow derived from Him is equally true with the axiom that all things return to Him. Furthermore, inasmuch as the shadow is God and nothing else, Ibn-'Arabí concludes that the shadow thus has two dimensions or realities—it is God Himself, and yet it is distinct, and thus remote, from God.[6]

Similarly, when Ibn-'Arabí asserts that the world of existence is God's shadow, he is not alluding to material existence; rather he is presenting the idea that existence is the form and design for the world of existence, the measure of things in their hidden state before their realization in the visible realm. The shadow is thus similar to the Platonic notion of the "forms" or "ideas" that give meaning to these abstract realities as they become manifest in specific

5. Muḥyiddín Ibn-'Arabí, *Fuṣuṣu'l-Ḥikam* (*Bezels of Wisdom*), pp. 101–2.
6. Ibid., p. 103.

representations. Ibn-'Arabí also interprets the Qur'ánic verse "lengtheneth out the shadow" as the extension of God's shadow in the form of these archetypes (again "forms," "ideas," "quiddities," or "essential reality") of all that has the possibility (*a'yánu'l-mumkinát*) of being created or of assuming a concrete expression.[7]

In this sense, we see a separation between God and the corporal world of existence. Yet, he confuses the issue in two ways. First, he believes that the archetypes of God or the knowledge of things are incremental elements of, or annexations to, God's essence and thus separate from that essence. The Báb refutes this assumption in forceful language, describing Ibn-'Arabí's conclusion in this regard as illogical because it implies joining partners with God, one of the most grievous violations of the theology set forth in the Qur'án.[8] Second, despite the various examples Ibn-'Arabí provides to prove the vast difference between God and God's shadow that encompasses the totality of existence, he contradicts himself and causes great confusion by offering the analogy of a transparent glass for the shadow: whereas a glass might manifest various colors of the light emanated from God (as with a prism, for example), a pure and flawless glass reflects the colorless light, God the Absolute. This analogy makes sense only if referring to the qualities of certain transformed souls among humankind, what Ṭáhirih alludes to in another poem in this volume (poem 64, verses 9–12), as the exemplars who illumine the whole universe:

Know Thou that the shadow of reflection that was formed
Was assisted by the rotation of the spheres!

Now, as the light becomes completely dispersed,
Countenances have dawned from these newly revealed rays of light!

Now they are reciting glorious utterances!
They have become united by the wonder of praising God!

No longer is there a mere shadow among the shadows!
Now the entirety of the universe is aglow with unsullied light!

---

7. Ibid., pp. 102–3.
8. See the Báb, Interpretation of the Mystery of Há, pp. 238, 239.

In these verses the shadow that was formed can be an allusion to the Manifestation of God Who unveils and sheds light on the world of existence, turning the shadows of pure ones into light.

Ṭáhirih, like Qeiṣary,[9] a well-known interpreter of Ibn-'Arabí, overcomes such misunderstandings by using the term "shadow of shadow" (*ẓill-i-ẓill*) in verses 34 and 58 of this poem, as well as in verse 12 of poem 7. "Shadow" in verse 12 refers to the station of the Manifestations of God, and "shadow of shadow" refers to the corporal existence, which is a shadow of the shadow of God. By means of this analogy, the connection between the Absolute and the world of creation is understood to be effected through the reality of the Manifestation of God. In Ṣúfí terms, through the manifestation in the World of Command (*álam-i-amr*), God's knowledge of all things—their archetypes (*a'yán*), their measure, and their form—are rendered discernible.

The reality of the Primal Point is thus like the shadow of God, and the realization of His knowledge in the realm of existence is like the shadow of that shadow. Such a perspective regarding this relationship disabuses the Ṣúfí view that by establishing a direct relationship with the transcendent God, the wayfarer can attain or even surpass the station of the Manifestation of God.

In this poem, through various terms and analogies, Ṭáhirih confirms the "indirect" or two-stage paradigm of God's manifestation of Himself. The first stage is the revelation of the Absolute in the intermediary reality of the Point, the Word, or the Logos, whereas the second stage signifies the revelation of that intermediary reality in the corporal world, or stated more specifically, that which bestows life and existence in the created world—the world of being. Ṭáhirih employs precise philosophical and mystical terminology to describe these two stages of God's manifestation, thereby representing the process of creation in both physical and spiritual respects. To the extent we felt would be useful, we have explicated her use of these terms in the footnotes to the verses.

In this poem, the sun symbolizes the Point from which emanates the illumination of the planets and their moons, but this process is distinct with each of the planets. It illumines the higher and lower spheres located above and below it,[10] and thus functions as a symbol for the Center of the Circle of

9. See Seyyed Ja'far Sajjadi, *Farhang-i-Lughát va Ta'birát-i-'Irfání,* p. 282.

10. As, for instance, we see in Ibn-'Arabí's *Fuṣuṣ,* seven spheres above the sun and seven below it (p. 75).

existence, the station of the Point. Each Manifestation of God thus manifests the Universal Reality according to the requirements of the era or dispensation in which He appears.

In addition to referring to the station of the Manifestations of God in general, verses 7–12 of the poem address the station of the Báb as the unique Manifestation of God in the Day of God. These verses resemble what the Báb proclaimed about His own station in the Súrih of Qadar in His Commentary on the Súrih of Joseph, where He refers to Himself as the light shining in Sinai, the Sun dawned in the dawning place of *'amá,* and the moon that was destined to shine from the station of the fire.[11]

We read in the Qur'án (25:10) that the sun is the light-giver and the moon is reflecting the sun's light. As such, the sun can be interpreted as God and the moon as the Manifestation of God, in the same way that for some Ṣúfís, the moon represents an intermediary between heaven and earth, and thus can allude to Muḥammad.[12] In another verse in the Qur'án (36:40) we read that inasmuch as the sun and moon have their respective places, they cannot reach each other, a notion that would seem to refer to the ontological distinction between God and His Manifestations. Yet we also read in the Qur'án (75: 9) that in the Day of Resurrection, the sun and moon will become joined together, a likely reference to the fact that in the Day of Resurrection, God will be fully manifest in the Temple of the Manifestation of God. The Báb, in the Commentary on the Súrih of Joseph, states that the sun and moon have become joined in His own being. Likewise, in various other places in this commentary, He proclaims that He is the sun or He is the moon.

The "mystery of *Há*" mentioned in verse 54 would seem to be a reference to the interpretations of the Arabic letter *há* in various writings of the Báb, particularly to the commentary of the Báb known as the "Interpretation of the Mystery of Há,"[13] even as verses 54–60 of the poem reflect certain concepts described by the Báb in this text. In verse 57 of the poem, the star of glory is portrayed as ascending and descending in the heavens as it searches throughout the constellations for the mystery of *Há.* Considering what the

---

11. The Báb, Qayyúmu'l-Asmá'.

12. Seyyed Hussein Nasr, *An Introduction to Islamic Cosmological Doctrines,* p. 163.

13. The Báb, Interpretation of the Mystery of Há, pp. 307–8.

Báb wrote regarding this letter, this image resembles the concept of the arcs of ascent and descent, though He does not explicitly designate this connection. Discussing the condition of human beings, He defines the descending levels of existence from the highest level to the lowest level, followed by the ascending levels from the lowest to the highest, assigning to each level a letter, which, according to the Abjad system, has a numerical value.

The descending levels begin with the universal spirit, followed successively by the universal soul, the universal nature, the universal matter, the universal form, and the universal body. These, in turn, are succeeded by further descending levels of the constellations, the various orbits of stars, the sun, the moon, and finally the four elements of fire, air, water, and earth, which together constitute the lowest level of existence.

We can thus discern a parallel between the Báb's analogies and the discourse taking place implicitly in this poem by Ṭáhirih. She employs symbols to represent in descending order the various levels of spiritual realms—the sun, the moon, the stars, and the earth. This hierarchy of levels of spiritual existence resemble what we read in the Báb's Commentary on the Súrih of Joseph: in his dream, the sun, the moon, and the stars prostrate themselves before Joseph, thereby symbolizing the spiritual realities of Fáṭimih (the sun), Muḥammad (the moon), and the Imáms (the stars). Put simply, this array of cosmological symbols alludes to the manifestation of the divine at different degrees and appearances at the various levels or stages of being. Within this context, we can better understand and appreciate the continuation of the poetic narrative.

In verse 54 of the poem, the sun of glory starts a search in the constellations for the Mystery of *Há*. In verses 55–60, the search continues from the highest level of the sun itself to the lower level of the moon, and, finally, to a falling star, which finds the mystery on earth at the lowest level of existence in the temple of Adam (His earthly or bodily form). Subsequently, the star resumes its ascending flight into the heavens and to the higher levels of existence whereby it beholds the "hidden mystery" in the eternal struggles of Adam, Who, in addition to being a Manifestation, also symbolizes humankind as a whole. When considered in its most ample application, this concept of the arcs of descent and ascent could be understood as alluding to the process by which the divine plan of God is borne out on every habitable planet.

From verse 61 to the end of the poem, Ṭáhirih continues describing the condition of Adam and His plight, thus an allusion to both the sequence of the tribulation of the Manifestations, and to the troubled history of humankind. In particular, of course, Ṭáhirih alludes to this critical turning point in human history and to the reality of the Point, the Báb Himself.

Although the letter *há* assumes various levels of meanings in the Báb's writings, in Ṭáhirih's poem, the letter itself—even as it is employed in the Persian Bayan [p. 193] and "the Interpretation of the Mystery of Há"—is an allusion to the Báb as the Primal Point.[14] Indeed, one observes that allusions to the letter *há* appear multiple times in this poem, and always with the same symbolic value.

Once the divine has been constrained by the limitations of the physical world, Adam begins weeping[15] in secret and in loneliness, like a fish floundering after it has fallen on the shore—another image we find in the Báb's writings,[16] as well as in other poems by Ṭáhirih.[17] Adam is struggling to return from the earthly material world to the vast ocean of divinity. Witnessing Adam's anguish and sorrows, God suddenly appears to Him, reminding Him that He has been created in His Own image, that there is no defect in His creation, and thence urging Him to manifest His spiritual station and powers within the limitations of the physical realm—a process that is the underlying meaning of "returning to paradise" and "reunion with God." God then urges Adam to become reconciled to His condition and this divine plan that He might over the course of time become united with the divine station that dwells latent within Him.

An aspect of the divine is that God is "Doer (without let) of all that He intends (*fa"álun limá yuríd*)," mentioned in Qur'án 85:16 and 11:107. Because the Prophets as representatives of God possess the same powers and attributes of doing and acting, Their action cannot be questioned, an axiom articulated by Bahá'u'lláh with sublime clarity. He affirms, "The essence of belief in Divine unity consisteth in regarding Him Who is the Manifestation of God and Him Who is the invisible, the inaccessible, the unknowable

14. See Nader Saiedi, *Gate of the Heart,* pp. 98, 226, 340 for a number of meanings of the letter *há.*

15. We see reference to Adam's weeping in the Báb's Commentary on the Súrih of Baqara (p. 45 of handwritten manuscript).

16. For example, in "Interpretation of the Mystery of Há," Qayyúmu'l-Asmá'.

17. See *Adam's Wish,* p. 55.

Essence as one and the same." He elucidates this verity, "By this is meant that whatever pertaineth to the former, all His acts and doings, whatever He ordaineth or forbiddeth, should be considered, in all their aspects, and under all circumstances, and without any reservation, as identical with the Will of God Himself."[18]

The subject of the action taken by the Manifestations of God is an important theme in Ṭáhirih's theological poetry and is repeated in numerous verses,[19] particularly those in the volume *Adam's Wish*. In the present poem, in verse 82, addressing Adam, God assures Him that the property of acting and doing is an essential endowment He possesses: "There is not a particle of imperfection in your creation! / Your animate (*fa"álih*, "active") essence is a perfect creation!" and in verse 94 Adam is urged to take action: "Establish yourself on the seat of Our throne of Authority / and manifest that vital ("active" or *fa"álih*) power latent within you."

The combination of the word "essence" (*jawhar*) with the word "active" (*fa"álih*) in verse 82 alludes to the specific quality of the Primal Will. "Essence" (*jawhar*) in Islamic philosophy generally does not refer to the essence of God. It rather refers to the first of the Aristotelian categories "substance" as opposed to the rest that are "accident" (*'araḍ*).[20] The first substance (*jawhar avval*) refers to God's Pen, the first creation of God, and refers to a reality that acts on behalf of God and also manifests God's attributes. The attribute of attraction (*ja<u>dh</u>b*) of the essence (*jawhar*) is referred to in verse 6 of poem 8. In His commentary on Bismilláh ("in the name of God),"[21] the Báb explains that God's actions appear from the Point (p. 1), as there is no direct relationship between the transcendent God and the world of existence. As such, in verse 94 we read: "Establish yourself on the seat of Our throne of Authority / and manifest that vital (highly active) power latent within you."

---

18. Bahá'u'lláh, *Gleanings from the Writings of Bahá'u'lláh,* no. 84.4.

19. For Ṭáhirih's direct references to the theme of action (*fi'l*) see in the present volume poem 7, verses 14–15; in this poem, verses 82 and 95; *Adam's Wish*, poem 7, verses 30, 112, 135, 143, 145–48,152, 162–64, 167–71, and 182; and in *The Quickening,* poem 9, verse 28.

20. Sachico Murata, W. C. Chittick, and Tu Weiming, *The Sage Learning of Liu Zhi, Islamic Thought in Confucian Terms,* p. 347.

21. A phrase in Arabic, that occurs at the beginning of the Qur'án, which in its complete form is translated as "In the name of God, Most Gracious, Most Merciful" (1:1).

In poem 7 of *Adam's Wish,* the title poem for that volume, there is a discourse about the fact that Adam, as a representative of God, has the free will to do whatsoever He wishes, but at the same time, He will not do anything that God does not wish. Adam's desire for the immediate perfection of humankind is allegorically a wish against God's Will, inasmuch as God wants humanity to grow and develop by stages throughout time. In the closing verses of the present poem, God tells Adam that the time for action has now arrived, and therefore He should now manifest His active transformative power. Thus, through the allegorical story of Adam, Ṭáhirih not only urges human beings to manifest the spiritual potential with which they have been endowed, but also, and more importantly, she is explaining the dual station of the Manifestations of God and the process by means of which each gradually, and in a timely fashion, reveals the fullness of His station. Even more particularly, Ṭáhirih in lucid terms, alludes to the sufferings of the Báb and the fact that the time for revealing His true station is at hand, a concept that we observe in the Persian Bayán (p. 95) where the Báb, like Muḥammad before Him, explains that in the station of the essential unity of the Manifestations of God, He may be regarded as Adam.[22]

POEM 14

Verses 4–6 explain how the intermediary realm of the Manifestation of God provides the means by which human beings can relate to God. Ṭáhirih thus describes the four aspects of the Manifestation of God that enable this process of worshiping God to come about. It should also be noted that these four aspects are mentioned by the Báb in the Persian Bayán (Section 5 of Unit 8, p. 285).[1]

The four manners of worshiping God are also mentioned in the Báb's Commentary on All Food.[2] The four terms the Báb uses are presented in this order: "glorification of God" (*tasbíḥ*); "praising God" (*taḥmíd*); "declaring the Unity of God" (*tawḥíd*); and "magnifying God" (*takbír*). These terms, or

22. See Bahá'u'lláh, The Kitáb-i-Íqán, pp. 151–76 for a complete discussion of "the station of pure abstraction and essential unity."

1. See also the Persian Bayán, section 17 of Unit 5 (pp. 180–81) with slight difference (*tawḥíd* changed to *tahlíl*).

2. The Báb, Tafsír-i-Kullu'ṭ-Ṭa'ám, pp. 229–30.

a variation of them, are mentioned sequentially in verses 4–6, and we have provided some explanation of them in the relevant footnotes.

Importantly, these four aspects of the Manifestation exist simultaneously in the Báb Himself in the form of the station of the Primal Will, the station of Muḥammad or "prophethood," the station of the Imáms, and the station of the "gates." In the Báb's writings, these four stations of His reality symbolize, among other things, the process of creation—in particular, the first four stages of the seven stages of creation. They also can represent the four dimensions of the human reality: the heart, spirit, soul, and body.[3] Ṭáhirih returns to the notion of the fourth stage in verses 16 and 17. Verses 7–9 portray the exalted and glorious station in the realm of Creation of those who respond to the call of the Manifestation of God.

While there are frequent references to color symbolism in Ṭáhirih's poetry, in this poem we find an association between colors and the concept of the veil. Each color manifests a certain aspect of the Absolute, while filtering out or obstructing other qualities, and thus functioning as a filtering device. In his hierarchical model of the six realms of being, Shaykh Aḥmad associates each of four of these realms with a veil (*ḥijáb*) of a certain color. The highest and most transcendent level is the luminous realm (*kawn núrání*), not associated with any color, the colorless realm of the Absolute. The next four that follow are in order of descent associated respectively with the white veil, yellow veil, green veil, and red veil.

These levels of colored veils correspond with the symbolism of "mystery" (*sirr*) in the Báb's writings. As we move from transcendence to immanence, it seems that the veils become thicker, darker in color, and more obstructive as they need to manifest the Absolute increasingly more in terms of earthly forms and attributes comprehensible to human beings. Considering the first four levels of the hierarchy (of the seven stages of creation), while the realm of God's Will (*mashíyyat*) is characterized as being a "mystery" (*sirr*), the next level lower, the realm of determination (*irádih*), is characterized as the realm of the "mystery of mystery" (*sirru's-sirr*). The subsequent level, "measure" (*qadar*), is assigned the attribute of the covered mystery (*sirru'l-mustatar*),

3. Refer to Nader Saiedi, *Gate of the Heart,* pp. 137, 296–98 for an explanation of these stages.

and finally the last stage is characterized as the mystery veiled with mystery (*sirru'l-muqanna' bis-sirr*). As such, it is reasonable to understand this verse of Ṭáhirih's in the Sh̲ayk̲h̲í and Bábí contexts as referring, as was the case with verse 21 of poem 11, to the appearance of the Báb from the three-fold veils:

Is this the hidden Mystery or the cloaked name
That has become manifest from behind threefold veils.

This symbolism has its roots in the Qur'án and in various ḥadíth̲s, and a brief and simplified explanation of how it functions based on various writings of Sh̲ayk̲h̲ Aḥmad can shed light on symbolism employed by both Ṭáhirih and the Báb. In the writings and teachings of Sh̲ayk̲h̲ Aḥmad, the color black symbolizes the earthly realm, the realm of multiplicities, while the color white symbolizes the transcendent realm of the divine. White also represents the utmost simplicity in contrast to the multiplicity of the contingent world. However, Sh̲ayk̲h̲ Aḥmad notes that some scholars believe that white is not even a color.[4]

Below white, and generally representing the divine Will (*mashíyyat*), is a level nearer to the world of existence and associated with the color yellow, denoting God's determination (*irádih*). As yellow becomes mixed with increments of black, there emerges the darker color green, closer to the material world, and representing God's design and measure of things (*qadar*). Below green is red, which is even more distant from the simplicity of the Absolute. It is the destiny (*qaḍá*) for things created, and, in relation to the spiritual regeneration of existence, it is the embodiment of the divine in the temple of the Manifestation of God. In light of this symbolism, the Crimson Point in verse 17 of the poem alludes to the appearance of the divine reality in the personage of the Báb.[5]

POEM 15

Ṭáhirih adopts certain cosmological symbols in verse 5 to denote the bright and sure future of the Cause of God. She employs the term *madár-i-'aksíyyih,* meaning "reverse orbit," a phenomenon which occurs when certain stars

---

4. Sh̲ayk̲h̲ Aḥmad-i-Aḥsá'í, *Sh̲arḥ Favá'id*, vol. 2, p. 356.
5. Ibid., pp. 358–59.

appear to be reversing their direction of movement, traversing backward in their orbit. When this occurs, the stars' light is less intense. This was traditionally regarded as a sign of misfortune and ill omen—a condition that Ṭáhirih says will not happen again in relation to the Cause of God as the Sun of Unity has appeared in the heavens.

In verse 53 of the poem, Ṭáhirih employs linguistic and grammatical rules utilized in Islamic literature and applies them to philosophical and ontological concepts about the relationship between God and His creation. The Arabic grammatical rules of how to derive the command "Be" (*kun,* "u" not being a letter but signifying pronunciation) from its root word—composed of *káf, váv,* and *nún*—dictates the omission of the letter *váv,* and thus the three-letter command changes to a two-letter word composed simply of *káf* and *nún.* This is represented in English translation by the combining of the letters "B" and "E" to produce the imperative "Be!"

Shaykh Aḥmad-i-Aḥsá'í, in his *Sharḥ-i-Faváid,* vol. 1, pp. 374–79, explains that the deleted letter *váv* actually exists, but is hidden, thereby symbolizing potentiality, a force, or an inherent process that exists in all things, however concealed it may be.[1] He employs various philosophical terms to allude to this ineffable and abstruse concealed reality: it is a reality which is devoid of materiality (*máddih*), form, or idea (*ṣúrat*); neither is it a quiddity or essence (*máhíyyat*), nor does it possess existence (*vujúd*). He then uses water as an analogy to explain this hidden reality. He explains that in a cloud, the water, which will become rain, is invisible and effable. The hidden reality is thus like that concealed water and symbolizes the source of creation, even as a verse in the Qur'án (21:30) observes: "We made from water every living thing."

Thus, in light of Shaykh Aḥmad's discourse on the hidden *váv,* Ṭáhirih's verse, "My once concealed *váv* hath appeared as *kun fa kán* (Be and it Was)" seems to apply this philosophical or theological concept to the spiritual concept of the renewal that occurs when the hidden potential for spiritual regeneration endowed by God is made manifest and its power fully released. In Ibn-'Arabí's symbolism, the hidden *váv* represents the Perfect Man, the intermediary between the divine and the world of creation. In this sense, Ṭáhirih would be referring to the reappearance of the reality of the Manifestation of God at this time in history, and to the spiritual regeneration this process leads to.

---

1. Coincidentally, this concept in various ways resembles the Chinese concept of the invisible Tao that exists in all things.

This verse of the poem might further allude to symbolism employed by the Báb regarding the hidden letter *váv* being manifest in the letter *há*. In the Panj-Sha'n (p. 88), the Báb explains that while the temple of the Primal Will (the physical dimension of the Manifestations of God) is manifest in the letter *há*, it is also like the hidden *váv*. The temple seems to be an allusion to the five-pointed star, which traditionally represents that human aspect of the Manifestation. Notably, the numeric value of the latter *há* is five, as is the numeric value of the word "Báb." However, the Manifestation of God Who appears in the form of a human temple also possesses the hidden divine reality of *váv*. In that sense the letter *há* represents the visible aspect of the Manifestations and the letter *váv* Their hidden divine reality. In short, it seems that the manifestation of the hidden divine mysteries in the figure of the Báb and the actualization of God's Will in this great Day are precisely the focus of this abstruse and allusive verse of the poem.

POEM 16

Ṭáhirih continues the discussion of the philosophical notion of free will, and in lines 26–30 explains how even the lowliest and weakest creation in the world of existence—a tiny ant—possesses a degree of free will. In particular, Ṭáhirih applies the concept of free will to the authority of the Manifestations of God, Ezra, Moses, and the tiny ant, which, though minuscule and normally unnoticed, here symbolizes the veiled appearance of the Manifestation of God in the earthly realm.

According to the teachings of the Báb and Bahá'u'lláh, the Manifestations of God perfectly incarnate the attributes and powers of God, but explicitly disdain any notion that They incarnate His essence or assume partnership with God—a major theme we also find in the Qur'án. They thus fulfill Their "destiny"—the mystery of *Qadar* (verses 37 and 38)—and thereby simultaneously occupy both the divine station and the station of servitude, a theme Ṭáhirih addresses in poem 7 of *Adam's Wish*.

She continues in this poem to stress the theme of the simultaneous existence of the absolute authority of God and His rationale for endowing creation with free will by interpreting the stories of King Solomon and Moses as recounted in two Súrihs of the Qur'án, each of which is alluded to with two of the "disjointed letters."[1] Súrih 23 (The Ant) begins with the letters *Ṭá* (T) and *Sín*

1. The "disjointed letters," "mysterious letters," or "disconnected letters" are combinations of Arabic letters that appear at the beginning of twenty-nine of the

(S), and Súrih 20 begins with the letters *Ṭá* (T) and *Há* (H), the alphabetic nomenclature Ṭáhirih utilizes as allusions to these Súrihs in verses 46 and 51 of the poem.

Ṭáhirih interprets the Qur'ánic verses relating to the conversation of the lowly ant with the powerful King Solomon, and the king's "attraction" (*ja<u>dh</u>b*) by the Queen of Sheba (Súrih 27). She also alludes to the stories of the enlightenment of Moses on Mount Sinai and His subsequent encounter in the guise of a humble subject with the powerful Pharaoh (Súrihs 20 and 27). Lines 31–42 interpret the story of Solomon's encounter with the ant, in which the ant symbolizes the Manifestation of God, Who, though lowly in the esteem of society, is empowered by the command of God to encounter those with the highest degree of authority, renown, and knowledge. Verse 38 clarifies that, although possessing an exalted station among the people is the result of personal choice (*i<u>kh</u>tíyár*), such a station does not mean one is entitled to be selfish or to assume partnership with God (*<u>sh</u>irk*). Ṭáhirih thus demonstrates that humble servitude and obedience resulting from one's own choice are essential conditions for acquiring and exemplifying the most exalted spiritual station, even as did Ezra, the ant, and Moses.

Line 43 continues describing how the story of the ant and Solomon is at this time manifest in the revelation of the Bayán and how the ant is awakening and enlightening Solomon so that he can search for and be "attracted" to the countenance of celestial beauty, as symbolized in his attraction to the Queen of Sheba. Ṭáhirih then concludes the poem by urging the reader to learn lessons from the stories of the past in order to appreciate how they foreshadow the events taking place in the present. She concludes with a prayer that God might cause Him Who manifests these mysteries to become recognized and accepted.

The language of this poem is thus highly symbolic. For example, the ant would seem to represent the human aspect of the Manifestation of God—what Bahá'u'lláh designates as the "station of distinction"—a condition in which the Manifestation is perceived as weak and insignificant in the eyes of the people, yet appears in the world with divine majesty, power, and wisdom, and represents the most exalted levels of glory and knowledge. Thus, the ant

---

114 Súrihs in the Qur'án just after the phrase "*Bismilláh*" ("in the name of God), but prior to the Súrihs themselves.

encounters and enlightens Solomon—who in Persian literature is an emblem of majesty (*ḥishmat-i-Suleymání*) and wisdom (*ḥikmat-i-Suleymání*).[2]

Likewise, Moses, fearing His own weakness and frailty (Qur'án 20:25–35), is commanded by God to encounter Pharaoh, overcome the emperor's power, and thence free the enslaved children of Israel (20:47). The authority and power the tiny ant demonstrates when facing Solomon, telling him "The source of my life in this world is Power! / Except for me, '*Kun fa kán*' would not occur" (verse 33, repeated in 36), foretells or perhaps recounts the manner in which Ṭáhirih's herself encountered and disdained the proposal of the king, Náṣirid-Dín Sháh, as she explains in verse 42:

> Were it to appear submissive before the king,
> This same one would have assumed as his witness "other than God."

POEM 37

The Báb provides different interpretations of this term in His Own works.[1] Also, in the Qur'án (67:72), in the description of the creation of Adam, God addresses the angels saying: "When I have fashioned him (in due proportion) and breathed into him of My spirit, fall ye down in obeisance unto him," a concept repeated in Qur'án 5:29. As such, by using the term "breath-possessing," Ṭáhirih is alluding to a being that possesses a soul—that is, all human beings on whom God has bestowed life. It might also allude to the philosophical notion of the Universal Soul, the manifestation of God's attributes and powers in the world of existence.

POEM 41

Abraham was commanded by God to build the Ka'bih, as in Qur'án 2:127: "And remember Abraham and Ismá'íl raised the foundations of the House (with this prayer): 'Our Lord! Accept (this service) from us: For Thou art the All-Hearing, the All-knowing.'" The mystery of *hám* also refers to Abraham; in addition to its assonance with the last syllable of "Abraham," (*Ibráhím*) the word *hám* connotes "being passionately in love." This type of highly enigmatic allusion to Abraham is also observed in the *Adam's Wish* volume, poems 1

2. Examples of this in the poetry of Ḥáfiẓ can be seen in *Mawlá'í*, pp. 117–18.

1. In the Qayyúmu'l-Asmá', section 18, "Súratu'r-Ra'd," and in the Interpretation of Bismilláh (see Nader Saiedi, *Gate of the Heart*, pp. 79, 136).

(verse 87), 5 (verses 26–27), 7 (verse 93). We also come across the association of Abraham's name with passionate love in Ibn-'Arabí's *Bezels of Wisdom.*[1]

After alluding to Abraham, Ṭáhirih refers to Moses, the Prophet Whose title in Islam is *kalímu'lláh,* "the one who was spoken to by God,"[2] an epithet derived from the fact that He was addressed by God on Mt. Sinai (Qur'án 7:143). Ṭáhirih then continues with the theme of "speaking" as it relates to "the Word" in the Bible (John 1:1), as a reference to Jesus, "the Spirit."[3] Then follows an allusion to Muḥammad with Ṭáhirih's reference to a few verses from the most important Súrih of the Qur'án, the Súrih of Unity (*Tawḥíd*).

In sum, by referring to the sequence of Manifestations in the Abrahamic line, Ṭáhirih effectively establishes the fact that the Báb combines the attributes and powers of all previous Prophets and that, most importantly, as the "Primal Point," the Báb is the source of God's Revelation to humankind as a whole.

POEM 42

The central focus of this poem is on the reality of the Manifestations of God, and in particular, "the Point" and its appearance at this historical juncture between the end of the Adamic Cycle and the beginning of the Bahá'í Cycle. But Ṭáhirih also alludes to herself and her own situation by employing the name "Zahrá" (a title for Muḥammad's daughter Fáṭimih), inasmuch as Ṭáhirih was considered by the Bábís to be the return of Fáṭimih, she who was prophesized to reappear on the Day of Resurrection. Finally, we should note that we have taken the liberty of deviating from the original by providing a culturally based translation of certain verses in order to convey the beauty and significance intended by Ṭáhirih for these verses. For example, the English term "Dawn-Breakers" was perhaps first used in relation to Nabíl's narrative, many decades after Ṭáhirih, and the terms "*Kawthar*" and "the Divine Plan" do not exist in the original poem.

---

1. Muḥyiddín Ibn-'Arabí, *Fuṣuṣu'l-Ḥikam,* p. 60.

2. Riaz K. Ghadimi, Behnam Rahbin, Ehsanollah Hemmat, *Riazu'l-Lughát,* vol. 8, p. 242.

3. "In the beginning was the Word, and the Word was with God, and the Word was God" (John 1:1).

POEM 43

Despite Ṭáhirih's implicit and explicit disagreements with certain Ṣúfí beliefs and practices, she enigmatically describes the process of the Revelation of the Báb with reference to certain elements of Ṣúfí philosophy. She alludes to the letter *nún,* not only for its value according to Ṣúfí interpretation described below, but also as a multilayered symbol. In verse 12 of the poem, she alludes to the circular shape of the letter as representing the orbit of the Sun of Manifestation. *Nún* (also meaning "ink") is seen in the first verses of the Súrih of the Pen in Qur'án 68:1–3: "*Nún.* By the Pen and by the (Record) which (men) write / Thou art not, by the grace of thy Lord, mad or possessed. / Nay, verily for thee is a Reward unfailing." Translators of the Qur'án have often interpreted the word "*Nún*" in this verse to be a letter in the Arabic alphabet, one of the many discrete letters, or "disconnected letters" as they are commonly known, that appear at the beginning of some Súrihs without any clear or obvious meaning. *Nún,* however, also means "ink" and "inkstand" (Dehkhoda), and certain translators of the Qur'án have adopted this meaning (e.g., Ali, Maulana Muhammad).

In verses 2 and 12 of this poem, the orbiting of the sun and the planets in the heavens seems to allude to the period of concealment prior to the imminent manifestation and its effulgence in the world below. This process is often symbolized by the shining of the sun through clouds of *'amá.* For example, in poem 1, verse 72, of *Adam's Wish,* we observe that the orbiting of the sun represents a period of waiting and anticipation: "How long must I cycle in the sky like the sun? / Make manifest the secret of Unity!" And in verses 160–62 of that same poem, we read:

My countenance is concealed in the heavens!
My splendor can be discerned in *'amá'!*

My mystery is hidden in *huvíyyat,*[1]
but discerned through the veil of *váḥidíyyat.*[2]

---

1. *Huvíyyat,* "the Divine." The mystery of the nature of the Prophet is ever beyond understanding.

2. *Váḥidíyyat,* "Unity." Though the nature of the Prophet is concealed, the evidence of His presence can be found where unity is apparent.

The circularity, then, of the letter *nún* as it is presented in verse 12, is associated with the realities concealed in the ink, or with that which is soon to be revealed. Likewise, in verse 2, the *rotation* of the mystery of concealment in the veiled station refers to the period of concealment prior to the effulgence.

According to Ṣúfí philosophy, the process of God's creation of the world of existence takes place in two stages of emanation: *fayḍ aqdas* is the first and *fayḍ muqaddas* is the second. Prior to the first emanation, creatures emanating from God are not yet differentiated, a stage symbolized in Ṣúfí literature with ink (*nún*) because ink contains all letters and words, even though they are only in a state of potentiality. Ink in this conceit is thus contrasted with the pen (*qalam*), the means by which the ink is employed to fashion letters, words, and meaning. It is in this sense that the pen is the device by which the realities concealed in the ink are made manifest. Likewise, through the first emanation, the identity or individuation of things becomes apparent because each assumes its unique form as an idea or an archetype (*a'yán thábita*), a notion quite similar to the Platonic idea of the metaphysical forms from which each expression of reality takes its distinct meaning.

In its mystical interpretation, the archetypes of all that exists originate in God's knowledge and therefore manifest God's Will and His design for creation. As such, we see in this poem that Ṭáhirih uses the phrase "that which exists" (*má yakún*) to refer to God, the Existing One. Verses 4, 7, 8, and 14 of the poem end with this phrase. In this sense, nothing exists except God—a mystical notion she also refers to in other poems. The phrase also resembles the ḥadíth "There was God and was nothing else with Him." Explaining this ḥadíth, an accomplished Ṣúfí said: "now is the same at it was," meaning only God exists.[3] This concept is also referred to in Poem 45.

As such, the identities that were in a combined or potential state (*jam'*) appear in the state of distinction or separation (*tafṣíl*). The ink can thus be interpreted as the realm of *aḥadiyyih* (Singleness), which is an expression of the absolute transcendence of God, and the pen can be understood to be the station of *váḥidiyyih* (Unity) of God, which is the station of the Manifestations of God. This is the stage when the created things exist as separate entities in the knowledge of God.

3. 'Abdu'l-Bahá's Commentary of the Ḥadíth of the Hidden Treasure.

Ṭáhirih uses the word "soul" (*ján*) in verse 2 of the poem to indicate this station, even as we read in the explanation of Ṣúfí terms,[4] the soul (*ján*) refers to the fixed entities or archetypes (*a'yán thábita*), the reality of the things that abide in the world of existence, realities that have emanated from God's knowledge in the realms of Unity (*váḥidíyyat* and *jabarút*). However, these archetypes have not yet appeared as existing entities in the world. They are still concealed within divine knowledge. This station is still a transcendent state that is referred to with the attribute of the glory of God (*jalál*), a glory that in its intensity separates God from His creation, and a station or condition that human beings cannot comprehend. Subsequently, a second emanation takes place, and God's beauty (*jamál*) becomes manifest in the realm of existence (verse 3 of the poem).

In verse 4 and the verses that follow, Ṭáhirih interprets the process of creation as the process of the revelation of the Manifestation of God (as we also observe in 'Abdu'l-Bahá's commentary on the ḥadíth of the Hidden Treasure). In this interpretation, the realm of ink—in which all realities are concealed in the darkness of ink itself—is a symbol for the period before the Manifestations of God reveal Their station and purpose.

With the revelation of Their station through the verses revealed by Them, words and meanings appear, as we read in the last verse of the poem: "O Thou who doth hear the verses of God, a fire hath descended from the heavens! / Because of what hath been uttered, the sun of Qadar hath now emerged from concealment." Also, through the process of manifestation, the attribute of the "glory" or "majesty" (*jalál*) of God is replaced with the attribute of beauty (*jamál*), something we also observe in poem 1, verse 32 of *Adam's Wish:* "The Veils of *Jalál* have been rent asunder! / Lo, every *Jamál* has now become resplendent!" The first four verses of the present poem are concerned with the symbolism of *jalál* and *jamál*, the transcendent and immanent aspects of the Manifestation of God.

4. Siyyid Ṣádiq Gawharín, *Sharḥ-i-Iṣṭiláḥát-i-Taṣavvuf*, vol. 3, p. 7.

POEM 45

As explored in the introduction to this poem, Ṭáhirih alludes to a complex ḥadíth in verse 3 and depicts the conditions that take place when God brings forth the reality of the Manifestation—He Who has been attracted to God. But even this immaculate reflection of the attributes and powers of God manifested perfectly in the Prophets does not alter the absolute singleness of God Himself. The interpretation of this ḥadíth by Siyyid Káẓim-i-Rashtí is that when the Muḥammadan Light (the Reality of the Manifestation of God) appeared before the presence of God and praised and worshiped Him, God said, "O my servant you are (both) the desired one and the desiring one; you are the best of my creatures, My Grandeur and Glory. If you did not exist (if it was not for your sake), I would have not created the spheres (the world of existence)."[1]

This explanation resembles the concept in Ṣúfí philosophy alluding to the condition that occurs when God witnesses His own beauty and is in love with His own Countenance. In this condition, the lover and beloved are identical, or in the analogy of the Maiden of Heaven, the Maiden is the divine aspect of the Manifestation of God Himself. In verse 3 of the poem, the Arabic phrase "is as He was" (*kamá kána yakún*) refers to what the famous Ṣúfí Juneid said when the ḥadíth of "There was God and nothing was with Him" was recited to him. He responded with "now is the same as it was" (*al'ána kamá kána*). This response refers to the notion that God is always transcendent. In relation to the station of the Manifestations of God, this would mean that in every era or dispensation, as an intermediary between God and His creation, the Manifestations always exhibit the attributes of transcendence and immanence when They represent perfectly God's attributes and powers in the world of creation.[2]

Verses 5–13 of the poem address the manifestation of God's Will in the world of creation through the lofty station of the Manifestation of God, thereby alluding to the station of *'amá*, the realm of divine mysteries from which descends or emanates the manifestation of mysteries in the created

1. Translation of Siyyid Káẓim, quoted in 'Abdu'l-Ḥamíd Ishráq-i-Khávarí, *Qámus-i-Íqán*, p. 1289.

2. Refer to 'Abdu'l-Bahá's Commentary on the Hidden Treasure and to Siyyid Káẓim-i-Rashtí's *Khuṭbiy-i-Ṭutunjiyyih* and to the explanation provided in Ishráq-i-Khávarí's concordance of the Book of Certitude (pp. 1282–89) (*Qámús-i-Íqán*) for a detailed elucidation based on these sources.

world (physical reality). When the Manifestation observes that He can know and reveal these mysteries, this reality rotates around the Empyrean and reveals these mysteries at each era according to the needs of that time. To perform this mighty function, the Manifestation appears in human form and willingly endures the calamities and sufferings of rejection and persecution while intentionally restraining Himself from employing the miraculous powers available to Him (verse 11).

Verses 12 and 13 are prayers by the Manifestation beseeching God to assist Him in ministering to the people of Islam that they might return to God. The concept of Return (*raj'at*) appears several times in the poem, referring to the Arc of Ascent, the return of the world of creation to its divine origin, or, in this era, the return of Islam to the spiritual purity of its origins.

POEM 55

There is a reason why Ṭáhirih uses the Arabic term *lás͟híyah* ("spotless" or "immaculate")—a term not obvious in meaning to the Persian reader. The explanation might lie in the fact that she is referring to the ideal seeker of truth, the highest station of holiness in which one sacrifices earthly life and thereby becomes reborn into a new life, possibly attaining the ability to bestow life on those who are dead, an interpretation based on a Qur'ánic verse. That is, the word *lás͟híyah* is used in Qur'án 2:71 in a passage alluding to the special attributes of the heifer that Moses has told His people God has asked them to choose for sacrifice. This story is believed to be the reason this Súrih of the Qur'án is called the Súrih of the Cow. In verses 2:67–71, after Moses tells the Israelites that God wants them to sacrifice a cow, they repeatedly ask Moses for a specific description of which cow they should choose, and He explains the attributes of the cow three times:

> They said: "Beseech on our behalf thy Lord to make plain to us what (heifer) it is!" He says: "The heifer should be neither too old nor too young, but of middling age; now do what ye are commanded!"
>
> They said: "Beseech on our behalf thy Lord to make plain to us her color." He says, "a fawn-colored heifer, pure and rich in tone, the admiration of beholders!"
>
> They said, "Beseech on our behalf thy Lord to make plain to us what she is, to us are all heifers alike; we wish indeed for guidance, if Alláh wills."

> He says, "a heifer not trained to till the soil or water the fields; sound and without blemish." They said: "Now hast thou brought the truth." Then they offered her in sacrifice, but not with goodwill.
>
> Remember ye slew a man and fell into a dispute among yourselves as to the crime, but Alláh was to bring forth what ye did hide.
>
> So We said: "Strike the (body) with a piece of the (heifer)." Thus Alláh bringeth the dead to life and showeth you His Signs, perchance ye may understand. (2:68–73)

In His final answer, Moses mentions that the cow should not have any marks on its skin (i.e., "without blemish"). Such a cow is then found by people and sacrificed.

The verses that follow refer to how the people killed a man and how God brings the dead to life. God tells them to strike the dead with part of the sacrificed cow, and that when they do so, the dead will regain life. It would appear, then, that Ṭáhirih is interpreting these verses of the Qur'án as the condition of utmost sacrifice of the believer and a dying of self that leads to a new life and increased powers. This interpretation is consistent with certain aspects of the Báb's explanation of these Qur'ánic verses in His own interpretation of the Súrih of the Cow. However, His interpretation includes several levels of meaning, referring to the cow as the undesirable conditions of self that must be eliminated, or as false vicegerency (*viláyat*), or as the rejection of the covenant of Muḥammad in which He designates 'Alí as His successor.

When Moses first tells the Israelites to sacrifice a cow, they respond: "Makest thou a laughing-stock of us?" (2:67) The Báb interprets this response as people saying to Muḥammad: "makest thou a laughing-stock of us" by killing our own selves and accepting the vicegerency of 'Alí?" Accepting the vicegerency of 'Alí can thus be interpreted as fidelity the believers must have in accepting and believing in the Báb Himself, what He expects most people will not do, or else will do only with hesitancy. In further interpretation of these Qur'ánic verses, the Báb indicates that indeed in this killing, there is life. These interpretations of the Báb thus support the notion that in verse 7 of this poem, Ṭáhirih is exhorting the seekers to be ready to sacrifice all their impurities or undesirable conditions.

POEM 57

Ṭáhirih alludes to certain important concepts and terminologies throughout this poem, and we have found that analyzing them sequentially in the order of the verses is not practical. What follows is an exploration of some of the concepts alluded to throughout.

The principle of the transcendent Oneness of God has been referred to in numerous Qur'ánic verses, such as 59:2: "Alláh is He, than Whom there is no other god;—the Sovereign, the Holy One, the Source of Peace (and Perfection), the Guardian of Faith, the Preserver of Safety, the Exalted in Might, the Irresistible, the Supreme: Glory to Alláh! (High is He) above the partners they attribute to Him," and 6:19: "Say: But in truth He is the one Alláh, and I truly am innocent of (your blasphemy of) joining others with Him."

The word "oneness" (*tawḥíd*) is not mentioned in the text of the Qur'án, though one Súrih (112) has been given the title "*Tawḥíd.*" But a ḥadíth attributed to Muḥammad states: "Oneness is the glory of paradise and of all worship [uttering] Oneness is adequate." Yet, what Muslim mystics have written about oneness can easily amount to volumes of books. Ṣúfís have defined more than thirty types of *tawḥíd,* of which, many have similar meanings while perhaps ten have fully distinct definitions. Some other mystics said it is not possible to understand the meaning of oneness and that the utmost knowledge of it is considering everything that you know as oneness as not being oneness.[1]

The discourse on oneness (*tawḥíd*) is present in several of the Báb's writings. In His interpretation of the Súrih of Oneness, the Báb explains that this Súrih is the soul of the Qur'án. In the Ṣaḥífiyi-'Adlíyyih (p. 21), the Báb refers to four aspects of belief in the oneness of God: the Oneness of Essence (*tawḥíd-i-dhát*), the Oneness of Attributes (*tawḥíd-i-ṣifát*), the Oneness of Actions (*tawḥíd-i-af'ál*), and the Oneness of Worship (*tawḥíd-i-'ibádát*). Yet the Báb emphatically emphasizes that, except for God, no one is able to understand the reality or essence of oneness (p. 22), but, nonetheless He asserts that all people are obligated to observe these four signs of oneness in the person that God has related to His own Self (the Manifestation of God). The Manifestation of God is therefore the perfect mirror reflecting the transcendent divine, though God's signs can be seen in various degrees and forms throughout creation.

To better understand or even make sense of many verses of the poem, the reader needs to attain some awareness of certain Islamic mystical terms and concepts. In verse 2, Ṭáhirih makes a distinction between the transcendence, the incomparable essence (*dhát-i-bí-mithál*) of God and the immanence of

1. Siyyid Ṣádiq Gawharín. *Sharḥ-i-Iṣṭiláḥát-i-Taṣavvuf,* vol. 3, pp. 292–94.

God in the world of creation as witnessed by those who are connected to God (*ahl-i-ittiṣál*), those who experience the ecstasy of nearness to God.

This resembles the Ṣúfí statements that "Oneness is to see the multiplicity in Unity and seeing Unity in multiplicity."[2] The Báb essentially says in this regard that the essence of the eternal, His manifestation is the same as His hiddenness, and His hiddenness is the same as His manifestation.[3] In this verse, Ṭáhirih seems to refer to the Ṣúfí term, the "Oneness of Essence" (*tawḥíd-i-dh̲átí*), which can be understood to allude to the mystic seeing only God and becoming oblivious to all else.[4] In verse 3, she points out that the existence of the whole of creation is possible only through the grace of oneness—an allusion to the Manifestation of God.

This concept—that the divine reality of the Manifestations of God is the source of the creation of the world and that the Point is the cause of creation—is observed in the Báb's writings. In the verse that follows, however, Ṭáhirih emphasizes that this does not mean that each created thing consists of a part of that oneness, a concept ascribed to Ibn-'Arabí by his commentators. Such an interpretation would effectively amount to a belief in polytheism (*s̲h̲irk*), the exact opposite of oneness (*tawḥíd*). The Báb rejects outright such polytheistic notions of the Unity of Being (*vaḥdadtu'l-vujúd*) proposed by some mystics.

In verse 5, Ṭáhirih reminds the bird, her own spiritual self, that she should truly deserve the claim of, or the station of, the mirrors (*maráyá'*)—a term the Báb primarily used for the Letters of the Living as they reflected the perfections of the Manifestation of God (the Báb Himself), but also in reference to other levels of believers as a hierarchy of mirrors, each reflecting the divine perfections.

In harmony with Ṣúfí understanding, mirrors here would refer to all things in creation, each of which reflects certain attributes of God. Yet understanding mirrors as alluding to all things should not be taken to imply that everything in creation is capable of reflecting all of the attributes of God. According to the Báb, and as Ṭáhirih points out in *Adam's Wish* (pp. 120–31), everything in the universe has the choice to obey or disobey God, and if this is symbolic in the Báb's writings, it can be understood as a fact in relation to human beings.

---

2. Ibid., p. 282.
3. The Báb, Interpretation of the Súrih of Oneness (*Tawḥíd*), pp. 2–13.
4. Siyyid Ṣádiq Gawharín. *S̲h̲arḥ-i-Iṣṭiláḥát-i-Taṣavvuf*, vol. 3, p. 294.

As mirrors, people have the choice to face toward God or turn in a different direction, or they can allow themselves to become covered by the dust of otherness, in which case they become incapable of reflecting God's attributes as God intended that they should. It is in this sense that the Letters of the Living as the first believers in the Báb have, through their own search and powers of discernment, discovered Him and have freely chosen to face Him directly, and thereby to reflect His perfections.

In verse 5, Ṭáhirih advises the Bird of Paradise to be truthful and faithful in her "claim" (*iddi'á*) and to reflect the glorious light of God. On the other hand, in verse 21 and the verses that follow, she goes back to the theme of verse 5 and asks the bird to carefully examine the "claims" (*mudda'á*) of the mirrors (*qavábil*) who are in the place of leadership—presumably those mystics, believers, or people in general, who are given the spiritual capacity to reflect God's attributes, but who are too attached to their leadership and therefore fall short of fulfilling their capacity. In verse 23, she says instead of facing toward the Point of Oneness, they are facing the point of polytheism (*s͟hirk*) and are enemies of the Point. And, in verse 24, she alludes to a cover (*ṭamás*) over their mirror (*qábil*), obliterating the light of God they need to reflect. She continues describing the failures of these mirrors who, though reciting, "There is not one worshiped except of God" (*lá iláha illa-Alláh*), fall short in carrying out this verity in their actions. Conversely, in verses 30 and 31 she refers to the holy mirrors that are glorious, reflecting the light of truth and spiritual realities.

In this way, Ṭáhirih is answering an important question concerning oneness and the relationship between God and creation, and resolves the confusion observed in Ṣúfí texts and concepts. Certain Ṣúfís believe everything is a mirror reflecting the attributes of God and understand the Unity of Being in the sense that all things are like drops of one divine ocean. They thus conclude that there is no evil action taken by human beings. However, Ṭáhirih uses the word "*qábil*" ("facing") and its plural "*qavábil*" ("those facing") for mirror, and she employs the concept of mirrors as meaning that everything in creation is facing or has the potential to face God to receive His bounties. In this same vein, we observe how in Ṣaḥifiy-i-'Adlíyyih (p. 21), the Báb refers to even the lowest level of creation, the realm of minerals, as "those facing" (*qavábil*) God. Ṭáhirih points to the choices that human beings as mirrors can make, the notion of free will that she addressed in *Adams's Wish*. Accordingly, each person's course of action regarding this capacity is based on their free will.

In verse 6, Ṭáhirih juxtaposes two types of belief in the unity of God, one being a superficial belief based on only uttered words, such as the recitation of the aforementioned phrase "There is no worshiped one except for God" (*lá iláha illa-Alláh*). This type of oneness, which is based on utterance alone, is called "otherness" (*g͟hayr*) by some Ṣúfís because oneness is a mystery that cannot be expressed in words; therefore, words are considered as being the "other" (*g͟hayr*).[5] We thus note how the word "otherness" appears in verses 7 and 8 as that which is not accepted in the banquet of God's nearness. The second type of belief in the unity of God occurs when God's unity is felt in one's heart and becomes a part of one's essential nature or soul. In such cases, the light of oneness destroys all darkness in the world of existence, for all that such a person beholds is God's essence and attributes—an "ecstatic unity" (*tawḥíd-i-ḥálí*), as defined by certain prominent Ṣúfís, and a term alluded to in verse 6.[6]

Verses 6 and 7 of the poem make reference to another type of oneness defined by mystic thinkers—the belief in the concept of oneness based on reason and rationality, where one becomes aware of the interconnectedness of all things in the universe.[7] Yet in Ṣúfí texts, we also read that the standard for oneness is beyond the capacity of the rational mind to comprehend.[8] The Báb rejects this rational approach of philosophers, who, through reason seek to prove the oneness of God. He asserts that it is not possible for the created one to offer any proof (*dalíl*) in relation to the essence of God.[9] Ṭáhirih also points out the insufficiency of proof (*dalíl*) in verses 6 and 7 of this poem.

In verse 8, oneness is described as pure light, in contrast to being only a shadow. The word light (*núr*) in this verse is in contrast to the words "sparks of fire" (*s͟harárát-i-s͟harar*) in verse 10. Ṭáhirih more often uses the images of fire and sparks in a positive sense. Here, however, that is not the case. We come across this contrast in Ṣúfí literature, indicating that while oneness is

---

5. Kas͟hfu'l-Maḥjúb, quoted in Siyyid Ṣádiq Gawharín, *S͟harḥ-i-Iṣṭiláḥát-i-Taṣavvuf*, vol. 3, p. 272.
6. Siyyid Ṣádiq Gawharín, *S͟harḥ-i-Iṣṭiláḥát-i-Taṣavvuf*, vol. 3, p. 285.
7. *Kímiyáyi-Sa'ádat*, quoted in ibid., p. 277.
8. Ibid., p. 37.
9. The Báb, Ṣaḥifiyi-'Adlíyyih, p. 17.
10. Siyyid Ṣádiq Gawharín, *S͟harḥ-i-Iṣṭiláḥát-i-Taṣavvuf*, vol. 3, p. 291.

light, polytheism—or taking partners with God—is likened to fire.[10]

In verse 22 there is a reference to the term "Oneness of Actions" (*tawḥíd-i-af'álí*), which means all actions of people take place by God's assistance and grace. In this verse, Ṭáhirih seems to be referring to people who consider their actions to be the result of their own efforts; as such, their attention is limited to a focus on their own achievements. In verse 25, she refers to another term used by mystics, "superficial" (*qis͟hrí*), literally "the husk" in contrast to "the core." The "husk of Oneness" in Ṣúfí literature refers to superficial belief manifested only in words and not accompanied by action.[11] In verse 25, the word *qawl* in conjunction with the word "deception" (*g͟hurúr*) is most likely a reference to Qur'án 6:112: "Likewise did We make for every Messenger an enemy,—evil ones among men and jinns, inspiring each other with flowery discourses by way of deception."

POEM 64

In its use of specific terminologies and concepts, Ṭáhirih's discourse highly resembles that of S͟hayk͟h Aḥmad-i-Aḥsá'í concerning the "epicycle."[1] The S͟hayk͟h, through a detailed philosophical discussion, alludes to the simultaneous existence of free will—the rotation of every particle of existence in its own direction and around its own center—and determinism, the dependence of each and every particle on the collective movement of the spheres.

Such has been the condition of the believers in the Báb, who of their own volition have followed His commands (alluded to in verses 9–12). The shadow with the nature of light, which, like an epicycle, was dependent on the larger processes of the rotation of spheres, has now turned into highly scattered particles, illuminating the countenances of the followers of the Báb and conjoining them into a single and coherent body. Over time, then, all the shadows are removed from the world of existence. Again, more literally, Ṭáhirih is referring to the spreading of enlightenment emanating from God throughout the world, in comparison with God's transcendent glory throughout the entirety of creation.

In verses 13–21, Ṭáhirih urges the reader to comprehend the station of the Manifestation of God, and she describes how the company of angels is waiting

---

11. Ibid., p. 289.
1. S͟hayk͟h Aḥmad-i-Aḥsá'í, *Faváʼid*, pp. 81–82.

for His permission to descend to earth and reveal mysteries through ecstatic melodies and to destroy instantly the powerful contenders—the Companions of the Elephant, an allusion to the story (from Qur'án 105:1) referenced in poem 34. Verses 19 to the end of the poem can be understood as Ṭáhirih's prayer for her own participation in this drama. Yet, considering imagery employed in other poems, the gnat in verse 19 and the particle in verse 22 can be symbols for the earthly presence of the Manifestation of God, Whose support the heavenly angels are prepared for, but Who has not yet manifested His true station. Therefore, Ṭáhirih prays ardently for Him to do so.

POEM 70

A discussion of the symbolic nature of the imagery of *jihád*—rare in Ṭáhirih's poems but more frequent in the Báb's writings—is beyond the scope of this volume. Yet a brief explanation is in order to clarify Ṭáhirih's intent from verse 18 of this poem, because certain opponents of the Bahá'í Faith believe that the Báb and Ṭáhirih had a politically motivated revolutionary mission, an accusation that is refuted by even a cursory survey of documented accounts in books such as *The Dawn-Breakers* and *God Passes By.*

In the first two verses, Ṭáhirih informs the reader that she is following the style of the Báb's writings, manifesting mysteries in a symbolic language, and examining tropes, the meanings of which have been hidden, and the intent of which can now be disclosed. The symbolic nature of the concept of jihád becomes evident in both the Báb's and Ṭáhirih's works, as do the choices each one made in response to those oppressive events that resulted in their eventual executions.

On her way from Iraq to Iran, 1,200 new followers offered to go with her and safeguard Ṭáhirih, but she declined.[1] The Báb also rejected the offer of support by Manúchihr Khán Mu'tamidu'd-Dawlih, the powerful ruler of Isfahan, for spreading His teachings. Responding to the ruler, the Báb said: "Not by the means which you fondly imagine will an almighty Providence accomplish the triumph of His Faith. Through the poor and lowly of this land, by the blood which these shall have shed in His path, will the omnipotent Sovereign ensure the preservation and consolidate the foundation of His Cause."[2]

1. See Nabíl-i-A'ẓam, *The Dawn-Breakers,* p. 272, fn. 2. According to several other accounts, the number has been recorded as 12,000.

2. The Báb, quoted in Nabíl-i-A'ẓam, *The Dawn-Breakers,* p. 213.

The Báb's earlier references to the law of jihád can be found in His Commentary on the Súrih of Joseph (sections 96–100). However, because the rest of this commentary has striking similarities to verses and imagery in the Qur'án, sometimes quoting the Qur'ánic verses word-for-word, it might be misunderstood by some as repeating and emphasizing the Islamic concept of jihád. Yet, qualities attributed to this law as expressed in the commentary emphasize the development of various qualities in the believers, which in fact were exemplified by Ṭáhirih and others. Among these qualities are detachment from the material world—including family, friends, home, and country—and sacrificing wealth and enduring martyrdom if necessary, relying thereby on God and being satisfied with His Will. This obeisance to the Will of God meant being prepared for opposition that soon would come, being fearless in the face of the ascendency and power of the opposing forces, maintaining patience in the face of calamities, and being ever ready for sacrificing one's own life, while supporting and protecting other believers.

There are other verses in these sections of the commentary supporting the fact that the law of jihád as alluded to by the Báb is intended to be entirely symbolic. Among these are the well-known passage from Qur'án 2:256: "Let there be no compulsion in religion." Likewise, the command to slay those who are servants to idols and Lát and 'Uzzá (two important idols worshiped by infidels referred to in Qur'án 53:19) is clearly symbolic.

This is not to say that there were not some Bábís who did take these references to the law of jihád literally, a misunderstanding that underlies why Bahá'u'lláh would later declare, "Strife and conflict befit the beasts of the wild. It was through the grace of God and with the aid of seemly words and praiseworthy deeds that the unsheathed swords of the Bábí community were returned to their scabbards. Indeed through the power of good words, the righteous have always succeeded in winning command over the meads of the hearts of men."[3]

POEM 72

One might wonder why the reference in the first verse of the poem to the Qur'ánic term (*fárat-tannúru*) is taken out of its Qur'ánic context and given a new meaning. Reading the Báb's works, we observe that this is, in fact, how in

3. Bahá'u'lláh, *Tablets of Bahá'u'lláh,* no. 7.6.

His interpretations of the Qur'án, He arrives at novel meanings for the verses and stories. Likewise, Ṭáhirih is fully aware of her alteration in the commonly accepted interpretations and beliefs regarding these terms.

The purposeful alterations, and even her reversal of commonly understood meanings, constitute one means by which Ṭáhirih causes the readers to reflect deeply about meaning and encourages them to move beyond the surface meanings of the holy texts, thereby gaining new spiritual insights. Nevertheless, these innovative usages are one reason that readers accustomed to traditional interpretations find the work of Ṭáhirih so challenging. Regarding this specific case of replacing the symbol of the water (that which destroyed the tribe of Noah) with fire and light (which is being manifest at this time in history), we can observe how purposefully Ṭáhirih makes such symbolic reversals, both here and in her other poems. For example, we encounter these same verses in lines 54 and 55 in poem 7 of *Adam's Wish* where Ṭáhirih provides a lengthy interpretation of the story of Noah as a symbol for what is taking place during the Revelation of the Báb:

> Sparks began to fly from that fiery Point!
> Instantly the waters transformed into flame!
>
> Behold that (same) flame burning in Noah's breast
> As Noah mounts the Ark with a troop of true believers.

And in lines 96 and 97 of the same poem we read:

> At times He will make Himself manifest in mere specks of dust,
> At other times through the ocean and its waves
>
> When the waters become tranquil,
> He may arise with a robe of fire.

In these instances, water and fire allude to different aspects of the reality of the Manifestation of God, Who appears in each era or dispensation with those attributes most appropriate for that age. Therefore, the Báb in His works alludes to His own reality with symbols of water, fires, and various other figurative images, all of which, when combined, represent the realities manifest in the Point.

Thus the Báb, in His Commentary on the Súrih of Joseph, asserts that God has willed that this Gate (the Báb) will reveal the mystery of the fire of the Point of water, or that God is aware of His humility before God both day and night on the axis of fire around the water.[1] Importantly, the Báb as the Manifestation of God discerns in the Qur'ánic verses what others cannot perceive. He thus provides authoritative interpretations of the Qur'ánic verses in a manner that only He understands. Therefore, in verse 3 of this poem, Ṭáhirih urges people to see the spiritual realities with the eyes of the Manifestation of God rather than through the views of those clerics and divines who purport to understand the true meaning.

The Báb Himself emphasizes this point in His Commentary on the Súrih of Joseph, advising people to look at the Divine Sign (*áyatu'l-aḥadiyyah*) with His eyes. For example, it appears that the Báb is making a delicate and beautiful allusion to the specific verse of the Súrih of Joseph He is interpreting: "Since the women did not see Joseph with the eyes of the wife of the ruler of Egypt, they blamed her for her loving affection for her Joseph, her lowly servant."[2]

1. The Báb, Qayyúmu'l-Asmá', section 58, Súratu'l-Ḥuzn.
2. Ibid., section 31, Súratu'l-'Izz.

Glossary

Aḥmad A title designating Muḥammad. In Qur'án 61:6, Jesus prophesies the coming of Aḥmad: "And remember, Jesus, the son of Mary, said: 'O Children of Israel! I am the messenger of Alláh (sent) to you, confirming the Law (which came) before me, and giving Glad Tidings of a Messenger to come after me, whose name shall be Ahmad.' But when he came to them with Clear Signs, they said, 'this is evident sorcery!'" Whereas Muḥammad is the Prophet's given name, Aḥmad refers to His divine reality or the eternal reality of the Manifestation of God. The names Aḥmad and Muḥammad both derive form the word *ḥamd*, meaning "praise"—a term Ṭáhirih uses to refer to the Manifestations of God, and in particular to the Báb.

'Amá' "'Amá' is defined as an extremely thin and subtle cloud, seen and then not seen. For shouldst thou gaze with the utmost care, thou wouldst discern something, but as soon as thou dost look again, it ceaseth to be seen. For this reason, in the usage of mystics who seek after truth, 'Amá' signifieth the Universal Reality without individuations as such, for these individuations exist in the mode of uncompounded simplicity and oneness and are not differentiated from the Divine Essence. Thus they are individuated and not individuated. This is the station alluded to by the terms *Aḥadíyyih* (Absolute Oneness) and 'Amá'. This is the station of the "Hidden Treasure" mentioned in the Ḥadíth. The divine attributes, therefore, are individuations that exist in the Essence but are not differentiated therefrom. They are seen and then not seen. This, in brief, is what is meant by 'Amá'." (From a previously untranslated Tablet of 'Abdu'l-Bahá, quoted in *The Call of the Divine Beloved*, note 8, p. 105.)

Arcs of Ascent and Descent An Islamic mystical model depicting the process of creation and spiritual growth in the form of a circle. The pinnacle of the circle is the starting point (and end point) of the divine origin of the stages of creation along the arc of descent, and this process ends at the bottom of the circle where the material creation of human beings is completed. At this point the process of spiritual progress begins along the arc of ascent and ends at the original divine pinnacle of the circle. In *Some Answered Question,* no. 81.9, 'Abdu'l-Bahá states: "However, those who have thoroughly investigated the questions of divinity know of a certainty that the material worlds terminate at the end of the arc of descent; that the station of man lies at the end of the arc of descent and the beginning of the arc of ascent, which is opposite the Supreme Centre; and that from the beginning to the end of the arc of ascent, the degrees of progress are of a spiritual nature. The arc of descent is called that of 'bringing forth' and the arc of ascent that of 'creating anew.' The arc of descent ends in material realities and the arc of ascent in spiritual realities."

Áyih (pl. Áyát) Alludes literally to the verses or utterances of God as revealed by the Manifestations, though it can also be taken more liberally as an allusion to the manner in which all creation manifests some attributes or "evidence" of the Creator. Additionally, *Áyá* can refer to a verse in the Qur'án.

Bá The second letter of the Arabic alphabet, *Bá* is a symbol for the appearance of the multiplicities of the world of creation from the unity of the transcendent God. Refer to the various interpretations of *Bismilláh* (In the name of God) by the Báb and 'Abdu'l-Bahá. For instance, a well-known ḥadíth attributed to Imám 'Alí and mentioned by the Báb in His Interpretation of Bismilláh (p. 48) says that existence appeared from the *Bá* of *bismilláh.*

Bayán This term can refer to two revealed works of the Báb (the Arabic and the Persian Bayán), the Revelation of the Báb, or it can simply mean "utterances." It is used by Ṭáhirih in these senses in various poems.

Bihjat Meaning "joy," "grace," and "excellence," Bihjat is the poetry title of Karím Khán-i-Máfí, a follower of the Báb from the city of Qazvin, Ṭáhirih's own hometown. He was a fellow poet and close friend of Ṭáhirih. While in prison in the house of the governor of Tehran, she often addressed poems and guidance to him, and he responded with his own poems. Ṭáhirih clearly relied on him to communicate with her followers and convey her poems to other believers. (Asadu'lláh Mázandarání, *Kitáb-i-Ẓuhúru'l-Ḥaqq,* p. 304.)

Crimson Point "The Crimson Point" is an allusion to the Báb. In the Commentary on the Súrih of Joseph, He attributes the color red to Himself in various metaphoric terms, such as the "Crimson Leaf" (*varaqatu'l-ḥamrá'*) in Section 82 (Suratu'l-A'ẓam), the "Crimson Pillar" (*ruknu'l muḥammar*) in Section 85 (Súratu'l-Ḥaqq), and in Section 2 (Súratu'l-'Ulamá'), the Báb refers to Himself as the "Mighty Crimson Light" (*núru'l muhayminu'l ḥamrá'*) that has shined in Sinai. The fourth stage of creation, Decree (*qaḍá'*), is symbolized by the color red in the Báb's writings. This is the appearance of the Manifestation of God in the form of a human being in the figure of the Báb, the lowest point in the arc of descent (See **Arcs of Ascent and Descent** above). This in turn symbolizes the appearance in the world of earthly existence, of the potential and seed for spiritual perfections in the arc of ascent. Further explanation is provided in Nader Saiedi, *Gate of the Heart,* p. 310.

Dust (*G͟habar*) This word, along with its derivatives, is used by Ṭáhirih in analogies she often employs, such as in verse 10 of poem 47. The image is also used in Qur'án 80:40, which describes the faces besmirched and darkened with dust or dirt in the Day of Resurrection. Like Qur'án 80:37–42, poem 15 refers to two kinds of people—those who recognize the Point and the ones who stay behind and are smeared with dust. Likewise, in verse 5 of poem 52, the phrase "darkened faces" (*savádiyán*) is a reference to Qur'án 80:40–41, alluding to those in hell: "And other faces that Day will be dust-stained. Blackness will cover them" and other similar Qur'ánic verses. This is in contrast to those in heaven in 80:38–39: "Some faces that Day will be beaming, laughing, rejoicing."

East nor West (*lá s͟harqíyyih va lá g͟harbíyyih*) A reference to Qur'án 24:3: "Alláh is the Light of the heavens and the earth. The Parable of His Light is as if there were a Niche and within it a Lamp: the Lamp enclosed in Glass: the glass as it were a brilliant star: Lit from a blessed Tree, an Olive, neither of the east nor of the west, whose oil is well-nigh luminous, though fire scarce touched it: Light upon Light! Alláh doth guide whom He will to His Light: Alláh doth set forth Parables for men: and Alláh doth know all things."

"Even nearer" A reference to Muḥammad's nearness to God in His Night Journey when the Angel Gabriel says to Muḥammad that if He approaches any closer, His wings will burn: Qur'án 53:9: "And was at a distance of but two bow-lengths or (even) nearer."

The Existing One (*má yakún*) This term literally means "that which exists." Furthermore, in verse 2 of poem 45, "text" or written lines can be a reference to Qur'án 52:3: "And a Book written on unfolded vellum" (Maulana Ali), which has been interpreted to mean heavenly books like the Qur'án

(Riaz K. Ghadimi, Behnam Rahbin, Ehsanollah Hemmat, *Riazu'l-Lughát,* Vol. 4, p. 130). In that sense, "that which exists" is a reference to the world of existence, which is likened to a book, the Book of Existence (*kitáb-i-takvín*). The Book of Existence is in accord with the Book of Revelation (*kitáb-i-tadvín*) based on 'Abdu'l-Bahá's expositions in *Some Answered Questions*, chapters 11 and 13.

Fiṭríyyih, Fiṭrí, Fuṭúrí "Original" or "inherent," therefore endowed by the Creator. See Qur'án 6:79, in which Abraham instinctively turns His allegiance from power manifest in creation (e.g., the Sun) to the Creator of all the heavens and the earth, vowing "and never shall I give Partners to God." These and related words are found in many of Ṭáhirih's poems in relation to Abraham. For further explanation, see *Adam's Wish,* p. 94.

Há The Arabic letter *Há* alludes to the exalted and transcendent aspect of the divine in verses 16 and 54 of poem 11. It refers to the divine attributes reflected in the sublime mirrors. However, *Há* has been given several spiritual meanings in the holy writings, among which is as a symbol for the essence of God. (See Bahá'u'lláh, The Kitáb-i-Aqdas, p. 178, note 28). The numerical value of *Há* is five, the same as the value of the word "Báb," and it can thus allude to the Báb.

Ḥadíth Sayings attributed to holy figures of Islam. These sayings do not appear in the Qur'án, but some are considered as authentic representations of words spoken by Muḥammad or the Imáms.

Ḥamd, Thaná' Both words mean "praising" and "laudation," but often, in the poems in this volume, these terms refer to the Manifestation of God, and in particular to the Báb.

Ḥaram An Arabic term designating the sacred sanctuary at Mecca where no blood may be spilled. It refers to the Ka'bih, though the Báb explains that the true "sanctuary" to be worshiped is the Manifestation of God.

Ḥuriyyih A term, the roots of which can be found in the Qur'án (44–54, 52:20, 56–22, and 55:72), referring to angelic female figures that reside in paradise and accompany the believers. In the Commentary on the Súrih of Joseph, the Báb refers to various qualities of their veils and attire as being beautiful, or coarse, or of silk, allusions to various degrees of the revelation of the divine. (See John S. Hatcher, Amrollah Hemmat, and Ehsanollah Hemmat, "Bahá'u'lláh's Symbolic Use of the Veiled Ḥúríyyih," *The Journal of Bahá'í Studies*, Vol. 29, no. 3, pp. 9–41.)

Ingathering (*ḥas͟hr*) The Day of Resurrection. See Bahá'u'lláh, *The Summons of the Lord of Hosts,* no. 2.25: "Verily, the day of ingathering is come, and all things have been separated from each other." See also 'Abdu'l-Bahá, *Selections from the Writings of 'Abdu'l-Bahá,* no. 207.2: "O ye beloved of the Lord! This day is the day of union, the day of the ingathering of all mankind."

Innamá "Indeed" or "verily." As is the case in verse 12 of Poem 1 in *Adam's Wish* and various poems of this volume, Ṭáhirih is referring to Qur'án 48:10, where it is made clear that the Prophet of God represents God Himself and thus speaks and acts on God's behalf: "Verily, those who were swearing allegiance to you, were indeed swearing allegiance to Alláh." The concept is further emphasized in verse 20 of the aforementioned poem in *Adam's Wish:* "Indeed, Aḥmad's hand was the hand of God" referring to the same verse of the Qur'án.

Ja<u>dh</u>b, Ja<u>dh</u>bih Attraction and allurement. The words play a significant role in discourse appearing in a majority of the poems of this volume. In some cases, such as poem 16, there is a particular focus on and repetition of the terms. While we have provided various English renderings of the words, the terms can refer to the well-known ḥadí<u>th</u> of "What is the Truth?" (*má al-ḥaqíqat*), a tradition referred to by <u>Sh</u>ay<u>kh</u> Aḥmad-i-Aḥsá'í and Siyyid Káẓim, and then subsequently interpreted by the Báb.

The Báb interprets the ḥadí<u>th</u> as describing five aspects of the truth, the fourth being the "attraction by God" (*jaz<u>dh</u>b'ul-Aḥadíyyah*). According to the Báb, "attraction" in this ḥadí<u>th</u> refers to the attraction of the seeker of truth to God's unity, and functions as one of the stages of the revelation of truth to the seeker of truth. Alternatively, the Báb has assigned the stage of attraction to God as alluding to the fourth year of His Revelation, at least in its temporal sense. In various poems, Ṭáhirih makes references to the other stages of Revelation mentioned in this ḥadí<u>th</u>. (See Farídu'd-Dín Rádmihr, "Má al-Ḥaqíqah," *Safíniy-i 'Irfán,* Vol. 6, pp. 137–45.)

Jalál Literally "grandeur," but in Ṣúfism, an attribute of God representing the powers of God, as opposed to those attributes of God that represent His virtues or character.

Jamál Literally "beauty." In Ṣúfism, the term alludes to a loftier and more mystical sense of the divine, much as it does in Platonic philosophy where it stands for "the Beautiful" or "the Good," the notion of the source of creation and essence of God.

Ka'bih The sacred point of Muslims' pilgrimage in Mecca and the *qiblih* (point of adoration) toward which they stand for their obligatory prayers. It is an allusion to the Báb Himself, and Abraham's construction of the *Ka'bih* by the order of God is alluded to in various poems of Ṭáhirih.

Káf and **Nún** Letters forming the word *Kun,* meaning "Be," representing God's command for creation to come into being. "Be and it is" (*kun fa yakún*), is a phrase that appears in many places in the Qur'án, such as in 2:117: "To Him is due the primal origin of the heavens and the earth: When He decreeth a matter, He saith to it: 'Be,' and 'it is.'"

Kawthar According to Islamic tradition, this a river or pond in paradise that Muḥammad viewed on His *Mi'ráj,* or Night Journey, in which He ascended from Mecca to Jerusalem and was shown firsthand various evidences of God.

Kun fa yakúnu "Be and it is" and **Kun fa kána** "Be and it was." In relation to God's authority and power, these terms allude to the process by which God has but to wish or will creation for it to come into being. See Qur'án 2:117, 3: 47, 3:59, and 6:73. More specifically, this alludes to the fact that creation comes into being through the Prophets, Whose power is demonstrated primarily through speech or utterance and through Their immaculate character. In the Persian Bayán, the Báb symbolizes the Primal Will by the first letter of *kun* (*be*). In Persian poetry *kun fa kán,* a shortened pronunciation of *kun fa kána,* has been used to represent the whole process of creation or the entire created universe. (See Ali Akbar Dehkhoda, *Lughat Námih,* 40:265.)

Maḥv "Effaced," in Ṣúfí terminology signifying losing one's own identity or one's separateness from God or the divine by acquiring divine attributes.

Manẓar-i A'lá The Most Exalted Vista. Originally a Ṣúfí term alluding to the station of nearness to God. (See Javád Noorbakhsh, *Farhang-i-Núr-Bakhsh Iṣṭiláḥát-i-Taṣavvuf,* vol. 2, p. 175.)

Mirrors (*Maráyá'*) A frequently employed symbol of the faithful followers who reflect the sanctity and fidelity of the Manifestation. It is a term the Báb primarily used for the Letters of the Living as they reflected the perfections of the Manifestation of God, the Báb Himself, but also to other levels of believers. In this sense, it represents a hierarchy of mirrors in which each mirror reflects the perfections of the higher level. (See Bahá'u'lláh, The Kitáb-i-Íqán, ¶151.)

Muṣṭafá "The Chosen One," a title of the Prophet Muḥammad.

Nún The images of "ink" (*nún*) and writing as alluded to in the poems of this volume are generally references to the first verses of the Súrih of the Pen in the Qur'án: "Nún. By the Pen and by the (Record) which (men) write / Thou art not, by the grace of thy Lord, mad or possessed. / Nay, verily for thee is a Reward unfailing" (68:1–3). Translators of the Qur'án have often interpreted the word *Nún* in this verse to be the letter of the Arabic alphabet, one of the many discrete letters, or "disconnected letters," as they are commonly known, that appear at the beginning of some Súrihs of the Qur'án with no clear or obvious meaning. *Nún,* however, also means "ink" and "inkstand" (Dehkhoda), and certain translators of the Qur'án have adopted this meaning (e.g. Ali, Maulana Muhammad). The mystery of Nún can be understood as the purpose for creation. Nún, the second letter of God's command *kun* (Be) is a symbol for God's determination (*irádih*) to create the world of being, according to Shaykh Aḥmad's symbolism in *Sharḥu'l-Favá'id* (Vol. 3, pp. 103, 283).

Paran (***Fárán***) Alludes to Mount Sinai, Ṭúr, where the radiance emerged in the conflagration of the Burning Bush and God conversed with Moses, and in general to the Holy Land, the terrain in which Jesus was born. The word appears frequently in this volume and is often referred to as the source of light. As regards the wafting of the Holy Spirit from Paran mentioned in Poem 41, see Qur'án 4:171: ". . . Christ Jesus the son of Mary was (no more than) a messenger of Alláh, and His Word, which He bestowed on Mary, and a spirit proceeding from Him: so believe in Alláh and His messengers. . ." Also, in 66:12, we find: "And Mary the daughter of 'Imran, who guarded her chastity; and We breathed into (her body) of Our spirit; . . ."

Primal Point (***Nuqṭiyi-Úlá***) A title of the Báb derived from the ḥadíth by the Imám 'Alí: "All that is in the Torah and the Evangels and the Psalms is in the Qur'án; and all that is in the Qur'án is in the Fátiḥa [the first súrih of the Qur'án]; and all that is in the Fátiḥa is in the Bismi'lláh [the opening phrase of the Fátiḥa]; and all that is in the Bismi'lláh is in the Bá [the first letter of Bismi'lláh]; and all that is in the Bá is in the Point [the dot beneath the Bá]; and I am the Point." Shoghi Effendi elucidated the station of the Báb with the following observation: "He Who communicated the original impulse to so incalculable a Movement was none other than the promised Qá'im (He who ariseth), the Sáḥibu'z-Zamán (the Lord of the Age), Who assumed the exclusive right of annulling the whole Qur'ánic Dispensation, Who styled Himself 'the Primal Point from which have been generated all created things . . . the Countenance of God Whose splendor can never be obscured, the Light of God Whose radiance can never fade'" (*God Passes By,* p. 3).

Qadar and **Qaḍá** *Qadar* is the third of the seven stages of creation addressed in the Báb's writings, with roots in Shí'ih and Shaykhí literature. It indicates

God's measure and design for all things in existence. *Qadar* is contingent on the second stage, God's determination (*irádih*), which in turn depends for its existence on the first stage, the Will of God (*mas͟híyyat*), but that Primal Will itself has no ontological relationship with the transcendence of God. As such there is no direct relationship between God and His creation. *Qaḍá* is the fourth stage of creation. The two terms often appear together, alluding to the realization of God's Will in the world of existence.

Rúmí's Reed (*Qaṣabih Rúmíyyih*) The word *Rúmí* is a title for Mawláná Jalálu'd-Dín Rúmí, the greatest Persian mystic poet. *Rúmí* means "from Rúm" as he lived in Asia Minor, which was once called *Rúm*, a territory in the eastern part of the Roman Empire. The famous first stanzas (35 verses) of the Mat͟hnaví of Rúmí recount how a reed (flute) bemoans its plight because it has been separated from its place of origin, the reed-bed. The reed has been interpreted to symbolize "the Muḥammadan Reality," sometimes called "the Muḥammadan Light," which is a reference to the spiritual reality of the Prophets of God in general and not solely to Muḥammad. This reality is alluded to by Bahá'u'lláh as the station of Essential Unity—a station that refers to the reality of the Holy Spirit, which reveals itself in different ages in the world through the intermediaries of the various Prophets or Manifestations Who have appeared successively and progressively during the course of human history.

The reed in Rúmí's poem has also been interpreted to symbolize the pen and the soul (see Siyyid Ṣádiq Gowharin, *Farhang-i-Lug͟hát va Ta'bírát-i-Mat͟hnaví*, Vol. 9, p. 192). The Manifestation of God is thus like a hollow reed—a reed from which the pith or self has been removed—that is being played upon by the Master Musician, God the Creator. In this sense, the Manifestations speak not through Their own wish, but rather They say only what God tells Them to reveal. The same relationship obtains with the pen, which inscribes whatever the author wishes and nothing of its own. Consequently, we see that in Poem 52 Ṭáhirih is urging the Manifestation of God to reveal His true identity or reality or light. In this sense, the Manifestation as reed sounds out the song of longing or love for the reed bed (the spiritual realm) from which it was plucked in order to become a means by which humankind can be informed about celestial reality. "Rúmí's reed" in this and other poems can also be a reference to Ṭáhirih herself by the same logic with which some interpret the reed in Rúmí's poetry to refer to Rúmí.

Seven Stages of Creation The seven stages of creation rooted in an Islamic ḥadít͟h are mentioned in several of the Báb's writings and in various S͟hayk͟hí texts. In the Persian section of the Panj-Sha'n (p. 27), the Báb mentions the seven stages of creation as the qualities that adorn the chosen believers in "Him Whom God Shall Make Manifest" (the station proclaimed by Bahá'u'lláh)—attributes that these believers shall make manifest in their dedication and actions.

Shaykh Aḥmad-i-Aḥsá'í A well respected Shí'ih scholar and philosopher of the nineteenth century, who, in his works, offered novel and non-literal interpretations of the concept of resurrection and of Muḥammad's Night Journey to the heavens. His non-traditional propositions led to his severe renunciation by some influential clergy, including Ṭáhirih's uncle Mullá Muḥammad Taqí Baraghání (Nosratollah Mohammadhoseini, *Kitáb-i- Ẓuhúru'l-Ḥaqq*. Vol. 3, p. 159). Despite this, Ṭáhirih ardently followed Shaykh Aḥmad's teachings regarding the immanence of the advent of the Qá'im.

Shirk Assuming partners with God, assuming names and attributes for the transcendent divine; or stated more simply, idolatry or polytheism.

Sinai and **Sinaitic** An allusion to God's revelation to Moses on Mt. Sinai and the pervasive influence of that image in the Qur'án and in the writings of the Báb and Bahá'u'lláh, as well as in the poetry of Ṭáhirih.

Siyyid Káẓim-i-Rashtí A student of Shaykh Aḥmad-i-Aḥsá'í, and his successor in teaching the advent of the Qá'im. He praised Ṭáhirih and she taught his students after his death. One of his principal teachings was that after the appearance of the Qá'im (the Báb) the Qayyúm would be made manifest: "for when the star of the Former has set, the sun of the beauty of Ḥussayn will rise." (Nabíl-i-A'ẓam, *The Dawn-Breakers,* pp. 41–42).

Sunnat This word is mentioned in various places in the Qur'án, such as in 17:77 or 33:38. It alludes to the manner or methodology with which God brings to pass His intentions for creation, even though that pathway may be veiled or seem illogical to ordinary people. More generally, it alludes to a pattern of behaviour that can be emulated by others. Much of what became the laws of the Sharia derive from what clerics and divines perceived to be examples or patterns of behavior demonstrated by Muḥammad's actions and methodology.

Thaná' We have translated this word as "praise," representing the divine aspect of the Manifestation of God. In this sense the verses of praise can be understood as divine verses.

Traces (*Áyát*) Used frequently, this word alludes literally to the verses or utterances of God as revealed by the Manifestations, though it can also be taken more liberally as an allusion to the manner in which all creation manifests some attributes or "evidence" of the Creator.

Ṭúr The name of Súrih 52 of the Qur'án, and a term mentioned in many Qur'ánic verses referring to Mt. Sinai where Moses beheld the divine fire in a tree. Ṭúr is important symbolically, not only as the place where God spoke to Moses, but also symbolizing the source of access to God and the beginning of divine guidance in the form of God's laws about personal comportment as regards social and spiritual norms.

Zahrá Meaning "bright" or "the one with an illumined face," Zahrá is the title of Fáṭimih, the daughter of Muḥammad, who holds a lofty spiritual station in Islamic tradition. Verse 15 of poem 42 refers to a ḥadíth recounting when Muḥammad was asked why He titled His daughter Zahrá, He answered: Because when she stood in her *miḥráb* (prayer chamber facing the *Ka'bih*) her light illumined the inhabitants of the sky as the light of the stars illumine the inhabitants of the earth (Muḥammad Báqir Majlisí, *Biḥáru'l-Anvár Majlisí,* Vol. 43, pp.12–13). Because Ṭáhirih's own name was Fáṭimih and inasmuch as she was known by the Bábís as the prophesized return of Fáṭimih Zahrá on the Day of Resurrection, she sometimes alludes to herself as Zahrá.

Bibliography

WORKS OF BAHÁ'U'LLÁH

The Call of the Divine Beloved: Selected Mystical Works of Bahá'u'lláh. Haifa, Israel: Bahá'í World Centre, 2019.

Epistle to the Son of the Wolf. 1st pocket-size ed. Translated by Shoghi Effendi. Wilmette, IL: Bahá'í Publishing Trust, 1988.

Gleanings from the Writings of Bahá'u'lláh. Translated by Shoghi Effendi. Wilmette, IL: Bahá'í Publishing, 2005.

The Hidden Words. Translated by Shoghi Effendi. Wilmette, IL: Bahá'í Publishing, 2002.

"Iqtidárát va Chand Lawḥ-i-Dígar." https://reference.bahai.org/fa/t/b/IQT/iqt-2.html#pg2. nd.

The Kitáb-i-Aqdas: The Most Holy Book. 1st pocket-size ed. Wilmette, IL: Bahá'í Publishing Trust, 1993.

The Kitáb-i-Íqán: The Book of Certitude. Translated by Shoghi Effendi. Wilmette, IL: Bahá'í Publishing, 2003.

"Ode of the Dove" (Qaṣídiy-i-Izz-i-Varqá'íyyih). A Provisional Translation by John S. Hatcher, Amrollah Hemmat, and Ehsanollah Hemmat. *Journal of Bahá'í Studies,* vol. 29, no. 3, Fall 2019.

Prayers and Meditations. Translated by Shoghi Effendi. 1st pocket-size ed. Wilmette, IL: Bahá'í Publishing Trust, 1987.

The Summons of the Lord of Hosts: Tablets of Bahá'u'lláh. Wilmette, IL: Bahá'í Publishing, 2006.

Tablets of Bahá'u'lláh revealed after the Kitáb-i-Aqdas. Compiled by the Research Department of the Universal House of Justice. Translated by Habib Taherzadeh et al. Wilmette, IL: Bahá'í Publishing Trust, 1988.

WORKS OF THE BÁB

Commentary on All Food (Tafsír-i-Kullu'ṭ-Ṭa'ám).

Commentary on the Súrih of Joseph (Qayyúmu'l-Asmá'). National Bahá'í Archives of Iran, manuscript 3.

Interpretation of Bismilláh. National Bahá'í Archives of Iran, manuscript 60 pp. 1–56.

"Letter to Ṭáhirih." National Bahá'í Archives of Iran, manuscript 91, pp. 145–52.

Panj-Sha'n. National Bahá'í Archives of Iran, manuscript 1, pp. 1–88.

The Persian Bayán (Kitáb-i-Mustaṭáb-i-Bayán-i-Fársí). National Bahá'í Archives of Iran, manuscript 62.

Prayer of Sorrows (Du'á'u'l-Ḥuzn). National Bahá'í Archives of Iran, manuscript 1, pp. 101–4, National Bahá'í Archives of Iran, manuscript 58, pp. 14–23.

Ṣaḥífiyi-'Adlíyyih. 42 typed pages. Np, nd.

Selections from the Writings of the Báb. Compiled by the Research Department of the Universal House of Justice. Translated by Habib Taherzadeh et al. 1st pocket-sized ed. Wilmette, IL: Bahá'í Publishing Trust, 2006.

WORKS OF 'ABDU'L-BAHÁ

Commentary on the Ḥadíth of the Hidden Treasure. Translated by Moojan Momen. *Bahá'í Studies Bulletin,* 3:4, pp. 4–35.

Memorials of the Faithful. Wilmette, IL: Bahá'í Publishing Trust, 1997.

Paris Talks: Addresses Given by 'Abdu'l-Bahá in 1911. Wilmette, IL: Bahá'í Publishing, 2006.

Selections from the Writings of 'Abdu'l-Bahá. Compiled by the Research Department of the Universal House of Justice. Translated by a Committee at the Bahá'í World Center and Marzieh Gail. Wilmette, IL: Bahá'í Publishing, 2010.

Some Answered Questions. Newly revised edition. Haifa, Israel: Bahá'í World Centre, 2014.

WORKS OF SHOGHI EFFENDI

God Passes By. Wilmette, IL: Bahá'í Publishing Trust, 1974.

Tawqí'át-i-Mubárakih. Tehran, Iran: Bahá'í Publishing Trust, 1972.

OTHER WORKS

Afnan, Muhammad. *Majmú'ihyi-Maghálát-i-Doctor Muḥammad Afnán* (Collected Essays), Dundas, Ontario, Canada: Intishárát-i-'Andalíb, 2013.

Aḥsá'í, Shaykh Aḥmad. *Ḥayátu'n-Nafs*. Karbilá. Iraq: Maktabah al-Mírzá al-Ḥá'irí, nd.

______. *Favá'id*. Istanbul, Turkey: Shirkat Iráníyyah, 1870.

______. *Kitábu'r-Raj'at*. Beirut, Lebanon: Ad-Dáru'l-'Álamíyyah, 1993.

______. *Sharḥu'l-Favá'id*. 3 Volumes. Beirut Lebanon: Mu'assisah Fikru'l-Awḥad, 2006.

Dehkhoda, Ali Akbar. *Lughat Námih*. https://www.parsi.wiki/, nd.

Gawharin, Siyyid Ṣádiq. *Farhang-i-Lughát va Ta'bírát-i-Mathnaví*. 12 Vols. Tehran, Iran: Intishárát-i-Zavvár, 1983 (1362 Sh).

______. *Sharḥ-i-Iṣṭiláḥát-i-Taṣavvuf*. 4 Vols. Tehran Intishárát-i-Zavvár, 1989 (1368 Sh).

Ghadímí, Riáz K. *Sulṭán-i-Rusul Ḥaḍrat-i-Rabb-i-A'lá* (*King of the Messengers the Báb, the Lord, the Most Exalted)*. Toronto, Canada: University of Toronto Press, 1987.

Ghadimi, Riaz K., Rahbin Behnam, Hemmat Ehsanollah. *Riazu'l-Lughát*, 10 Vols. Toronto, Canada: University of Toronto Press.

Ḥáfiẓ, Shamsu'd-Dín Muḥammad. *Diván-i-Ḥáfiẓ*. Tehran, Iran: Kitáb-i-Pársih, 2011 (1390 Sh).

Hatcher, John and Amrollah Hemmat. *Adam's Wish: Unknown Poetry of Ṭáhirih*. Wilmette, IL: Bahá'í Publishing, 2008.

______. *The Poetry of Ṭáhirih*. Oxford, England: George Ronald, 2001.

______. *The Quickening: Unknown Poetry of Ṭáhirih*. Wilmette, IL: Bahá'í Publishing, 2011

The Holy Bible. Nashville, TN: Thomas Nelson Publishers, 1984.

The Holy Qur'án. 'Abdullah Uusuf Ali (trans.). Elmhurst, NY: Tahrike Tarsile Qur'án, Inc., 2001.

The Holy Qur'án. Mawlana Muḥammad Ali (trans.). Columbus, OH: Ahmadiyyah Anjuman Ishá'át Islam Lahore USA Inc., 1995.

Hornby, Helen. *Lights of Guidance: A Bahá'í Reference File*. New Delhi, India: Bahá'í Publishing Trust, 1994.

Ibn-'Arabí, Muḥyid-Dín. *Fuṣuṣúṣ'l-Ḥikam (Bezels of Wisdom) Ta'líqát by Abu'l-'Alá 'Afífi.* Beirut, Lebanon: Dáru'l-Kitábu'l-'Arabí, 1980 (1400 AH).

______. *Tafsíru'l-Qur'ánu'l-Karím,* Vol. 2. Beirut: Darul-Undulus, 1968.

______. *The Universal Tree and the Four Birds.* Translation and introduction by Angela Jaffray. Oxford, England: Anqa Publishing, 2006.

Ishráq-i-Khávarí, 'Abdu'l-Ḥamíd. *Qámus-i-Íqán (The Íqán Concordance).* Tehran, Iran: Mu'assisi-yi Maṭbú'át-i-Amrí, 127 BE.

The Koran. J. M. Rodwell (trans.). NY: Ivy Book / Ballantine Books, 1993.

Madelung, W. "Ká'im Ál Muḥammad," Bearman, P. (ed.). Encyclopaedia of Islam (Second ed.). Brill Reference Online, 2022.

Majlisí, Muḥammad Báqir. *Biḥáru'l-Anvár Majlisí,* Vol. 43. Np, nd.

Mawlá'í, Muḥammad Surúr. *Tajallíyáti-Usṭúrih Dar Díván-i-Ḥáfiẓ.* Tehran, Iran: Intishárát-i-Ṭús, 1989 (1368 Sh).

Miller, William. "Ad'iya wa-ash'ár, Collection of Bábí Writings and Other Iranian Texts 1846–1923." Uncatalogued Bábí Manuscript in No. 218 Microfilms. Princeton, N.J: Princeton University Library, 1890 (1307 AH).

Mohammadhoseini, Nosratollah. *Ḥaḍrat-i-Ṭáhirih.* Madrid, Spain: Fudacion Nehal, 2012.

Murata, Sachico. *The Tao of Islam.* Albany, NY: State University of New York Press, 1992.

Murata, Sachico and Chittick, W.C. and Tu Weiming. *The Sage Learning of Liu Zhi, Islamic Thought in Confucian Terms.* Cambridge, MA and London: Harvard University Press, 2009.

Nabíl-i-A'ẓam. *The Dawn-Breakers: Nabíl's Narrative of the Early Days of the Bahá'í Revelation.* Wilmette, IL: Bahá'í Publishing Trust, 1999.

______. *The Dawn-Breakers.* Translated into Persian by Abd'u'l-Ḥamíd Ishráq Khávarí. New Delhi, India: Mir'at Publications, 2010.

Nasr, Seyyed Hussein. *An Introduction to Islamic Cosmological Doctrines.* NY: Sate University of New York Press, 1993.

Noorbakhsh, Javád. *Farhang-i-Núr-Bakhsh Iṣṭiláḥát-i-Taṣavvuf.* 4 Volumes. Tehran: Cháp-i-Marví, 1993 (1372 Sh).

Plato. *The Republic.* Translated by Benjamin Jowett. Digireads.com Publishing, 2008.

Radmihr, Farídu'd-Dín, 2003. "Má al-Ḥaqíqah" in *Safíniy-i-'Irfán,* Vol. 6, pp. 123–51. Darmstadt, Germany: Asr-i Jadid Publishers, 2003.

Saiedi, Nader. *Gate of the Heart: Understanding the Writings of the Báb.* Toronto, Canada: Association for Bahá'í Studies and Wilfred Laurier University Press, 2008.

______. *Logos and Civilization.* Bethesda, MD: University Presses of Maryland, 2000.

______. "Tafsír-i-Bismilláhi-r-Raḥmáni-r-Raḥím" In *Pazhúhish Námih,* No. 6, 1999 (1377 Sh).

Sajjadi, Syyid Ja'far. *Farhang-i-Lughát va Ta'birát-i-'Irfání.* Tehran, Iran: Kitábkhánih Ṭahúrí, 1971 (1350 Sh.)

Steingas, F. *A Comprehensive Persian-English Dictionary.* New Delhi, India: Munshiram Manoharlal Publishers, 2000.

Original Manuscript

[٤٠] در نسخه اصل بداء ها هم درج شده
[٤١] در نسخه اصل نوريات هم میشود خواند
[٤٢] در نسخه اصل كنون از بيان هم درج شده
[٤٣] در نسخه اصل ناركن هم درج شده
[٤٤] در نسخه اصل لوح هم درج شده
[٤٥] در نسخه اصل سيف هم درج شده
[٤٦] اعراب مطابق نسخه اصل ميباشد
[٤٧] بر حسب نسخه دانشگاه پرينستون
[٤٨] بر حسب نسخه دانشگاه پرينستون
[٤٩] در نسخه دانشگاه پرينستون بتكلم است
[٥٠] بر حسب نسخه دانشگاه پرينستون
[٥١] در نسخه دانشگاه پرينستون ار است
[٥٢] بر حسب نسخه دانشگاه پرينستون

[١] در نسخه اصل واضح نیست
[٢] در نسخه اصل واضح نیست
[٣] در نسخه اصل واضح نیست
[٤] در نسخه اصل واضح نیست
[٥] در نسخه اصل محدیّت است
[٦] در نسخه اصل ازکان است
[٧] در نسخه اصل با عززا است
[٨] در نسخه اصل واضح نیست
[٩] در نسخه اصل واضح نیست
[١٠] در نسخه اصل سرلندیب میباشد
[١١] در نسخه اصل شد میباشد
[١٢] در نسخه اصل شعاو است
[١٣] در نسخه اصل واضح نیست
[١٤] در نسخه اصل ذکری است
[١٥] در نسخه اصل اندار است
[١٦] در نسخه اصل بایدت است
[١٧] در نسخه اصل تشانین است
[١٨] در نسخه اصل امرآ است
[١٩] در نسخه اصل لسان است
[٢٠] احتمالا قائنن بوده (جمعِ ازفاآن)
[٢١] کلمه "الله" که در حاشیه اضافه شده بود حذف گردید
[٢٢] در نسخه اصل نطاری است
[٢٣] در نسخه اصل واضح نیست
[٢٤] در نسحه اصل ابا است
[٢٥] در نسحه اصل قیبیل است
[٢٦] در نسحه اصل مأل است
[٢٧] در نسحه اصل لهبای است
[٢٨] در نسخه اصل واضح نیست
[٢٩] در نسحه اصل متناع است
[٣٠] در نسخه اصل واضح نیست
[٣١] در نسخه اصل واضح نیست
[٣٢] در نسخه اصل ظهوش میباشد
[٣٣] در نسخه اصل رفعائی میباشد
[٣٤] در نسخه اصل واضح نیست
[٣٥] در نسخه اصل اسرارا میباشد
[٣٦] در نسخه اصل ر میباشد
[٣٧] در نسخه اصل فناده میباشد
[٣٨] مصرع در نسخه اصل واضح نیست
[٣٩] در نسخه اصل طا رف است

نازل آمد بتو از سرمد مدّ مدّ و مدد
ریز برریز که آیات شکور است امروز
تا بیاید بتو آن جلوه فطاره نزیل
برباید ز تو آن حکم غیور است امروز

عرشهٔ عرشه حق گشته مصدر آیات

آن بآن در شرف نور ظهور است امروز

خواهد او[۵۱] تیغ کشد عالم و آدم بکشد

لیک فائش بتمنّا که غفور است امروز

باید آید بعیان سرّ غفاریت تو

سرّ وهّاب و جوارات بظهور است امروز

بایدت عفو که بد شیوه تو عفو عفاف

اسم اعظم ز تو او برّ شکور است امروز

بهجتا گیر ز ما منظره از نور بهاء

ریز در جام تظهّر که ظهور است امروز

در تظهّر تو بیاور ز شئونات بدیع

از قلم ریز بلا مطل که سور است امروز

دان[۵۲] بایقان یقین چشم همه روشن شد

از ظهور تو که اشراح صدور است امروز

ریز در جام شکر ریز باعزاز عزیز

زانکه حین در صرح صرح بلور است امروز

بایدت آنکه نمائی تو بالحان بدیع

شرح آیات الهیّه که نور است امروز

هان نگر واقف منظر که ستاده حیران
منتظر بهر تاذّن بظهور است امروز
باید آئی تو ایا بهجت ما در تغرید
ثبت تثبیت نمائی که ضرور است امروز
نازل آید ز تو آیات بدیعیّه بفاء
زانکه آیات توام شرح صدور است امروز
گوی با احرف نوری بتغرّد ائید
زآنکه حق در شرف صدر زهور است امروز
ریز در جام من ای طایر طوبی منظر
تا که گویم بعیان حق فطور است امروز
طیر قدسی که گشاده پر و بال زرّین
در ترصد بنقاریّه نقور است امروز
واندگر محو ستاده که بیاید اذنش
و از نفیخات رواحیه بصور است امروز
هان نگر طرف دگر قائم قیوم نگر
که مصدّر بمصادر بصدور است امروز
گوی الله اله هو محبوب جمیل
یوم ایفای عهود است و غفور است امروز

بهجتا درک نما نقطهٔ صدریّه فا
خواهد او جلوهٔ عفویه غفور است امروز
ظلم کردند همه بر همهٔ خود بیقین
سر فکندند همه[٤٨] نشر نشور است امروز
باید آئید شما احرف نوریّه منیر
بگذشت از همه خلق ضرور است امروز
عیسی مریم آن روح مجسد بجهان
چون گذشتی بظلم قلب بنور است امروز
باید آئید شما معشر احرف بعیان
هر یکی عیسی مریم که ظهور است امروز
ذکر از غیر نباید که نمائید عیان
بلکه او خود بنمائید که نور است امروز
هان ایّاک ایا بهجت با شور و سرور
حکم تو حکم صبائی فطور است امروز
دیگرت ذکر نباید بقلم[٤٩] از اغیار
بربا ظلمت ایشان که ظهور است امروز
آنچه مخلوق بود از همهٔ کون و مکان
از سما[٥٠] آمده مختار صبور است امروز

(۷۵)

هان که از مرکز قافیّه ظهور است امروز
جمله آیات الهیّه بشور است امروز
حکم نازل شده از شطرهٔ دیوان قدر
غیر آیات عمائیه بکور است امروز
لیک باید که حروفات برآیند ببلج
غلب تغلیب نمایند که نور است امروز
از نظرهای صفی پاک نمایند جمیع
زآنکه زیشان برز سرّ غفور است امروز
ذکر از غیر نیاید که نمایند بقبح
زآنکه انوار خدائی بظهور است امروز
باید از طرف نظر محو نمایند همه
عفو فرمای شوند[۴۷] حکم شکور است امروز
پس بباید که گذشت آیدشان شان جمیل
ذکر ناید ز سوی زآنکه سرور است امروز

که حق ظاهر آمد ز طرز قدر   فناء گشت کل سوی سر بسر
هر آنکس که محجوب باشد ز او   باظلال افکیّه در بند او
ایا غافل از حال و احوال ما   بیا و نگر عزّ اجلال ما
که بگذشته از ماسوی سر بسر   بیک نظره محو جمال ازل
نگر شور حشری بدیوان ما   دگر امر نشری باعیان ما
بنظم بهائی کنون در نظام   بسرّ خدائی عیان فیض عام
بیا نِشستَنِ[٤٦] بر بسیط جلال   مرفع نما طرز عزّ وصال
که تا آنکه مشهود آید تو را   جلالُ جمالُ بهاءُ ضیاء
الا ای تغافل نموده شعار   بهوش آی از شدّت انتظار
بعز بهاءُ صفاءُ ضیاء   مرفع نما پرده امتناع
که تا اینکه بینی جمال بیان   مظهر شده از مقام عیان

(٧٤)

تربص تربص بیا چند چند   ترمّس ترمّس ایا هوشمند
عیان طلعت حق ز اطراز نور   نگر یوم اظهار بعث قبور
قیام قیامت مقوم بر امر   نظام نظامت منظم ز امر

(۷۳)

(هوالله الملک المحبوب)

ز مشرق بانوار قدسی عیان	کنون شمس عزت باعزاز و شان
بذکر خداوند دارای فرّ	گشوده لسان با ضیاء شرر
بعالم در انداخته شور و تاب	که گویا نشور استُ یوم الحساب
ایا طائر قدسی خوش نباء	شنو رمز لاریبی از رنّ نای
باغنان جذبا ربا اهل هوش	که طمطام قدرت کنون در خروش
شنو سرّهای نهانی بآن	عیان ساز فی الان بطرز بیان
که شمس ازل در شرر آمده	مبلّج بسرّ قدر آمده
بطرفی عیان زهره با ازتهار	بازهار حرفیّ جذوات نار
عیان مشعله در فروز ضیاء	مرفع حجاب از جمال بهاء
بعالم درافتاده شور و شرر	ز اقباس طوری شمس قدر
بینداز اکنون ز جذوات نار	فروزان نما مشعل استنار
که تا آنکه بینند اهل فروز	رموز الهی نموده بروز
حجابات محرق ز جذوات او	حروفات منطق ز آیات او
نمانده باستار سرّی نهان	همه سرّ اسرار گشته عیان
هر آنکس که بگذشت از ماسوی	بآن دید او وجه عزّ بهاء

تو را نیست گر چشم او یاب باک ولیکن تو را هست عقل فراک
نگر این چه شور است در عالمین فتاده بشرّاریت او ببَین
گروهی گذشتند از ماسوی ستاده بکف جانها در فدا
ندارند جز دوست مقصد دگر جهان در گرفته ز ایشان شرر
ندارند مقصود جز ربّ خویش گذشتند از خویش و پیوند خویش
چه دیدند ایا واله بی خبر چنین در گذارند بس شعله ور
اگر چشم خود را گشائی بآن به بینی کنون سرّ رجعت عیان
به بینی دگر جمله اسرارها عیان گشته فی الحان ز استارها
نمانده دگر سرّ در پردهٔ همه ما سوی محرق از شعلهٔ
اگر انقطاعت شود رهنما بیابی کنون سرّ کیهان خدای
منور بانوار حقی شوی مقوم باقوام عالی شوی
ره استقامت شود جاذبت بسوی اقامت شود صادفت
ولیکن نه بینم تو را در مقام که آئی کنون منقطع از لئام
تضرع نما شیوه ای هوشیار توسل باحمد و آلش بدار
که تا آنکه مشهود گردد عیان وجود شهادت بطرز بیان

تغـنی سرای از نــوای حجــاز | کـه تا قصـبه رومیـه در نیـاز
برارد خـروش از نـوای بطـون | بالحــان بــدعی بغــنج فنــون
بیـارد صراحی پـر از مشـک ناب | ربایـد ز کل جملگی هـوش و تاب
بگـو از مقامـات قـدسی عیـان | بگـو از طـرازات غیـبی بیـان
بگو از جمالات رخشنده گـون | کـه تا آنکـه ظـاهر شـود سرّ نـون
بگو ز انچه دیدی باذن خدای | بادلیّـــه ثامــــن ایا رهـــنما
ولــیکن ز اسـرار غیــبی مگــو | که تا آیـد این قصبه در جسـتجو
ز جـوهر عیـان آرد او سـترها | ز جـذبت بـرون آرد از قبرهـا
منــور بانــوار قــدس جـلی | همــه در ثنایــت بــذکر خفــی

(٧٢)

نگر یوم بدع است و حق در ظهور | بفوران عیان گشـته تنّور نور
بچشـم حقیقـت عیـان بنگریـد | به بینید آنرا چه کس او ندید
ولـیکن بچشــمش ایا هوشـیار | نگر تا چه بینی عیان زینهار
بچشـم دگـر او بسـی محتجـب | باطراز عزت نهان بس عجب
لطیف است و الطف ایا هوشیار | غریب است و اغرب بسـرّ مدار

ز نورت منور شده کن فکان		مطلــع مســمیّ ز کمّ بیــان
چه اسماء مشهود در انشراق		چه آیات منطوق در انطباق
نه بینند جز وجهۀ پاک تو		نه بینند جز وجه اعلای تو
منور ز انوار قدست همه		معزز باعزاز عزت همه
بیانی ندارند جز ذکر تو		لسانی ندارند جز ذکر تو
الهی بجاه و جلالت که آن		بسی ظاهر است از طراز بیان
بده اذن از فرط الطاف نور		که تا ظاهر آید سماء ظهور
نقاب از جمال خدائی کشد		کشد تیغ[۴۵] قهار جمله کشد
نماند بجز وجه فعّالیت		بجز عدل و انظام نضاریت
که جز تو ندارم هوای دگر		مقام نباشد بجای دگر
الـه الـه الـه		بجز تو نباشد گواه و پناه
توئی ملجام ای خدای جهان		توئی محرمم ای عزیز کیان
رهانم رهانم رهان		بسوی نضار الهی رسان

(۷۱)

بذکر خداوند دارای فر		گشا طیر طوبی کنون بال و پر

که تا ظاهر نماید سرّ اسرار بدیعی را
بگوید آنچه را فی الان شهوداً در فلق آمد
بگو الحمد لله عزیز قادر قدار
که یوم وعد او الان برشح ما فتق آمد

(٧٠)

بطرز بیانی و رمز عیان عیان آرم اسرار از کن فکان
بگویم ز اسرار غیبی کنون نمایم همه ماسوی سر نگون
بخوانم خداوند دارای فر بسرّ خدائی نماید بصر
نه بینم بجز وجهتش در عیان زدایم همه زنگ را از بیان
براندازم احجاب را سر بسر که سوزان تر آمد بسی بر شرر
الهم برآرم تو این مدعا که تا آنکه مشهود آید دعاء
شنو دعوتم را بحق نبی نگر کربتم را بجاه ولی
الهم توئی قادر و مقتدر توئی ناصر نصر و بس منتصر
بجز ذات پاکت ندارد وجود همه ماسوی بر سوی نیست بود
ز تو نازل آمد بهاء و ثناء ز تو ظاهر آمد دعا و عطاء

برار آن رنّه نحلی بریز از آن شراب صاف
شفای کل امراض است در جانم فدا گردان
بیـار از دف آن نائی کـه نایاب اسـت در عـالم
به آفات وفات وفائیه ز نو عالم بپا گردان
الــه قــادر اقــدر نصــیر ناصر انصــر
چه نار است این شعال است بنورت اختفا گردان

(٦٩)

جمیـع ماسـوی در سـکر بینم یا اله الحـق
مگر آیات حقیّه ز اشراق سنا منطق
فتاده گو بعالم شور حشری یا اله العزّ
مگـر آن جذبـه مطلـق بجـذب مـافتق آمـد
الهــا قــادرا عــلام حی محــیی ناصر
مگـر آن رشح بدعیّـه بشـور مسـتبق آمـد
بـلی یا ناظـر محبـوب در ایـن آن بنظر مـا
شـؤنات کمالیـه بنطـق منطبـق آمـد

کـــه تا مشـــهود بیـــنی نقطـــه جـــذبت
رهـانی کل ذرات از کشاکشهای این طـرار
لسان جمله را یا رب بذکرت رطـب فرمائی
که تا صادق به بینی جمله را یا عدل و یا نصار
بحمدت ختم فرمایم کنون این مقطع عزت
بـذکرت جـذب بـنمایم همـه الـواح یا نصـار

(٦٨)

بـــذکر قـــادر محبـــوب منـــور عـــالمی گـــردان
که تا مشهود از بنیان شـود آن عدلهٔ فاران
بیـــاور از بهائیـــات قدســـیه در اینعـــالم
پس انگـه از ثنائیات مشعشع عـالمی گـردان
بگـو از حمـد محبوبی کـه قـدار است و بس قـادر
جمیع عـالم است از وی بشـور و نشـر در صعدان
ثنـایش را بیـان فرمـا بعـز قـدس فـردوسی
بهایش را بجان آور عطایش را عیان گـردان

که دریابی مرا از فضل خود ای کردگار من
که تا آرم بجذب حمد تو این سرّ صعقانرا

(٦٧)

بتکبیرت عیان گردد سراسر جملهٔ اسرار
بتقدیست نمایان وجه پاکت یا علی العال
بذکر پاکت ای رب عزیزم مطمئن گردان
که تا ظاهر نمائی آنچه را در خبئه زینهار
که ذکرت باعث احیاء نور عالمین باشد
نباشد غیر او موجود اندر عرشهٔ انضار
باو موجود کل ماسوی از نقطه بدئی
ایاب کل بسوی وجهتش یا قادر و غفار
الها حمد محمودی تو را شاید باین نعمت
کزو مشهود آید کل امداد از مقام قال
الهی حق ذات پاک بی مثلش
نظر فرما ز الطاف نهان یا قادر و قدار

١٢٠

ولیکن طیر طوبائی بدان این قصبه رومی
نیاید در افاقه جز بیابد سرّ فاران را
تو گر داری ز جذبات شهودیّه عیان آرش
که تا مشهود تو گرداند آن طلعات جذبانرا
تو ای سامع بینداز آنچه داری از سوی از دست
که تا یابی عیان سرّی که یابی معنی آنرا
بدان ظاهر شده آن کنز مخفی از همین قصبه
و لیکن غافلی عالم نیابد جذب دیانرا
خداوند احد دارای فرّ و قدرت حشمت
بنزد تو بسی واضح که دارد سرّ وعدانرا
ولیکن خلق تو غافل از این آیات حقانی
فتادند در مقام بعد و افکندند بنیانرا
بذکرت ای خداوندم لسانم رطب فرمائی
که تا ظاهر نمائی سرّه مستور سرّانرا
الها حق ذات پاک اعلایت اله الحق
که شان پاک او آمد مطهر جمله شانانرا
بهر روزی تو در جلوه بیاری جلوه دیگر
نموده از جذاب خویش روشن کل امکانرا

حق غصنهای رفیع لمیع — حق آیهٔ طالعه از بدیع
که از فضل و الطاف ای کردگار — رهانم ز ما لاتحب در مدار
بجبّت الهی عیان بینیم — بسرّ بهایت بیان بینیم
اله عزیز قدیر بصیر — توئی بارء کل عزیز قدیر
بجز ذات پاکت ندارد وجود — توئی بود و کل سوی نیست بود
لسانم بذکرت مرطب نما — که تا ظاهر آری عیان سرّ ها
لک الحمد یا اله الثنآء — لک الفضل یا ربی الحق بهاء

(٦٦)

بحمد قادر محبوب زدایم زنگ امکانرا
ربایم جملهٔ همزات آرم سرّ[٤٤] اعیانرا
نه بینم غیر محبوبم بعالم باعثی دیگر
ز نور امر او سازم مشرق وجه بنیانرا
بیار ای طیر طوبائی از آن الحان جذبائی
که تا در آفق و وجد آری رجال صدر رضوانرا
ببین عالم فتاده صعق مسکور از ندای تو
دگر باره نگر دریاب این بیهوش سکران را

بنظمت بعالم بیارم نظام		زمام جوارت نمایم ذمام
نه بینم بجز وجهتت در بنا		نجویم مگر آنچه داری رضا
باثبات اثبات آرم ثبات		باقرار آیات آرم حیات
زکاس ملطف بنوشم بجان		برون آرم آن سرّ ز طرز بیان[۴۲]
همه کون و امکان منور کنم		منضّر منصّر مسیّر کنم
الهی بحق گواهان عدل		که باشند در محضرت لا عدل
ستاده بشور و نشور بهاء		عیان سرّ رجعی ز ایشان هیا
که گویا مظهر شدند از نداء		ستادند جمله بعز و بهاء
که دریاب این ذرهٔ مهمله		عیان قدرتت آید از عطّله
ندارد بجز تو معین و پناه		تو بر وحدت او توئی بس گواه
الهی مطهر ز اغیار کن		ز اغیار اغباریش باز کن[۴۳]
توئی خالق ماسوی سر بسر		تو ستار و غفار مَلِک ما نصر
بحق لوائت بـبزم بیان		بحق ثنایت بطرز عیان
حق اول از کائنات بدیع		همه ماسوی نزد وجهش خضیع
حق ثانی ای کردگار محیط		که کینونیت حق ز او شد پدید
حق ثالث ای کردگار ظهور		که ناطق بود او بسرّ فطور
بر او ظاهر آمد لوای صمد		از او باهر آمد عطای احد
حق رابع ای کردگار ودود		که آمد باو بود ازمام و جود

شنو ای مطرز باطراز نور ... ز آیات غیبی بلحن فطور
که الیوم یوم جزاء وفا است ... زمام اموری بدست خدا است
نباشد منفس کسی در مقام ... مگر ذات پاک علیّ علام
بدان جمله آیات وعدی گذشت ... همه سرّ اسرار مطوی گذشت
نباشد بستری عیان وجهۀ ... نیابی ز عالی نهان قبسه
همه شور شرار شد آشکار ... بکل نور انوار شد در دیار
جهان در جهان جمله در نار شد ... زمان در زمان طی باظهار شد
ز دهری نمانده اثر در عیان ... که دیهور شد ظاهر از کن فکان
ز سرمد سرّ مدّی شد آشکار ... که مدت نباشد باظهار کار
صنیع است رب ازل در عیان ... مر او راست شان فعالی بشان
هر آنرا که خواهد خدائی دهد ... جلال و عزاز ثنائی دهد
مقوم باقوام عدلی کند ... منطق باسرار رجعی کند
نباشد بجز وجهتش در بناء ... بنائی بناء عظیم ثناء
اله قدیر عظیم جلیل ... کریم نبیل قدیم جمیل
رهانم ز همزات غبریه شان ... بسوی نماط مرفع کشان
ز کاس محبت بنوشم بجان ... زداید ز من زنگ غیری نشان
که محو آیدم ماسوی از نظر ... بصحو الهیّه آرم شرر
بجذبت عیان آرم اسرارها ... بعدلت قوام آورم عدلها

ستاده سروش سواء هیئتان | که تا اذن اید ز رشح بیان
سرایند با جذب و شوق بهاء | رقائق بدرنند با دف و نای
شوند از سماء عمائی نزیل | ربایند فی الان همه آل فیل
بعوضه بعضو صغیرش بجان | فتاده مقطع بطرف جهان
نماند بجز ذات پروردگار | احد ناصر آید کنون در دیار
بصدقش ظهور بها آورد | بحقش شهادت ثنا آورد
الهٌ الهٌ اله | توئی بر چنین ذرّ مهمل گواه
ندارد بجز تو معینی دگر | نباشد ورا دیگری از نصر
رهانش الهی ز کید زمان | الی بسط احسان و عدلت رسان
بتاجید باشد چه ما لایحب | فتاده بسطح صعیدت عزب
طلوعش عیان ساز ای کردگار | که تا ظاهر آید کنون سرّ کار
الها دگر صبر و طاقت کجا است | که تا آورد استوایش کجا است
رهانش خداوند دارای فر | کشانش الی بسط عدلی نضر

(٦٥)

بذکر خداوند جان آفرین | نمایم عیان سرّ غیبی یقین
بیارم ز کاس محبت کنون | ربایم ز مرآت وهم و ظنون

(٦٤)

الا ای مطـرز باطـراز نـور	بـرون آی فی الحان ز اججاب نور
مرفـع نمـا جمـله اججـاب را	مظهـر نمـا سرّ البـاب را
بیـار از صراحی مشـکین ناب	ربا از همه حاضران هوش و تاب
بیـار و مینـدیش از ماسـوی	که ظاهر شده سرّ حق از بداء
ز طرز مشیت گذر در مقام	ز همـز ارادت ربا هـان زمـام
قدر را بینداز در پیچ و تاب	قضـا را نگـر زو مرفـع حجاب
باذن خداونـــد دارای فـــرّ	مقطـع نمـا طـرز اذن و اجـل
کتـاب بیـانی بیـان در عیـان	نهار است اسبق بلیـل زمـان
بدان ظل عکسی که بد منوجد	ز تـدویر افـلاک بـد مستـمد
کنون جمله شد در نهایت شعیع	ز ایشـان مطلـع وجـوه بـدیع
بنطـق بهـائی منطـق شـدند	بسـرّ ثنـائی ملفـق شـدند
نباشـد دگـر ظـل از ظلیـات	جهـانی سراسر همـه نـوربات[٤١]
تو را گر هوائی بود از هوا	مرفـع نمـا ایـن طـراز بهـاء
نگـر مـاه سیما سـوائی مقـیم	سـتاده باعـزاز باشـد قـویم
نـدارد نظـر جز بـآیات حـق	بسـرّ عمائی کنـون در نطـق

(٦٣)

بحمد خداوند دارای فر گشایم لسان و نمایم شرر
بگویم ز اسرار جباریش عیان سازم آن سرّ قهاریش
که افکنده شور نشوری بجان نمانده بجز وجه او در امان
لهیبات شراره از هر طرف گرفته همه کون و امکان بطرف
نه بینم کنون ذی نفس در امان همه شعله در جان و در الامان
بسوزند از نار بس تابناک همه در فتاده بتیه هلاک
ندانم چه روز است ای کردگار که عالم پر از شور شرار دار
اله جلیل عزیز قدیر مبین سمیع علیم بصیر
بحق گواهان که در استقام ستاده خرامان بعز مقام
نیالوده باشند از همزیات مصفی ز هر غبر در کاینات
مشعشع نضاران اعلی مقام ملمع وجوهان با استقام
نه اندیشیان از همه ما سوی مقوم قوامان با ابتهاء
اله بحق چنین سروران که پاکم نما از غبرّ زمان
کشانی بسوی نماط شعیع مصدر نمائی باعلی رفیع
حق این سواهان نیکو سیر ستاده بامرت کنون سر بسر
نجویند جز استعانت ز حق نگویند الا بحق و رضای بحق

اله الحق لک الحمد حبیب قادر اقدر
رهانم از کشاکشها رسانم بر مقام ها
که از عکس همین نقطه بیاورد عالمی موجود
دلیل وجه باقی جلوهای نظر از او بود
که تا آمد عیان سرّش بناگه از طراز عزّ
بعالم عالم دیگر ز نو ابداع او فرمود
ز انکه اهل این عالم نبودند حامل سرّی
همه مطروح در قعر مذلت نیست و نابود
ایا طائر بخوان آیه ز اهل ذکر
که تا کشف حجاب عزیت بینی تو از مقصود
بگو آن سرّ مستوری بلحن حق مفطوری
که ان الله خلق بدعا لحمد السرّ مستوری
حدیث از صادق آل الله آمد در عیان ظاهر
بیومیکه نبود جز ذکریاتش هیچ مذکوری

نگر دیگر نگر باشد بساط بسطیه از وی
مبسّط در سریر او عزّ قدس او ادنی
نگر دیگر نگر صهبای قدرت در تشعل بین
که گویا عین نار است او که نازل از شجر فی الهاء
نگر دیگر نگر ثلج فؤاد است او مطرب بین
نگر دیگر نگر باشد هوای عطری روحاء
نگر دیگر نگر سرّ سکون است او عیان ظاهر
مصدر گشته او اندر نماط عزت اعلا
نگر دیگر مقام نطق ما بگذشت
همان حرفیکه باشد عزت منطوق او انجا
اله قادر چشم دگر باید مرا فی الان
که از غیریت اغیار او باشد مصفاها
چرا راه دلیل آمد در اینعالم کنون مسدود
بچشم خویشتن باید به بینی وجهه اعلا
تعالی الله جمیل ربنا المحبوب نضار
مصدر بر نماط خضریه با عزّ و با اعلی
لک الحمد اله قادر قدار رب هو
جمیل اجمل محبوب ذا لطف بدیع هو

عجیب است سرّ این نقطه بسی اعجب بسی اعجب
که عالم در شرر افتاده از وی از ره اسناد
ز عکس جلوه جذبش بود موجود در ابناء
بنای صنعت مصنوع و صنع صانع ایجاد

(٦٢)

نگر ای طیر طوبائی کنون در منظر اعلی
عیان بین سرّ ماوائیّ ز جذب نقطه بیضاء
باستیدار از سرّش نگر افلاک عزیّه
باستبدار از وجهش ببین این طارق[۳۹] خضراء
نگر دیگر سرادق بین زسرّش در سرا بر پا
ملئلاء بس مشعشع از رفاع ستره حمراء
نگر دیگر نگر وجه عمائی در بروز آمد
که گویا سرّ اسرار است گشته ظاهر النّداء
نگر دیگر نگر عرش الهی منوجد از وی
باعزاز و برفعیت مصدر در بساط ها[٤٠]

همه معدوم بس معدوم همه محروق بس محروق
باضمحلال طرفی بین بطرف نظرهٔ فاران
بدان ای سامع آیات که الفاظ است در ابداع
ولیکن جمله معنایش بود تازه در این تبیان

(٦١)

بذکر قادر اکبر دگر آن آیدم امداد
که تا ظاهر نمایم سرّ اسرار از ره ابداد
بود دیگر حبیبم حمد مطلق در عماء قدس[٣٨]
ز عکس جلوهٔ وجهش بنام نقطهٔ ایجاد
که کل ماسوی موجود از این نقطه گردیده
بسرّ قدرتش ناطق بهر بنیاد و هر امداد
تعالی الله عزیز قادر محبوب هو اعلی
که کل ماسوی را باشد این همان بنیاد
نباشد غیر او موجود در احجاب رفعیّه
نه بینم غیر او موجود در الواح استمداد

(٦٠)

ایا محبوب بس محبوب توئی مطلوب محبوبان
فدایت انچه را خود مبدعی در حین هم در حان
بجز خود را فدای خود نه بینم قابل ای محبوب
فـدایت نفـس محبوبـت ایا عـالم بهـر بیّـان
چه عالم بینم از عالم مبرا در همه اوصاف
همین باشد همان وعدی مسطر در بیان آن
اله قادر اقدر لک الحمد و لک الانصـر
همـین آن سرّ مشـهود اسـت فتـاده[٣٧] در بنائیـان
که خواهـد در ظهور آید بجذب طلعت محبوب
بوجـد و در وجـود آرد همـه آیات طرخیـان
همین رجع است یا محبوب بعالم کردۀ ظاهر
همین کر است یا مطلوب ز آدم کرده باهـر
ایا صـانع بصـنع الطـف محبـوب در عـالم
عیان بینم همان صنعی که بدعا کرده ظاهر
کجـا آیات قبلیـه کجـا آیات بعدیّـه
کجـا اشراق وجهیـه کجـا الـواح عزیّـه

غنی انت یا محبوب عن کل السوائیات
و انت الظاهر الفعال والاتی بما هو شاء

(۵۹)

عیان بین عالم اعلی ایا ناظر بنظر حق
نهان بین جمله اسماء بخباء جبتی مطلق
دگر بنگر بطرف سرّ ببین سرّ شهودی را
که در ستر خبا باشد بنظر وجهۀ مطلق
نگر در منظر اخضر دگر با نظرۀ دیگر
به بین آن سرّ تبیانی فتاده در فلق مرتق
نگر در جمله آفاق چه آید در نظر دیگر
بدان آن سرّ مشهود است فتاده در بساط حق
و لیکن حق خود ای حق مکش دم اندر این دم دم
که باید بغتته آید عیان این سرّ در انطق

ستاده بس منشط با جلال و عز حقانی
نگر نازل شده امرش ز بین مطلع طوبی
نگر ای ناظر منظر بطرف دیگر از عالم
ملمع وجهتان بنگر ز نظر وجهۀ اعلا
دگر بنگر بطرف سرّ عیان بین جلوه دیگر
که گویا اسم اعظم او بود در مطلع اسما
ستاده او بکف دارد همان عضاب شراره
بگو الله اکبر ربنا المعبود ها ابداء
بخوان ربّ محبت را در این آن ای بهائی سرّ
که ابواب عمائی جمله را مفتوح در اعلا
اله یا اله قادر اقدر
نظر فرما ز احسان مخلّص از سوی فرما
بگردان جمله اورادم تو ورد واحدی در شان
که تا بینم عیان حالم بنزدت سرمدی الله
که تا آنکه مسکر بینم این مرات نورانی
نه بینم جز جمالت را مشعشع از طراز هاء
بگویم آنچه را تعلیم فرمودی تو در ابداع
لک الحمد البهاء المبهاء الجامع الاعلی

۱۰٦

احرف توحید بین بس جلوه‌گر
از حقایقهای نوری سر بسر

(۵۸)

بحمد کردگار ظاهر مشهود در ابداع
مطرز آرم این الواح نورانی در این انشاء
عیان گردانم آن سرّی که مستور از بداء آمد
منور عالمی گردانم از وجهش در این ابداع
تعالی الله الله ظاهر و موجود در عالم
که صنع الطفش ظاهرتر از هر شئ در ابداع
تعالی الله که از نظرات وجهیه بسوزد او
همه افکات نشئیه ز اهل غره سوداء
نمانده جز ثنایش اندر این عالم بطرز عز
همه انظار عزیّه فتادند در جنان ها
ایا ناظر بنظر رب نگر در منظر اخضر
عیان بین سرّ اقنع را بطرف شمسه اعلی

جمله را در قید افعالی ببین
طره را در تیه اضلالی ببین
نقطه شرکیه را بین شعله ور
از قوابلهای قالی سر بسر
لیک از هر شمیهٔ در انعکاس
بینیش بر وجه قابل در طماس
بعض را آخذ بالفاظ قشور
آن دیگر ملتصق بر این غرور
امّتی در انهمال و انعطال
قبضتی در انطراح و اشتعال
عالم عالم از شرار و کفر و شر
سوخته بینی تو بی دون شرر
لیک لفظا قائل قول اله
لا اله محض کفر و اشتباه
هان ایا ناظر بانوار جلی
سوختی تو ماسوی را بالسّوی
بعد تحریق سوی بین جلوه را
از مرائیات قدسی در بهاء

پس بنظر حق بآيات بهاء
خرق احجاب جلالی را نما
تا به بينی وجهۀ مطلب عيان
از مقام عزّ با صد عزّ و شان
وارهی از ماسوای و ماعدا
محو افتی بر بساط انّما
ها که محو آئی بنظر کردگار
درک بنمائی کنون اسرار کار
اينکه توحيد خداوند بيان
نيست او محض تنطق از لسان
بل کرور اندر کرور اندر کرور
غير معدود معدد از کرور
لفظ را از لفظ لفظی قائل اند
آيه را از عکس قمصی مائل اند
نيستند از سرّ وحدت با خبر
جمله عين شرک و کفر اندر ستر
تيز فرما ديده و بين مدعا
از مرايای قوابل در رعاء

لیک این توحید عین وحدت است
قامع بنیان شرک و کثرت است
باید آئی صادق اندر ادعاء
از مرایای بهائی با ضیاء
حالیا باشی تو در وحدت دلیل
نی ز قال همس و لمز و قال و قیل
زانکه بزم وحدت تو بس جلیل
شان غیریت نباشد زو دلیل
نور صرف است و ز عکسیت بری است
بزم حق است ز غیریت بری است
گر تو را شور و هوای وحدت است
میل پرواز همای عزت است
وارهان خود را ز اغبار غبر
پاک فرما از شرارات شرر
روی برتاب از همه افّاکیان
در ترفرف آی بر افلاکیان
غیر حق را بی وجود و هیچ بین
جمله را ز اعمال خود در پیچ بین

نگــر ای طــایر طــوبی بالــواح بیانیّــه
عیان آید تو را سرّی که محوت کرده از ابداء
نظر بنمودم ای محبوب من در کلّ لوحیات
ندیــدم در مفائیــات چنــین جــذبیت حزقــاء
مگر از تو که در عالم بیاوردی چنین امری
که عالم محترق از وی نماید هیچ از اشـیاء
بسـی محویه ز امـر او بصـحو آور اله الحـق
که تا بینم عیان وجهت ز طرز سرّت یا الله

(۵۷)

(بسم الله الرّحمن الرّحیم)

طــایر طــوبی بالحــان بیــان
بازگــو از داســتان قدســیان
اول از توحیــد ذات بی مثــال
در توجّــد آر اهــل اتصــال
زانکــه از توحیــد عــالم منوجــد
جمــله عــالم ز فیضــش منوجــد

منــور طلعتــان بنگــر مســوی هــیکلان دیگــر
ستاده صف بصف در خدمت محبوب ما قرّر
نگر دیگر عیان بنگر چه بینی کو تو در منظر
ولـیکن دم مکـش الان کـه تا آیـد بعـزّ و فـرّ
کــه بایــد بغتتــه آیــد عیــان سرّ خداونــدی
نباشـــد دیگـــری الان موجـــود از ره دیگـــر

(۵۶)

اله الحق حبیب الصدق یا محبوبی الاعلی
جذیب العین طری السّـر هو فی المنظر الکبری
عیـان بیـنم بعـالم سرّ اسراریکــه در مطلـع
چه او نبود دگر چون او قدیم و قادر و اعلی
الهی کیست این محبوب و این جذاب شور افکن
فتــاده از هــوایش جملگــی بــر نار یا الله
همی جوشند بسی سوزند خوش آیندشان آید
که سوزند در هوایش در چنین نار بدیع الله

(۵۵)

توئی شاهد بجز تو نبودم شاهد دگر موجود
ندارم جز توئی مقصد بکونین یا اله الحق
ز[۳۶] فضل افضلت باشم منطق در چنین روزی
که عالم جملگی موتی مصعوق اند اندر بق
زهی غافل به بینم نفس خود را اندر این بنیاد
که اغفل از ویش نبود بکل ماسوی بنیاد
توئی قادر اله الحق توئی ناصر بهر حالم
توئی محبوب ای مطلوب تو ناظر باقبالم
رهانم از کشاکشهای قالیه اله الحق
رسانم بر بساط عزّ حالیه اله الحق
که تا بینم عیان من جمله اسرار حقیّه
بنظر آیم ز اشهار و ز اعضارت بوجدیه
ایا طالب که باشی در مقام لا شیه موجود
نگر اندر بساط قدسیه از جلوه معبود
چه آیات بهائیه مکون از بهای او
چه اشراق ثنائیه مشرق از ثنای او

مگر از نو پدید آمد بنائی در بنا فی الحال
که بانگ نوش در نوش است اندر مقعد اعلی
مگر آن جلوهٔ غیبیّه خود را عیان کردی
که از قبس جمال او بسوزد جملهٔ غبرا
مگر آن طرز عزیّه که بود ملفوف از قدرت
مبسّط گشته از امرت کنون در مصدر اعلی
مگر آن جوهر مکنون که مکنون از ازل آمد
عیان کردی ز فضل خویش در اینعالم غبرا
مگر آن سرّ مخزونی که عندت بود او مخزون
نمودی آشکار از فضل و منت یا اله الهاء
مگر آن نقطه غیبیه کو مستور در نزدت
باستیدار آوردی بنظر خویش یا الله
بحق ذات پاکت یا الهم وارهان از کل
کشانم سوی بیت رفعتت یا ربی الاعلی
اقل من آن یا ربّم نباشم مهمل از محبوب
بیابم لذّت قربت بقدر قدر او ادنی

اله قــادر قــدار یا نصــری نگــر حــالم
بده نصرت که تا ظاهر نمایم سرّ تو در حان
بحمـدت جلـوه‌گـر آیم در ایـن آنات حقـانی
نمـایم جمـله را مصعوق و سـکران از جمالیـان

(٥٤)

ثنـای عـالی صـادر ز صـدر مصـدر اعـلی
سزد صـاعد شـود بـر صـدر قـرب ربّ او ادنی
حبیـب اسـت حمـد محمـود اله قـادر یکتـا
که جز وجهش نبوده هیچ شئ موجود از اشـیا
مشعشع جلوه قدسش بود از لـوح خضـریه
مطلـع آیـۀ عـزش ز طـرز قمـص او ادنی
چه عالم اینکه از شورش فتاده در ثناء یکسـر
سرور حشـر در عـالم شرار قـبس در دنیـا
مگـر سرّ قیامـت آشـکارا گشـت در عـالم
بیامـد وجهـه مطلـوب از شـطر عماء هـا

تعـــالی الله اله قـــادر قـــدار بـــل اقـــدر

جمال الله آن وجهیکه طالع گشته در سرطان

بحـــق ذات پـــاکم غـــیر ذاتم را نبـــد یارا

که تا حامل شود امرم در اینعالم باین تبیان

شنو تغرید جذبایش بسوزد جمله را یکسـر

منم آن نار غیبیّه که بد مستور در ستران

مـنم آن نار شـعّاله مـنم آن قـبس فعّـاله

مـنم آن عـدل عـدّاله نبـاشم در مقامیـان

مـنزه از همـه اغیـار باشم در همـه تبیـان

مقـوم باشم از حـکم صمـد در جلـوه در هـر حـان

هر آنکس کو هوایم را نموده اختیار از امر

ستاده در قیام حکم مقطع از دل و از جان

پس آنکـه شعله افکیّـه گشـته سـنخش را

مجـذب تا فتـاده نقطـه اصـلیه در سـتران

بیایـد از نـدایم در مقـام اخـذ حـق خـود

بگـیرد آنچـه را بردنـد از آیات افکیّـان

بدانـد اینکـه الیـوم او مطهر از جمیع غـل

مصـدر آیـد از امـر الهـی بـر طـرازیان

باظهار صنیعی در بداع آوردم این عالم
ز سرّ صنعتم ناطق نمودم آدمی در حان
که در تنزیه و تکبیرم بکوشد از ره ذلت
که تا آید مظهر سرّ خلقت در صناعیان
نظر بنمودم از الطاف محضه در قوابلها
ندیدم هیچکس موجود از جمله بداعیان
که بتواند تحمل او نماید سرّ ظاهر را
تقوّم شیوه اش آید بطور عز بدعیّان
نظر برداشتم از عالم دوری بگذشتم
بتسبیح و بتهلیلم نمودم جمله را بنیان
نهان بنمودم آن سرّم ببطن علقه صفراء
که تا امد عیان وقتش بخمسین الف در دوران
نمودم آشکار آن سرّ قیومی بیک سطره
تعالی الله از این قدرت جمال الله این تبیان
همان بودم من ای سامع بطرز احمدی ظاهر
ولیکن در علق حکمم بسی مستور در هر شان
پس انگه عالم دیگر نمودم از بداء ابداع
عیان و ظاهر آوردم همه اسرار در تبیان

اله قـادر اقـدر تـوئی عـالم بلحـن او
بجز تو نیست یک نفسی که یابد سرّ از تبیان
بحقـت جمـله احجـاب را مرفـوع فرمـوده
همـه اسرار را[٣٥] مکشـوف آورده بطـرزیان
چگوید گو ایا نازل بارض بدع در این آن
کـه تا شـاهد نمـایم بـر بیـانش کل بابیـان
لـک الحمـد اله قـادر قـدار هـو اقـدر
باذن نازل از شـطر عـماء در نـزد هائیـان

(٥٣)

منم ان نار نوّاری که بودم از ازل مستور
منم ان سرّ اسراری که بودم از ازل منظور
منم موجـود و جـز ذاتم نبوده موجد دیگـر
بوحـدت متصـف آیم بـنزد نقطـه احمـر
بدان ای نقطه شرار شور افکن در این ایام
کـه جـز ذاتم نباشـد هـیچ شـئ موجـود در تبیـان

تعالی الله الله سمیع قادر اقدر
چه آیات الهیّه مظهّر گشته از تبیان
شنو ای ناظر نضریه هان تغرید جذباتش
که عالم در خروش آمد زعکس طفح ناریان
امان جویند اهل بزم از شراریش در حین
ولیکن قاطع امن است از بهر عکاسیّان
شنو تدبیر خفیاتش بقدر منظر اعلا
که در تهیاء خروج است او باذن قادر دیّان
شنو اصیاح هیایش بعکسیات افکیّه
فتادند جملگی موتی چه دیدند صدق بابیان
بگو الله احمد ربنا القدار جبار
فهذا هُو هُوَ یوم صعیب اصعب فی الحان
شنو بار دگر ای منطرح در لجهٔ لاهوت
هویت ظاهر از ستراء طرز هاء بائیان
چه گوید گر عیان تا نار غیبی آشکار آید
مرفع شو و بردار این نظر از جمله افکیان
غنای تو بسی محبوب امده در حین
لقای تو همین مطلوب ادنی شد بانیّان

اله یا اله یک نظر فرما ز فرط لطف
که تا مستخلص آیم از شئونات سوائیان

(۵۲)

بیا ای قصبهٔ رومیّه شرار در تبیان
عیان بین وجههٔ محبوب خود را در عمائیان
مرشح آن غمام نضریه آمد باذن الرّب
بالواح بیانیه لاحیاء العظامیّان
بدان یوم قیامت گشته ظاهر لاشک و لاریب
نمانده جز همین نقطه بعالم در خبائیان
تعالی الله چه شرار است و شور افکن بعالم این
زهی قدرت ز او ظاهر تعالی الله از این اعیان
ز بعد یاس کلیّه مظّهر رایت نصری
بطرز ذلت اکبر مطرح در سوادیان
نگر ای ناظر اکبر بجذب طلعیه آمد
بلوح حکمت این نقطه ز بین جمله طرحیّان

هر انچه دیدی ای ناظر گذر از وی در این ساعت
که بشری آیدت نازل ز طرف بلدهٔ سبحان
نگر الله اکبر با جلال و فر شده لامع
حبیب الله کو طرز هویت را بود بیّان
بسوزد جمله سبحات از برقیه وجهش
مشعشع عالمی گشته ز طلع آیه بر خلقان
بگو الحمد هو محبوب ربّ قادر اجمل
که آورده ز نو صنعی چنین در سطحه صعدان
که کل ماسوی معدوم صرف آمد بیک جلوه
که ظاهر گشته از وی بر طراز شمسه عدلان
اله حق این زیبا سوائیان مه طلعت
که عالم از وجود ذی وجودی در وجودش آن
ربایم از مقامیات سودیه در این ساعت
رسانم تا مقام عزت و قدرت ملیک الشان
بجز تو نیست مقصودم بجز تو نیست معبودم
توئی شاهد باحوالم توئی ناظر بهر تبیان
بذکرت یا اله نغمه سرایم اندر این سطره
که تا از جلوه مطلع منور صعدهٔ غبران

گویا که بود احمد شاهنشه با تمکین
از شطر دگر اعلی در منظر و در میسر
الله که آن جلوه معروف به این آن شد
کز نور رخش عالم در بهجه و در منظر
این حضرت زهراء است در عرش نضاریه
از عکس جمال او عالم ببهاء و فر
یا رب بحق زهراء فرمای نظر بر ما
تا انکه بطرف نظر آیم بطریق انضر

(۵۱)

الا ای سامع از ایات حقیه بفضل حق
سراپا هوش شو از ما نزل از قبسه مشرق
که در اشراق آمد شمس حکمت از عماء قدس
که تا تطهیر تو آید ز ما اشهدت فی الاسبق
اها ها با خبر از ما نزل از سطره شرقی
که لا شرقیّه ظاهر و لا غربیّه از حق

بنگـر تـو ایا ناظـر با نظـره طرفیّـه

در سـتر بهائیـه ایـن کیسـت بایـن منظـر

بـرگـوی بلحـن بـدع از نقطـهٔ جـذبانی

بربـود تـو را اکنـون در منسـطه[۳٤] احمـر

ای طـایر قدسـیّه وی نظـره بدعیـه

ایـن جلـوه حسـنیه بربـود مـرا یکسـر

گـویا همـه عـالم از عکـس رخـش پیـدا

جـز او نبـود دیگـر در منظـرهٔ اکـبر

با طـرز بهائیـه با جلـوهٔ حقیّـه

در بلـج و ضـیا آمـد در مسـطع و در مصـدر

بنگـر تـو ایا ناظـر با نظـرهٔ حقیّـه

دارد زکـه او سـیما برگـوی بمـن یکسـر

ای طـائر قدسـیّه وی جلـوه حقیّـه

بسیار عظیم امد این نکته و این مسطر

محـو امـده ام از کل از مـا بـرزت فی الحـان

افتـاده ام از رفـرف از حکمـت ایـن اقـدر

ایـن قامـت زیبـائی ایـن طلعـت جـذبائی

ایـن منطقـه و ایـن نور در منظـر و در مسـطر

(٤۹)

ای خداونــد عزیــز ذوالمــنن قــادر و قیــوم و حیّ ممـتحن
یاب از فضلت که بس شرمنده ام از خجالت سر بزیر افکنده ام
تا بکی باشم اسیر و دسـتگیر الامـان یا قـادر و حی قـدیر
سوختم یاحق بیاب از فضل خویش پاک فرمایم خدا از کمّ و بیش
نفس جزّاعـه مـرا بی قـدر کرد آتش طوریّ حق را سرد کرد

(٥۰)

از رشحـهٔ کافـوری برریـز در ایـن مصـدر
یا آنکـه بنـور نار بـربای کنـون یکسـر
برگوی تو آن سرّی کو مستسر اندر هاء
در وجد و ولج انداز احباب بنون یکسـر
از جذبـهٔ فطریّــه بــردار کنــون پـرده
بـربای هـر آن مطروح در سـطره و در مسـطر
از رنّ نحولیّــــه از دف نوائیّــــه
در شـور نشـور انـداز اوراق ثنـا یکسـر

تا آنکه حجّتت بعیان آید از بداء
ظاهر شود ز ذرهٔ ذرات در دعاء
حق حقیقتت که بود ظاهر و ظهیر
باقی نمانده ام ز مریان مستسیر
درگیر از کرم که برآیم ز تیه حبل
تا بر فراز قدس معرّا ز غبر حبل
شاهد توئی بآنچه برشح آید از بداء
سوزد جمیع ما برزت من صدور هاء
الله شاهدی که بهر آن از خفا
سوزد مرا جمیع عطیات بی بهاء
درگیر از کرم که الهی و مقتدر
تا انکه خالص آیم از اقطار مغتبر
شاهد توئی که انچه کشیدم من از بلاء
در راه حبّ و جذب تو آمد بابتداء
سهل است یا خبیر رهانیدنم بآن
از آنکه فضل افضل تو در بیان عیان

هر آنکس کو ندایش را شنید و محو خویش آمد
بیامد از جذاب حق بفرّ نور برهانی
سوای از انچه بودی اوفتاده در خبای غبر
باو امداد مهلیّه منزل از عکیسانی
که شاید اینکه آید در مقام تزکیه کامل
به بیند آنچه او ظاهر ز قمص عزّ سبحانی
که در اجلال حقیّه مصدر بر نماط قدس
ز نورش جمله آفاق در اشراق سطعانی

(٤٨)

ای داوری که داوریت داد بیکسان
آید ز تو اعانت و امداد بیکسان
شاهد بجز توام نبود ای اله من
زیرا که غیر تو نبود عدل و داد من
گردیده ام بدور مهائیّه در فلک
گردیده ام نزیل الی مقعر سمک

(٤٧)

بنظم و انتظام آور کنون رشحات سینائی
مکشف هان نما در این سطر آیات تبیانی
بگو از ما بدء بدعا مصدر بر سطیح ارض
که یوم وعد حق ظاهر کنون از شطر رفعانی[٣٣]
بگو از صنعت بدع لطیف خالق اکبر
که از نو آمده بارز ز طور امر سبحانی
جمیع ما سوی معدوم از ظل بدای او
نمانده غیر او اندر مقام عز قدسانی
هر آنکس کو مخالف آمد از عکس جمال او
یقین بربایدش این امر نازل از صراحانی
بدان نار است نازل از سماء امر در این آن
محرق انکه را او منکر است از امر حقانی
بیامد نقطه فتانه هان از ستره سوداء
رباید انچه را بیند سوی از جذب طلعانی
چرا زیرا که امرالله نازل گشت در اسبق
بنور رفعت و برهان ز شطر بیت رفعانی

(٤٦)

الله بعد از این قبول آمد عیان شمس افـول
در شـعلهای ناقبـول بـر زمـره اهـل یقـین
باریـد اتـش از عیـان از رودهـای افکیـان
بر اهل بلد نوریان ارباب فرّ و عزّ و دین
ظلمی که نابودی بدهر نشنیده گوشی در اثر
گشته عیان از این شرر با نزلیـات نار بیـن
الله یا رب حکـیم یا حیّ و محبـوب قـدیم
دریاب از فضـل عمـیم ایـن زمـره ناقـابلین
ای طائر طوبی مقام باعث باحیای عظام
بـردار پـرده از کلام انا الی الله راجعـون
بشری نزیل از آسمان از امر محبوب بیان
بـر زمـره مشـائیان فـافهم بجذب الراشـدین

الله یا رب الثنـــاء یا حـــق بالنـــداء

الله قـــائم در مقـــام مختـــار در نظـــم نظـــام

آمـــد ز اسرار عـــماء از شـــطره رجـع یکـــون

شـــاهد باسرار زمـــام عـــالم بســـرّ مـــا یکـــون

دیـــد او ز اسرار قـــدر و از آیهـــای مستتـــر

کشف عیان گردیده سرّ عاری ز هر ریب منون

دید آنچه خواهد از خدا ظاهر ظهورش[٣٢] از بداء

آیـــد عیـــان از بلدهـــا با غـــنج اغـــماض جفـــون

پس دور زد بـــر فلـــک نـــور از جذبـهٔ رب غفـــور

آورد او آیات طـــور بـــر طبـــق مـــا هم یطبقـــون

کـــرد اختیـــار او از وفـــا تغمـــیس در بحـــر بـــلا

تطهـــیر از کل ســـوی با غنجهـــای نارگـــون

گفتـــا اله مقتـــدر با نصـــر و فـــرد منتصـــر

باشم میـــان مِـــن اذن ذرّ فاقبـــل رحـــیم الراحمـــون

یا ربّ حـــلّ وهم مقـــام در رجعـــت اهـــل ســـلام

دریاب از فضـــل عظـــام انا الیـــک راجعـــون

ای قصـــبه رومیـــه حـــان بـــردار پـــرده از میـــان

بـــربای الـــواح بیـــان کل لدیـــک قـــائمون

برخــوان از لحــن بــديع از آبهــاى فطريــه
برباى اوهام و ظنون از طلعت شمس يقين
سمعـا الهـى بالبـداء احـرق حجـابات البـداء
آتى اليـک يا حبيـب فى هيئـة الاصـاعبين

(٤٥)

چون گشت سرمست ازل عارى ز اوهام علل
نوشـيد او بى غشّ و غـل از صـافى مـاء بطـون
ديـــد از شراق وجهيـــه آيات قـــدس حقيـــه
انـدر حجـاب خفقيـه با سـطرهاى مـا يكـون
نزديـــک شـــد با ابتهـــا از جـــذبهاى با بهـــاء
تا شـد درون پردهـا ديـد او كـما كان يكـون
پس محـو آمـد از نظـر از طـرف نظـر آمـد اثـر
بربــود او را بالنظـــر از كل مـــا هم يعملـــون
بدريـد يكســـر پردهـا نازلشـد از طـرف عـماء
با اشتراق و اضتواء شد مستوى بر ملک نون

این قامت با استوی با جلوهای با بهاء
سوزد جمیع ماسوی از نظریات افکین
یا رب عیان بینم کنون سرّ ازل آمد برون
از طرز های مشرقه با اعتزاز بالیقین
الله رب یا جمیل محبوب حیّ یا جلیل
ذاتیّتت ظاهر شده از سطحه غرب زمین
الله محبوب قدیم حی حبیب یا کریم
کینونیت باهر عیان بر صفحهای بارقین
الله یا رب البیان یا جذبهٔ طلع البیان
نفسیّتت گشته عیان از جذبهای آتشین
الله این با اقتدار باشد بامرت استوار
غیر از تو او را در نظر ناید دگر از سائرین
الله از رشحات نور عالم پر از نور ظهور
یا ربی الحی الغفور دریاب کل طرحیین
الله یا جبار عدل عالم پر از نار شرر
از عکسهای ظلیه موّاح نار ظالمین
ای طائر طوبی مقام آر از سماعیات ما
بردار احجاب غبیر از طرزهای مشرقین

ای طائر طوبی نزیل از نور کن در ابتلاج
بر گوی از ما اشهدت من لا اقدّی فی البطون
ای سامع آیات حق ناری است نازل از سماء
آمد برون از مانطق شمس قدر از مابطون

(٤٤)

چون در مقام اصطفاء قائم باقوام وفا
شاهنشه ملک بقا شد نوحه گر حان آفرین
بنگر بنظر صافیه اندر حجاب ناریه
کاز سطرهٔ عدل صفا آمد برون سرّ یقین
برخوان بلحن فطریه عالم ربا از ماسوی
گردید حق خود نوحه گر از بهر شاه بی قرین
هان گر تو را شور صهبا است بشنو نداءالله را
از سطره عدل قفا است در استشراق یقین
الله یا حی قدیم محبوب حق هو رفیع
ساعت نمودی آشکار اندر عیون ناظرین

الله با جـــذب بهـــاء با اســـتنار و اضـــتواء
در اهـــتزاز و ابـــتلاج آمـد عيـان نـور بطـون
از نظـرهٔ طـرف نظـر انـدر حجـاب منسـطر
عـــرش اله مقتـــدر در اهـــتزاز از مـــا يكـــون
از اهـــتزاز عرشـــيه و از ســـطرهاى حقيـــه
كـــرسى رفعـــت در ثنـــا آمـــد ز اسرار بطـــون
تا كـــه ز نـــور ناريـــه طـــالع ز كـــرسى بهـــاء
شـــد آســـمان در اشـــتراق از شرقـــهٔ با شرقيـــون
ســـبحان محبـــوب قـــديم آمـــد بنظـــر حقيّـــه
ســـلطان قيـــوم قـــديم كل لديـــه معـــدمون
از شرقـــه نـــور كلام بربـــود كل را بالـــتّمام
كى حامـــل سرّ مقـــام محبـــوب كل عـــارفون
خـــواهم ز محبـــوب ازل رب قـــديم لم يـــزل
تا در مقامـــات وفـــا آيم باظهـــار بطـــون
بايـد مـرا تقـويم امـر از امـر محبـوب قـديم
تا ظـــاهر آيـــد بـــر همـــه سرّ الى الله راجعـــون
الله از ايـن اقتـدار گشـته عيـان از شـاه ديـن
بربـود كل مـا سـوى از وهم و اوهـام و ظنـون

کی اهـل عـالم بشـنوید سرّ خـدائی شـد پدیـد
از شـطر ایـوان قضـا ظـاهر جـمال مـا یکـون
این روز آن روز لقا است ظاهر ز طرز انما است
این جلوهٔ کیهان خدا است بارز ز سرّ کاف و نون
هر که شناسد حق وی باشد ز او بی شک و ریب
آنکس که باشد در حجاب شد در جهنم سرنگون
پس ز این نـداء با صفاء شد شور در عالم بپا
آمـــد جمیـــع ماســـوا در ابـــتلاج مـــایکون
نا گـــه ز شـــطر غربیّـــه آمـــد طلیـــع جذبیـــه
نازل بـــنزد هـــیکل قـــائم بامـــر مـــا یکـــون
در دست او لـوح بـداء مسطور از نـور و ضیاء
کی پادشـاه کـن فـکان مختـار بـر مـا یـبرؤن
بنگـــر بنظـــر حقیّـــه انـــدر صحیـــف نزلیـــه
الیـــوم یـــوم وعدیـــه انا الیـــک مرســـلون
هـــر انچـــه داری در نظـــر ای کردگـــار مقتـــدر
ظـاهر نمـا از طـرف نظر از طرزهـای کی یکـون
الله از ایـــن نائـــره در دور آمـــد دائـــره
در بلـج اشراق آمـده شمـس القـدر از طـرز نـون

نگر که از بلجیات مطهفش الیوم
جواهرات ملاءلاء نضار لرزد و ریزد
نگر که ز آنچه بخواهد بان ز مجدیّات
برون ز مصدر نضار نار لرزد و ریزد
نگر که ماه بطون از بطون این مقطع
بسان قطرهٔ نیسان ظهار لرزد و ریزد
بنوش ماء وداد از صراحی جذبت
که از سماء کنون بانهار لرزد و ریزد

(٤٣)

(یا حبیب ادرکنی)

تا از طراز امر حق امد برون سرّ بطون
با اشتراق و اضتواء شد مستوی بر ملک نون
بس دور زد با اجتذاب اندر طراز احتجاب
تا که عیان گردد بجان از جلوه سرّ بطون
تا که ز اطراز جلال گشته عیان وجه جمال
در جذبهٔ شور وصال با غنج الحان فنون

بانقطاع یقین دان که ایستاده کنون
همان نقطه که با احمرار لرزد و ریزد
بسطح صعد منور نگر تو طلعت زهراء
که از صفاء بروقش مدار لرزد و ریزد
نثار مطلع بالعیان کنون بنگر
ز عرشیات جواهر نضار لرزد و ریزد
مشو تا غافل از این سرهای منکشفه
که از قلم بنواریّه نار لرزد و ریزد
بدان مدار جهان بالیقین عین مدلست
که از مقام بداء باقتدار لرزد و ریزد
و گر تو را بعیان آمده جذاب بدیع
بدان ز طفح همین نامدار لرزد و ریزد
جمیع آنچه بود در سماء و فوق سماء
بسطح ارض لاجلش مدار لرزد و ریزد
نگر بقامت قیوم قائمش اکنون
که نقطهای بها با استوار لرزد و ریزد
نگر که از چه عیان بنگری کز این[۳۱] مرکز
که ماء مدیّه زو بانهار لرزد و ریزد

رسید نالهٔ قدّوسیه چه بر ناقور
زلازلات باو باظتهار لرزد و ریزد
نگر چه شور فتاده بعالم بالا
رشاحیات سبوحی نضار لرزد و ریزد
بدان که از جذبیّات نظره محبوب
صبائیات مسلسل مدار لرزد و ریزد
نگر که عکس[٣٠] همین جذبه از برون جمال
بسان شبنم گل در بهار لرزد و ریزد
طراز قامت زیبا سوائیش بنگر
که از مقام بهاء باستوار لرزد و ریزد
نگر که جام بلورین ز عکسه وجهش
میان عین معیّن نضار لرزد و ریزد
نگر بطرف نظر کز ید جمالیّه
زجاجیات بلا اختیار لرزد و ریزد
نگر اگر تو ز اهل وفاء ابهائی
که آیه از ید با اقتدار لرزد و ریزد
بیار جذبت غیبیّه ای نکو سیما
که تا مدار بلا اختیار لرزد و ریزد

آدمـی از تـو در میـان آمـد نـوح از جلـوه ات بجـان آمـد
بانی کعبــه سرّ هــام آمـد مــوسی طـور از کلام آمـد
از شفاعت کلام را بنیان
آن کلامــی کــه روح را بانی شــد مجسّــد ز نفــح فـارانی
زاقــــتراب ظهـــــور ربانی گشته حاکی که عیسی است عیان
ذات پاکت منزه و صمد است لم یـلد وصفت از ممدّ مـد اسـت
حدّ مولود را چه وصف و حد است ذات پاکت مطهر از حـد آن

(٤٢)

هو

سرشـک از رخ ان گلعـذار لـرزد و ریـزد
چنانچه شبنم گل بانهار لـرزد و ریزد
ز عکس قمص بهایش فتاده شور نشور
ز طفح رشح بـدایش مـدار لـرزد و ریـزد
شنید صیت بلایش چه مصطفی در خلد
سرشـک از رخ ان نامـدار لـرزد و ریـزد
برنّه چونکه برآمد صدای نحل بزاری
صراح خمریه از ابتـدار لـرزد و ریزد

فیوض سرمدی گشت آشکارا　　همه آلاء فردوسی مهیّا
نظر کن عرش رفعت را مزّین　　بانوار هویت گشته روشن
ز رکن اوّلش عالم منطّق　　از او صبح ازل گشته مفتق
ز رکن ثانیش عالم مروّح　　که ابواب ثنا گشته مفتّح
ز رکن ثالثش عالم منضّر　　بانوار بهاء گشته منور
ز رکن رابعی در سرّ قاطع　　ز رمز جامعی وز نور لامع
بفوران آمده اشجار انوار　　بصیحان آمده طمطام اسرار

(٤٠)

بگو از داستان عشق بخروش　　که می آید ازار بغی او جوش
که امکان گشته مغلوب و هراسان　　عیان گشته همه آیات تبیان

(٤١)

نقطه بدء را بنائی تو　　الف لین را خبائی تو
اصل تقویم را قوائی تو　　عین تعیین را عیانی تو
زانکه حقت نموده والی شان

(۳۷)

که عالم پر از شور شیراز شد	جهان در جهان حجله از ناز شد
نماند بجز ذات پروردگار	عیان ذی نفس در مقام مدار
نگر تیز با چشم با اعتبار	که عالم پر از نار شد در دیار

(۳۸)

بیار از صراحی صهبا شراق	ملاءلاء نما جام از اسطباق
بتدویر کاس بلورین عیان	نما سرّ سبعی عیان از طباق
بجذب الهی بلحن صباحی	بیار و مدار آنچه داری لحاق

(۳۹)

بیا ای طالب درد الهی	طلب کن آنچه از اسرار خواهی
که فتاح ازل بگشوده ابواب	بجلوه آمده وجهش ز هر باب
بیامد سر زمان و طی شد ازمان	عیان شد سرّ حق از عین تبیان

ایا غافل از سرّ غیب الهی نگر آنچه فا الحان بازمار بین
جمال ثنائی ز استار عزت ملاءلاء مشعشع بانوار بین
بنقر نوائی نوائی تو بنواز کنوز صباحی بانوار بین
غمام سنائی مغمّم باکفار قطیر حراقی باقطار بین
بیا ای صبائی ببزم خدائی که آن سرّ مستور ظهار بین
بیار ای مغنی ز غنّ ثنائی که عالم پر از قبسه نار بین
برافکن نقاب غباری ز آیات برانداز احجاب و گو نار بین
شناور بطمطام ناری بیاور شئونی که در ظهر استار بین
هیا شمس حکمت مکرکر بعزت جمیع سوی جمله در نار بین

(۳۶)

ز رشک ز غیرت بپرداختم رموز نهانی عیان ساختم
باسماء سیما سموات عزّ به پیچیدم و جمله انداختم
بجذب خدائی طلع الازل همه طرزها را بیان ساختم
توگر سالکی از مسالک بیا بجز حق مبین شئ کانداختم
که تا آنکه بینی سراسر جلال عیان از جمال بهاء ساختم
بیا و میندیش از عکسها که از قبسه جمله برداشتم

(٣٤)

بنوا آمده حان طیر منا　　شور افکنده بذرات بهاء
اهل سجّیل ز سنگ سجّیل　　اوفتاده بشرار و بدعاء
لعن نازل ز سماء امر است　　از لسانیکه خودش اصل دعاء است
سورهٔ فیل بود شاهد صدق　　قد ارانی الحق ما لم ترها است
کید تضلیل نگر با شاهد　　آمده اهل دعا در دعوا
هان که نازل شده از شطر سماء　　طیر مشهود ابابیل عماء
باخبر باش ایا ناطق صدق　　گشته نازل ز چه آیات سوی
بین حجاره ز کلامت موجود　　گشته مشهود بانت الاعلی
زیر از فوق نگر پس آندم　　جمله احجار سواری بنوا
شمس نازل ز سماء عزت　　ظل معدوم باشراق ضیاء

(٣٥)

مطالع ز مطلع بانوار بین　　مساطع ز مسطع باظهار بین
سناء سنائی بدفّ نوائی　　باحراق اقدس باحرار بین

یوم بداء است این سرّ قضا آشکار
آمده از نو عیان شمس قدر در دیار
ریز ایا طائر قدسی ماوی مکین
از شرریات نار در قدح آتشین
شمس ازل بین کنون در شرف ارتفاع
در طلعیات وجه با نظر امتناع[٢٩]
طرف نظر در نگر ماه هویت ببین
در جذبیات نور جاذب اهل یقین

(٣٣)

برگوی باین آن تو ایا طائر طوبی
این شور و شرر چیست بعالم شده برپا
گویا که عیان آمده در سطره خضراء
آن جلوه حقیّه مستوره بابداء
رشحات ثنائیه مرشح ز غمائم
جذبات بهائیه ملئلا ز عماء هاء

یا ربم دریاب کو افتاده ام در تیه غم
با گرفتاری اسیر قوم اشرار شرر

(۳۱)

مظهر بهاء قدرت با عز بهاء نشسته
شاهنشه صدر اعلی با فر ثناء نشسته
از نضرهٔ طرفی طرف عالم همگی ربوده
اهل عزّ و فرّ آنها جمله جابجا نشسته
در مصدر صدر دیوان جز ذکر بیان امرش
دیگر نبود عیان شئ در مجدالعلی نشسته

(۳۲)

(حقّ هو حقّ لا اله الاّ هو مبدع الاسماء بدیع)

از شرریات نار عالم امکان بجوش
آمده طمطام نور در صیحان و خروش

(۳۰)

از حرم برگوی ای طوبی سیر در این سطر
ریز در جام ز مشك نابیه بار دگر
تا رهم این شئونات همازیّه به آن
بر فراز آیم باوج شمسه رفعاء قدر
پس شوم وارد ببلد ایمن رب غفور
از شراریات قبسیّه بسوزم سر بسر
تا نماند از من از کل مقامات بدئی
قدر ذرّ ذر نماند دیگرم از من اثر
چون باین حالت بیابیّم خداوند لطیف
از تلطّف از تنظر از تکرم از نظر
نازل آید از مقام رفعتت یک رشحهٔ
آن حقیقت منوجد آید بامرت از قدر
پس بدور آید ز جذبت یا اله المبتدع
حاکی آید از مقامت یا ملیک المنتصر
یا الها وجه بنماید شود او رهنما
پس بسوزد ماسوی از جذبتش یا مقتدر

بگـویم از صراحیـات امـر قـادر اکـبر
که تا در شـور و شر آینـد اهـل بـلدهٔ ابهـام
نیندیشم دگر از هیـچ شـئکه کو بـود مرکوز
بیندازم جمیع منکـرین در طلّهٔ سـودام[۲۸]
که تا یابند آن سرّی که کو رای العیـان آمـد
بلا کشف حجب ظـاهر بقمص قـادر علام
که تا یابند سرّ سـطوت حق از بـدای حـق
که در قیـد و محن افتـاده انـد اینفرقـه از آثام
اله قــادر اقــدر ملیــک ناصر انصــر
بیاب از فضل و احسانت قرین فرحه و اغمام
بحقت یا الهی پاک فرمایم ز هر شـانی
که او ناقابل آمد نزد تو یا قادر علاّم
بفهــمان ای خداونــدم ز آیات بهائیّــه
کشــانم یا ربم در صــدره طوبیــه در انجــام

سوختم از لهبهای[٢٧] عکسیه در تیه
دیگرم نبود قرار و دیگرم تاب الم
یا الها پاک فرمایم از این آلایشات
برکشانم تا بساط عزّ یا رب الحیات

(٢٩)

بذکر اسم پاک ذوالجلال الحی و الاکرام
نگارم من کنون این صفحه را از نضرهٔ انظام
بگویم از جلالیات با عز خداوندی
برون آرم کنوز مخفیه از قطعه ایّام
بگویم انچه او مستور در صدراء نوراء بود
بشور و اهتزاز آرم جمیع لوحهٔ الطام
بگویم آنچه را مغمور در خباء بنانیّه
بیارم انچه را منظور از اعلا و از اعدام
بگویم از نهانی امر کو محجوب در احجاب
که تا آرم سمائیان بوجد و شور از ارمام

(٢٨)

هوالحبیب و نعم الحبیب بیا ای طیر زرین عز بگشا بال

از صحیفه نزلیه برگوی ای طیر عماء
در نزیل عالیه بربای یکسر ماعدا
دیگرت تاب تحمل از نزیلات بدیع
تا بکی ای نازل از اغصان بس رفع رفیع
عرش را بنگر بنور وحدت حق مستقر
کرسی رفعت ز او اندر مرایا جلوه گر
شمس عزت رو نماید از قباس اندر فلک
سیر فرماید بعکس خویش سرعا از فلک
تا نماید جلوهٔ بدعیّه را او آشکار
از مرایای بهائیه باعزاز و وقار
یا الها حق ذات پاک بی مانند خود
یا الها حق نفس عال بی پیوند خود
یک نظر فرما ز انوار خفیه یا اله
وارهانم از شئونات غبیره یا اله

(٢٧)
در وصف نرگس

چشمت گشوده نگران بر جمال دوست
یعنی عیان نگر که سوی نیست هست او است
سنبل حکایت از لفظات شعریّه
دارد ولی چه سود ز شرّار ناریه
حاکی ز زلف پیچ عیان گشته بباغ
لیکن چه سود بر طرفت آشیان زاغ
مشهود گشته اید شما جمله با شکوه
بیرون نموده اید جواهر ز غصنها
اما چه سود والی والا بدشت کین
افتاده بی معین و نصر بین مشرکین
الله یا ربا بنما یا اله حق
تا انکه پاک آیم و آیم بجذب حق

جز او منگر در همه ذرات وجودت
از او بنگر جمله آیات بداء را
بی او نبود شئ عیان ظاهر و موجود
از او بعیان جمله ذرات بداء را
شاهد بودم آنکه سوایش همه معدوم
از وی بعیان سرّ قضا را و بدا را
آگاه نمود از شرف منطقة الحق
مجموع سوی مستوی عرش عطا را
الا کل شئ ما خلا الله باطل
و کل نعیم لا محالة زائل

(٢٦)

بر ریز قلم از ثمر نخله رضوان تا آیدم از جذبه مخفیّه باعیان
بردار کنون پرده ز رخسار و میندیش تا آوریم در ولج و لجه باین آن

ای جوهریکه گشته منور ز نور حق
از چشمهٔ ظهور تو شاراب کاسیان
برخوان خدای قادر محبوب خویش را
تا ظاهرت نماید ز اسرار کن فکان
الله قادر هو محبوب لم یزل
دریاب طاهره تو ز الطاف بیکران

(۲۵)

بی پرده نگر وجه مطلوب عما را
از شعشعهٔ وجه ربوده است سوا را
جز او نبود شئ دگر ظاهر و موجود
کز غیر بدی خالق او غیر خدا را
الله که خالق نبود غیر خداوند
او خالق و او بارء و او کل سوا را
بردار کنون پرده ز ابناء مبنّئ
اقرب بود از حبل ورید قربا را

ای واقف از رموز که کرده ز نور وی
بشـــنو نـداء را و ربا خـود ز خـود بـآن
آمـد بطـرز عـزت مشـــهوده جلـوۀ
کو در مقـام عزیّه بودی بجـان نهـان
وصفش بود ز چون و چرا عاری از ازل
بـودی ز کلّ مـا نشـاء فی المشـائیان
بنگـر جمیع مـا ظهر از سرّ مـا بـداء
محروق گشته از شرق ضؤ وجه آن
بنگـــر جمالیـــات باطـــراف بیـــت او
با جلوهـای نضـریه محرق بایـن و آن
بنگر بطرف عین دگر یا حبیب من
آنچـــه بزاهـــرات ز زهرائیـــان عیـــان
باب حـــرم نگـــر ز شمـــوس بهائیـــه
در انقطـاع محض سـتاده ببلج هـان
بنگـر بطـرف نظـر ایا واقـف رمـوز
باب وصول منقطع آمد ز این و ان
درکـوش در مقـام دعـاء با ثنـاء فـرّ
قـدوس ربنـا و هـو الحـق فی البیـان

٦٠

الحمد هو جميل عزیز بصدر قوس
ما لیس دون حد جلالت مآل ما
یا رب بفضل خویش بیابم بامر خویش
پاکم نما ز انچه منافی بحال ما
الحمد هو جمیل حبیب بطرز عز
قد اشرق الشعاع و ایّد جمال ما

(٢٤)

ای طائری که آنچه به بینی بطرف آن
از آیهٔ مرشّحه آن بین کن فکان
بیرون بیاوری تو ز انوار سرمدی
ظاهر کنی جمیع بطون از طراز جان
برگو ز ما رایت ز آیات حکمتی
تا در سرور وجد بیایند هائیان
از جنت شهودی ظاهر باین صعید
برگو که رشح مدّیه نازل ز هامتان

حمدت که وصف ذات علیّست عال او
باشد ز نور وجهۀ او اتصال ما

داریم بر لسان بیانش بهر بیان
غیرش نبوده ذکر بداء مآل[٢٦] ما

دریاب از کرم که بیابیم حظ خویش
آریم در عیان بیان سرّ حال ما

البته قادری تو بهر بدء در بداء
آور بنظم و نثر کنون سرّ قال ما

حق حقیقت تو خداوند کردگار
بردار پرده آر بیوم وصال ما

الله منم مقر بایات بدعیه
کز سرّ دین حق محمّد ص جلال ما

ان سرّ که بود در ستر سطریه ستیر
بیرون ز پرده گشت تعالی جلال ما

پس سوخت از نضار بروقیه در عیان
ان شعشعی که او محجئه آمد جمال ما

الله شاهدی که توام ناصر و نصیر
جز تو دگر نباشد و دیگر بیان ما

بعضی قتیل[٢٥] و بعض دگر در قیود حبس
آفاق بالتمام بر ایشان عماء شده
راه مفر نباشدشان از طریق حبّ
در قید حبس قلب و کبد هم سوی شده
آیا نبود سنت غیر بدیل حق
الان در مقام بیان رهنما شده
صفا بصف ستاده بصف ماه طلعتان
جانها بکف قتیل براه خدا شده
میدان یقین که آمده بیرون ز پرده راز
امثال در مثال ز هم جان جدا شده
بعضی ستاده بر شرف و عز و امتناع
آن دگر بعزّ خودیت هباء شده

(٢٣)

الله شاهدی تو بهر حال حال ما
بیرون ز وصف چون و چرا شد مقال ما

بالله گشت وارد مدین بنوع خفاء
عالم ز شور نور پر از شعلها شده
دریاب سرّ اگر تو از اهل مشاعری
این جذب کیست کان چنین دلربا شده
بنگر بنظر صاف ایا ناظر مبین
در سنت الهیه کان رهنما شده
بود است جذب حبیّه میزان دین یقین
ز جذب حق محق ز معاند سوی شده
آنکس که او ستاده باثبات حقّیه
تا آنکه بند بند ز او هم جدا شده
باکش نبوده قدر ذر از بند ابتلا
در کل حال داعی ذکر خدا شده
گوید بهر لسان انا[٢٤] العارف البیان
تا انکه ماسوی ز ثباتش سوی شده
ایا نبود سنت غیر البدیل حق
الان بصفّ طف بعیان برملا شده
از مال و جان گذشته بحال سرور و وجد
در راه حق بجب ولا مبتلا شده

الله بیــاور بعیــان جلــوهٔ محبــوب

تا آنکـه ربایـد و زدایـد همـه باری

(٢٢)

عـالم تمـام مطـرء نظـر خـدا شـده

جز او سـوای او بسـوائی هبـا شـده

اسرار دین احمدیه در بروز و کشف

بیـت الحـرام مظهـر قـبله نمـا شـده

از نظره جذاب خود شـاه کن فکان

بربـوده آنچـه را ز سـوائی سـوا شـده

هر کس که لایق آمده از نظر طرفه

صـافی ز غـلّ و غـشّ غبـار و هبـا شـده

او قابل است آنکه شود حامـل بیـان

از حمل او عیان است که قبله نما شده

بـردار پـرده را و نگـر در وراء سـتر

آن کیسـت متکی سـبب طـا و لا شـده

الله چه عالم شده از تازه مظهّر
آفاق پر از نور و نیار است بناری
الله عیان گشت مگر وجه خفائی
از آنکه ربوده است ز ما ثبت قراری
دیدیم چه آن جلوه غیبانیه خفیاء
محویه نداریم دگر ثبت قراری
از شعشعه وجه جمالیه آنشاه
در سوخته شد جمله ما قبسه ناری
الله توئی شاهد احوال الهی
جز تو نبود دیگرم اثبات مداری
دانم بیقین رب عطوفم و کریم
این جذبه نیاید ز شؤنات غباری
بل وجهه مطلوب مطلّع ز عماء شد
در سوخت همه کون و مِکان جمله بناری
الله توام شاهد محبوب بعالم
جز تو نبود نصر دگر ثبت قراری
دریاب که نایاب بعالم شده الان
آن نقطۀ حمریه کز او ثبت قراری

گـویم بلحـن فطریـه مـن فـاش بـر مـلا
دیـن اسـت حـبّ کار بانجام عـام او
آنکس که متّکی شده بر قول و فعل خویش
بنگر بآن که سوخته از یک کلام او
دین است حب احمد و آل علی بآن
معنیّ دین همین و تمام است کلام او

(۲۱)

الله ز الطـــاف نهانیــــه نظـــاری
تا انکــه بیـــارم بعیـــان نقطــه باری
گـــویم ز مقامیکـــه مـــنزه و مجـــرّد
از مثـل و مثـل از شرر شـور و شراری
ذکری نبـود جـز هـو محبـوب جمیـل
در نـــزد شـــهانیکه مصـدّر بســـراری
از شعشعهٔ وجه ربایند همه عیب[۲۳]
جز ذکر ندارند دگر شان و مداری

(۲۰)

ای صـاحب مقـام کـه او لامقـام او
ای بانـــی کلام کـــه او لا کلام او
فرمـای یکنظـر تـو ز الطـاف مخفیـه
بـر ریـز جرعهٔ کـه مسلسـل نظـام او
تا آنکـه بالعیـان شـود آن نقطـه بـداء
بی پـرده بی حجـاب مجردسـت نام او
آرد بجـذب طلعیـه در سـطحهٔ صـعید
آن سروری که بانی نظم و نظام او
بالله دیـن بـود ز نظـار وی اسـتوار
عـــالم باو مقـــوم اصـــل قـــوام او
معنـای دیـن محبت آن شـاه بی قـرین
از حـــب او تمـــام باتمـــام نام او
بـردار پـرده را تـو اگـر شـاهدی بـآن
شـاهد بادعـای مـن اسـت التیـام او

بر ریز تو از جام بلوریّه می ناب
تا غنّ صراحیّه بیابی تو ز اعیان
بر ریز و شکر ریز ایا طایر قدسی
بی پرده نگر وجه ملمع تو ز ستران
بر ریز و میندیش که آمد و نیامد
دیگر بعیان مثل تو ای سرور خوبان
بالله عیان بنگرم از طرف نظاری[۲۲]
جز تو نبود دیگر و دیگر بهمه شان
از شعشعهٔ وجه ربودیّ زدودی
هم زنگ غباریّه و هم دین و هم ایمان
بالله که ایمان نبود محض تلفظ
بل جلوهٔ حقیّه تو اصل ز ایمان
دین است همان حب تو ای قادر محبوب
بالله که غیرت نبود در همه تبیان
تعجیل بفرما تو ایا قادر محبوب
بالله که غیرت نبود در همه تبیان
تعجیل بفرما تو ایا قادر منصور
در رفع اظلات و اکتات باین آن

میریـــزد ازل عرشـــه نضـــار جـــواهر

از شعشعه او قبله نما شد چه بجا شد

بـــرگیر ایا ســـامع آیات الهـــی

این پرده که او ستر بباشد چه بجا شد

تا آنکـه بـه بیـنی بعیـان جلـوه غیـبی

از ستر همین پرده خودش وجهه نما شد چه بجا شد

(۱۹)

بـرگیر قـلم قصـبهٔ رومیّـه فتّـان

بر ریز باین سطر تو انوار ز فاران

برگـوی بالحـان فطوریـه ز اسرار

بـربای ز مـرآت شـهودیهٔ نضـران

ذرات غباریّه که گشته است محجّب

از جلـوهٔ غیبیـهٔ آن سرور خـوبان

بنگر که فتادند همه صعق و مکدر

نایاب اثر هیچ ز ایشان و باین آن

۵۰

کن مقوم قوام را ز قوام پس منظم نظام را ز نظام
زانکه تو خالقی و کون مکان جمله در نزد تو بود اعیان
[۲۱]جز توام نیست چاره بنما حکم محکم مرا بجا بنما
حق خود ای خدای رب ودود تو نسازم ز درگهت مردود

(۱۸)

آن جلوه غیبیّه عیان شد چه بجا شد
آن نقطهٔ اصلیه بیان شد چه بجا شد
از نظرهٔ طرفیه آن شوخ شکر ریز
آتش بعیان شعله نما شد چه بجا شد
از غمزه سکریّه آن فتنه دوران
آن نقطه عیان خویش نما شد چه بجا شد
از منطقة الجذب درخشید چه این نور
عالم همه چون طور سنا شد چه بجا شد
در مصدر اصدار مصدر چه شد آنشاه
در زهزهه آن عرش بها شد چه بجا شد

(١٧)

حمـد تابنـده از طـراز بهـاء　　حمـد مشـرق ز وجهـۀ اعـلا
وصف حق آمده بدهر و زمان　　از ازل او مشعشـع و تابان
لوح الواح زو منضر گشت　　روح ارواح زو ملـوح گشـت
زانکه او خلق اوّل است بـدهر　　قبل از او شئ نابده در دهر
اوّل اسـت او بنقطـه ایجاد　　اخر است او بلوح استعداد
ظاهر آمد عیان و در ظاهر　　باطـن اسـت او ملـئلاء باهـر
حق او بس عظیم در امکان　　حظ او بس جسیم در اعیان
یا ربا حق حق آنکه او را بود　　مایۀ وجـد بـود و سرّ وجـود
حق آنان که غصن این شجرند　　حـق آنانکـه اصـل ایـن ثمرنـد
یک نظر کن ز غایت الطاف　　وارهـانم ز هـرج و مـرج گـزاف
چشم ما را به بند زین عالم　　گـوش ما را به بند زین عالم
قلـب مـا را محلّ نـور نمـا　　صدر ما را تو اصل طور نما
وجـه مـا را باقتبـاس آور　　اصـل بنیـان را اسـاس آور

پس نگر دیگر نگر بین بی حجاب   آیهٔ نمله ملألاء از حجاب

کرد تعلیم او سلیمان بهاء   تا بیابد وجههٔ طلعیّه را

خوان بایات فطوری طاء و سین   از کلام پاک رب العالمین

بعد تنبیه سلیمان از بیان   بس تبسم کرد او چون یافت جان

بایدش جذب اثر جذب اثر   بایدش مرآت قایم در نظر

پس لسان بگشود از سرّ شهود   خوان حق را تا که آرد در وجود

آیهٔ طلعیّه غیبیه را   کشف فرماید حجاب خفیه را

رب وفقنی لاعمل صالحا   خوان بلحن فطرت طا سین و ها

پس نگر سرّ اجابت در ظهور   آمده از امر محبوب شکور

و تفقّد الطیر یا مستمع   تا بیارد وجه غیب ممتنع

طیر باشد جذب سلمانی عیان   آن بود تعلیم ذره در بیان

هان بخوان از آیهای فطریه   پس بنوش از کاسهای خمریه

پس بخوان از قصّه شهر سبا   باز آر از جذبهای انّما

آتیان بنگر بطرف حینییان   گوی الله عزیز فی البیان

یا ربا حقّ حقیقت یا اله   سرّ فطری را عیان کن یا اله

هان نگر ای سامع از آیات حق　　تا بیابی سرّ حق از ما طبق
در نگر در کل ذرات نشور　　کی بود یک ذره مهمل از فطور
ذره صغری بود اندر عیان　　حامل اسرار ربّ کن فکان
گر جمیع عالم از کل سوی　　جمع آیند تا که بربایند ورا
از مقام اختیارش ذرهٔ　　در حرکت ناید از عدل ذری
هان نگر دیگر نگر با چشم تیز　　تا به بینی وجه عزت یا عزیز
خاضع آمد ذرهٔ با اقتدار　　نزد انکه او بود اندر مدار
سلطنت باشد مرا جان در عیان　　غیر من نبود دگر در کن فکان
غیر خود را هیچ نایابد اثر　　سلطنت را داند از خود بر عسر
گر سلیمانی بیاید آشکار　　برگشاید او لبان[19] اندر مدار
سلطنت باشد مرا جان در عیان　　غیر من نبود دگر در کن فکان
هان نگر ای طایر طوبی نظر　　ذره باشد آیهٔ سرّ قدر
انیّت از وی دلیل وحدت است　　قامع بنیان شرک و کثرت است
گوید او حالیّة قالیّة　　غیر من نبود عیان از قاعنن[20]
پس نگر دیگر شنو سرّ خدا　　گر بگوید غیر این سوزد ورا
نار امری از مقام کن فکان　　زانکه این تکلیف او آمد عیان
گر ذلیل آید بنزد پادشاه　　پس گرفته غیر حق را او گواه
هان نگر باشد عیان سرّ فطور　　از جمیع مابدی از جذب طور

کردگارش گشت ظاهر از بدیع   پس نمودش آیهٔ قدرت صنیع
دیگرت جائی نباشد اعتکاف   در مقام قشر صورت در معاف
بایدت تلطیف سرّ ای بیخبر   تا بیابی جذبهٔ طوری شرر
از عزیر آمد عیان سرّ خبیر   عزم او گردد عیان نور منیر
ربط نبود بین مولا و اثر   جملگی قائم بفعلش از قدر
پاک باشد ذات واجب از علل   نه برون آید ز او نه او اثر
هر چه خواهد ظاهر آرد از بدیع   صنع او تام و مسوی هم منیع
قدر امر او نباشد ناقصه   تام باشد در مقام ثابته
ای قلم از جذبهٔ ربّ ودود   آر از پرده برون سرّ وجود
گوی با صوت بلند بس رفیع   تا بیاید سرّ رجعی از بدیع
گوی با لحن مظهر از یقین   لا اکراه فی الدین یا جاعلین
بلکه باشد سرّ غیبی آشکار   آنکه خواهد در جذابش در دیار
آشکار آید باجذاب منیع   یابد ان سرّی که باشد بس رفیع
آنکه او محجوب در احجاب شد   باعث تخسیر از هر باب شد
ظلم نبود در مقام اختیار   حق را با غیریت باشد چه کار
نیست تکلیف کسی الا اتی   انچه حق داده است بر او از عطا
پاک باید بود از غیر و غیر   تا بیاید طلعت غیبی منیر
اختیار آمد دلیل وحدتش   اضطرار او عین بغض و عکستش

غیریـت را نبـودی ره بـر بیـان عکسیت مطروح صرف آمد بجان
غیر او محمود صرف و باطل اند صمّ بکمّ غیرتـت را زائـل انـد
گر تو خواهی آیه از آیات حق تا بیابی نور امرش در سبق
اینکه جز او نبود اندر نشاتین[۱۷] بالـغ خـاتم بامـر العـالمین
نیسـت تکلیـف احـد ابـراز او جـدی آیات صمـد ارمـاز او
یا طـریح انـدر بسـاط فائقـه ان لله امـراً[۱۸] هـو بالغـة
خوان و دیگر دم مزن اندر مدار تا بیـابی سرّ رجعـت آشـکار

(١٦)

حمـدت ای داور بـود زیـب بیـان غـیر او نبـود بعـالم در عیـان
جملـهٔ عـالم ز نـورش منوجـد طـرّه آدم ز عکسـش مستـمد
باشد از رشحات وی این رشح نور باشـد از قبسـات وی طـور ظهور
ای یهـودی در مقـام امتحـان آی از خود هان برون شو پاک هان
علـت معلـول را مقصـود بـین جلـوه طوریـة را مشـهود بـین
دان عزیـر او آیـهٔ وحـدت بـود از بـداءش باء در رجعـت شـود
بـود او کم در مقـام معرفـت او طلـب میکـرد غـیر مابـدت

نوریان با شور جذب انجذاب　　در مقام نصر یا ربّ الایاب
یا الها حق خود ای کردگار　　سرّ خود ظاهر بفرما آشکار
امر غیبی کو نهان در نار بود　　حامل او طلعت مختار بود
احمد او را داشت در صدره نهان　　کاظمی از شور وی در آسمان
گشت ظاهر بغتة ای کردگار　　عالمی تازه نمود او آشکار
شاهد او نفس پاکش در عیان　　قائم قیوم و حیّ لامکان
آنکه او چون جمره سور غبیر　　مانده اندر تیه جزوی با اثیر
بنگرد در آیهای نزلیه　　تا بیابد جلوهای حقیّه
آنکه او محجوب صرف ناپدید　　منجمد در قعر حسبانی پدید
گوید اینکه نبودم اثر خبر　　از چنین امری که آید در اثر
بایدش تبصیر از آیات حق　　آیهای مستطر اندر سبق
آیهای قدرت پروردگار　　پس بخواهد او به بیند آشکار
آیها در بطن قرآن العظیم　　در تظهر آمد از وجه عمیم
بنگرید یا زمرهٔ افّاکیون　　ایّ حدیث بعد الله یؤمنون
باشد این آیه دلیل وحدتش　　قامع بنیان شرک و کثرتش
باشد این آیه نزیل از آسمان　　بهر قلع و قمع کل مشرکان
باشد این آیه همان سرّ سریر　　کو مظهر از مرایای قدیر
نفس او باشد دلیل وحدتش　　قامع بنیان شرک و کثرتش

احمدی بینم باجلال و کبر   کاظمی در صدرهٔ صدری مقر
جملگی در نصرت و در دعوت اند   حالاً قالاً جذیب وحدت اند
یا ربا دیگر عیان بینم عیان   واو غیبیّم برون از کن فکان
در نهایت از غضب آمد اله   در ید او آیه نارت گواه
یا ربا مقتول دیدم آن امام   از شراریّات ناری انام
یا ربا رجعت نمود پس گشود   جمله ابواب غیبی بر انام
یا ربا پس اینگروه خاسره   در مقام سکر فحشائی تمام
جمع گردیدند همچون کوه کوه   درربودند جمله الباس نظام
یا الها دیگر این شور و نوا   از کجا آید بگوشم یا علام
چیست دیگر این نوای با نوا   کیست این مه طلعت عالی مقام
گوئیا بربوده گردید از ازل   چون بدید او آیهٔ ارجعی نظام
یا الها نصر فرمایش کنون   تا نماید جمع کل را سرنگون
یا ربا بردار ز احجاب غبیر   تا بیاید طلعت نار منیر
تا بکی محبوس در قید بلا   تا بکی مطروح در تیه عنا
یا الها حق این زیبا لقا   آر از پرده برون خیر الثّناء
عالمی را سر بسر از نور کن   جملگی را بر فراز طور کن
یا اله الحق یا حق المجیب   یا حقیق الحق حق یا حبیب
ناریان باشند در شور و شرر   از عکوسات غباریّ قتر

آنچه را باید بوهابیتت — باید[16] آن را داند او از حکمتت
تا بکی باشم بزندان بلا — دستگیر و توامان با ابتلا
رحم فرما ای خداوند بیان — وارهانم از شئونات زمان
برکشان تا بر مقام رفعتت — پس نما آیات عز و شوکتت
یا ربم دریاب از احسان خویش — وارهانم از شئون جان خویش
بر بساط عزّ وصفت مرتفع — هان فرما یا اله الممتنع
زانکه فضلت مایهٔ جان من است — سرّ عدلت اصل سیجان من است
ای اندر نمطه وسطی عیان — ای مبرا از شئونات زمان
برفروز آثار غیبیّه کنون — عالمی را پس بفرما سرنگون
گوی از آیات غیبی در ظهور — آور از اسرار رب لایزول
بایدت تخلیص از کل شئون — تا مصفی آید آن ماء البطون
این نظرها افک محض باطل اند — نیست و نابود و جعّل عاطل اند
کی تو را شور و هوای وحدت است — میل پرواز و هوای عزت است
برگشا بال و فراز آی بر مقام — تا بیابی لذت رجع مدام
گیر از من منظره با نور و فر — پس نگر در وی ز آیات قدر
لیک دم درکش ایا عالی مقام — تا برون آید ستیر الایتهام
یا علی الحق یا ربّ البیان — یا منیع العز یا حق العیان
بنگرم در منظر با استنار — جمله آیات قدرت در نضار

در مقـــام سرّ ایجـــاب آمـــده خیـل املاکی بایـن باب آمـده
ای ملایک جملگی ساکن شوید در مقامات ثنـاء مـاکن شـوید
زانکـــه تاب اســـتوار اقتـــدار از شـما نبـود بشـطر ایـن دیار
نیست مقصود وی ای ارباب هوش آنچه را یابید از فتراک هوش
در تـنزل پـس بیائیـد از سـماء حـول بیت عزّتش انـدر دعـاء
پس عیان خواهید دید و پس شنید آنچـه را مقصـود او باشـد پدید
یا الهـــا یا جلیـــل المقتـــدر مـــا نمـی فهمـیم رنّات سـهر
لیـــک یا ربّ العزیـــز بالبیـــان جز تواش نبود دگر ذکر لسان
گوید و گرید بطرف این بداء اوفتـاده او طـریح انـدر دعـاء
یا ربا نصـرش بـود از نـزد تـو غیر تو نبود ورا جز حب تو
یا ربا گویـــد بالحـــان بـــدیع یا سمیـع و یا علـیم و یا منیـع
حق من در نـزد تـو باشـد نهان نـه بـنزد زیـد و عمـر و ایـن آن
یا ربا از فضـــل افضـــال بـــدیع یا سمیـع و یا علـیم و یا منیـع
حق من در نزد تـو باشـد نهان نـه بـنزد زیـد و عمـر و ایـن و آن
یا ربا از فضـل افضـال بـدیع آفریـــدی جمـــله ذرات بـــدیع
جد و جهد و سعی بنمودن اله یافتند از جدّ خود یک مشت کاه
از کرم باشـد بـدور ای کردکار خواند من را حق خـود انـدر دیار
حق من باشـد عظیم ای مقتـدر زانکـه فقـر صرف باشم در سـطر

(١٥)

ای قلم از قصبهٔ رومیه آر　　قبسهای طوریه اندار[١٥] مدار
گوی از ما اشهدت کینونتک　　تا براری از سباحیان دمار
گوی از آیات غیب ممتنع　　یا بیانی سرّ طرز مرتفع
خیز از جا ای قلم با شور و فر　　در مقام کشف اسرار اثر
دیگرت نبود مدار عکسیه　　نایدت از فضل حق آن ظلّیه
شمس وحدت گشته ظاهر در سماء　　ناطق از اسرار پنهان خدا
دان که آمد عرش ربّ کردکار　　در تزهزه از نوای این هزار
جملهٔ عالین باستعلا شدند　　خیل کرّوبی باستبداء شدند
پس سمائیان بجوش و اجتذاب　　جملگی در غلق شور و اضطراب
کی خداوند رحیم دادگر　　قادر قیوم حیّ منتصر
ذرهٔ از تو فتاده او نجیر　　در میان کلّیان او دستگیر
اذن فرما یا اله المقتدر　　تا مشرف ما شویم اندر سفر
شاید آنکه باید از منّ رحیم　　نازل آید از طرازات قدیم
هان شنو این قصهٔ با شور و فر　　آن ندائیکه مظهر از قدر
باشد این با وی ملیک المقتدر　　پای تا سر هوش باش ای منتظر

گردیده ظاهر از ستریات اختیار
نازل شده بنقطه احمر بعز و شان
الله اعظم است ثنایت اله من
الله اکبر است دگر مر تو را بیان
دریاب از کرم تو خداوند مقتدر
افتاده ذرّهٔ ز تو در فیٔ امتحان
الله بار باد گرش ناصر و معین
نبود بجز تو یا احد رب عالمین
دریاب تو اله من از فضل بیکران
افتاده ام بتیه ضلالت بغیر بین
الله یاب از کرم و فضل بیحدت
زانکه توئی عزیز و نصیریّ و هم معین
غیر از تو نبودم دگری[١٤] ناصر ای اله
دریاب از کرم که توئی ربّ عالمین

رخشـید وجـه او ز نضارات وجهیـه
مشـروح صدر اوسـت بانوار آثیژان[۱۳]
قلبش مقام عـزت و رفعت بنور حق
نازل ز او رشـاح نواریّـه در عیـان
یا رب ز کیست طنطنهٔ عزت و جلال
کافـاق جملگی بـه تنـور ز نـور آن
الله کیسـت اینکـه جمیـع عمائیـان
در نـزد طلعـتش بفتادنـد صـعقیان
پس عرشیان جمیع خضیعند یا حبیب
در نـزد او خـدای جمیـع سـوائیان
یا رب ز نور وجه بهایش کنون عیان
کـرسی اقتـدار باشراق شـد بیـان
عـالین و پس کروبی و دیگر سمائیان
در سجده و دگر بنظار دگر بجان
یا رب جمیع کون مکان در شراق نـور
پس منتظر بنصرت او خیل کن فکان
الله یار باز کـه اجـلال آمـده
گویا که ذات پاک علیّت بعز و شان

(۱٤)

شاهنشهی که در همهٔ کون و هم مکان
نبود ز غیر او بعیان ذرهٔ عیان
از امر او ببلج وجودیّه در شراق
از دون عرش تا بمقامیکه لاعیان
پاک و منزه است وجود شریف او
از غیر ماسوی و ز اهماز همزیان
از عکس قمص نور جمال وی آشکار
تسبیح کردگار بهر شان و هر زمان
نور جمال طلعت او عین حمد حق
اثبات وحدت آمده او را بعزّ و شان
الکبریاء وضع ز آیات عزّتش
الله اکبر است لقاء ورا بیان
آنکس که یافت رشحهٔ از کاس حب او
آمد مطهر از همه ذرّات افکیان

گر واگذاریم بحق ذات پاک تو
نبود تو را شعار[١٢] نه اینهم تو را دثار
زیرا که ارحم آمدهٔ در مقام رحم
بل رحم منوجد ز مقامات اقتدار
دریاب از کرم تو کنون ذرهٔ طریح
زیرا که جز تو نبودش ای رب کردگار
گر یابیش سزد که بیابی اله من
گر واگذاریش که نیاید شد این مدار
الله یاب از کرم و فضل بیحدت
تا آنکه آیم نه بیندیشم از غیار
زانکه توئی نصیر من ای کردگار من
غیر از تو نبودم دگری رب کردگار
عالم فناء صرف بود یا حبیب من
امداد از تو میرسد و کون در مدار
گر آیهٔ طلیعه برون آید از حجاب
سوزد جمیع کون و مکان از قباس نار
الله یک نظر ز لطیفات نظریه
چونانکه پاک گردد عیان ارض با نضار

(١٣)

ای داوری که داوریت دار بیکسان
نازل ز نزد تو بود امداد بی کسان
عالم پر از شرر شده یا قائم عظیم
غیر از تو نبودم دگر امداد یا قدیم
شاهد بجز توام نبود در مقام امر
یاب از کرم که رفته زدستم عنان امر
گر واگذاریم تو خداوند کردگار
سوزد جمیع جمع ز اقباس پر شرار
الله یا اله حبیب قدیر حیّ
دریاب از تفضّل و احسان بی شمار
تا انکه در قوام بیایم بامر تو
آرم هر انچه نازلم آمد باین دیار
الله شاهدی که بجز او نباشدم
دیگر معین و یاوری از کل این دیار

تا بکی در عالم پر شور و شر
دور باشی تو ز مقصد دورتر
شو مکین بر مسند تمکین ما
قوهٔ فعاله را ظاهر نما
امر ما بیرون شده از کاف و نون
گشت ظاهر سرّ انّا راجعون
گو انا الحمد المجمّل بالجمال
گشته ظاهر از مقام اعتدال

(١٢)

هو المغرّد علی اغصان شجرة القدّوس

زحمد خداوند عرش عماء
منور نمایم جمیع سواء
بتغرید جذبی بیارم کنون
همه سالکان از خفایا برون
منم طیر طوبائی لم یزل
از الواح عزت شوم جلوه گر
بنغمه سرایم بسرّ عیان
بجلوه درآیم بوصف کیان
همه کون و امکان نمایم خبیر
باغنان قدوسی بی نظیر

آن خلافی را که با ما داشتی
در مقام صلح آر و آشتی
فیض را تعطیل نه تعطیل نه
حکم را تاخیر نه تاخیر نه
گشتهٔ محجوب از احجاب خویش
بسته از یک باب صد ابواب خویش
طرح غیریت خودت انداختی
خویش را محجوب از ما ساختی
تا بکی محبوس در ابدان شدن
بر حدود و بر جهت اعیان شدن
آدمیّت را نمودن اختیار
بابیت اسمت بلوح اعتبار
هان که امر مبرم ظاهر شده
حکم محکم آیهٔ قاهر شده[۱۱]
برکن الباس حدود بس قیود
خویش را افکن تو در دریای جود
فاش بین ایندم همه اسرارها
در ضیاء و در بهاء استارها

گفت یا ادم منم ربّ رحیم
از تجلیّ محیی عظم رمیم
طلعتم مستور باشد در هواء
جلوه ام منضور گردد از عماء
در هویّت گشته سرّم مستسرّ
از حجاب واحدیّت مشتهر
اسم پاکم از احد ناید بحد
جلوه ام گشته ملاءلاء از صمد
شان ذی شانم نیاید در گمان
قدر ذی قدرم مرفع از بیان
تا تو را از نور خود افراختیم
با بهاء عز مقمص ساختیم
نقص درخلقت نباشد ذرهٔ
صنع تام و جوهر فعّالهٔ
در کمال استواء با سواء
نطق بنما از جلالیات ما
جذبهٔ غیبیّه را اظهار کن
نقطه محویه را ابراز کن

کــو کجــا آن رشحهــای ناریــه
کــو کجــا آن جــذبهای باریــه
کو کجا فـردوس و جنـت در عیان
سرّ قـــدوسی مـــلاءلا از بیـــان
کـــو انـــیس با وفـــاء با ضـــیاء
گشـــته او مســـتور از مـــن آه آه
بـود او را گریـه شـغل و کار و بار
تا نمانـــده ز او اثـــر در ابتـــدار
چونکـه یاس از نفـس او را دلیـل
در نزهـــزه آمـــد و همـــس جلیـــل
ناگهـــان وجـــه منـــیر کردگـــار
جلـــوه گـــر گردیـــد از شـــطر دیار
با هـــزاران جلوهـــای با بهـــاء
فـــیض لطفـــش بی حـــد و بی انتهـــا
کشف فرمود او حجاب از وجه خویش
(در خط اصل همین یکفرد نوشته بود)
بـــس مـــروح او بـــنفخ سرمـــدی
دردمیـــده در عظـــام ممتـــدی

۳۰

تا که ساکن گشت اندر ظلّ ظل

یافت سرّ حقیقت مستقل

اینکه سرّش مستتر در خاک شد

زین سبب در سیر بر افلاک شد

دید او رمز نهانیهای او

آن کشاکشهای بی پایان او

آدمی از جلوهٔ او آدمی

صحو و مسکور و دمادم در دمی

بر صعید خاک با رنج و عنا

همچو ماهی در تبلبل از بلا

آه حسرت شغل او باشد مدام

کوه سرانديب[۱۰] او را شد مقام

خفیة اندر تضرّع با خضوع

شمس وحدت از کجا یابد طلوع

بود او را ذکر طرز حال و قال

یاد آن یوم و ممّا لایقال

از کجا افتاده این حوت کئیب

بر صعید ذلت و حسرت غریب

بشنو ای طیر عمائی راز او
در پس این پرده این آواز او
جلوه ربانی انوار او
جذوهٔ فارانی شرّار او
پس نهان کرد او رخ و شد او نهان
درحجاب غیب اندر لامکان
شد مکان از وی مکون در جهان
چونکه خود دید او نهان شد در کیان
شد زمان در دور از تدویر او
دهر در تدهیر از تدبیر او
بر فلک شمس ثناء با بهاء
شاید انکه پی برد بر سرّ هاء
پس قمر از او ملمّع در عیان
گشت سائر در بروج آسمان
چون بهر برجی رسید و وارهید
جلوه اش را در مقامی تازه دید
نجم عزّت گشت سائر در بروج
در فراز و در نشیب و در هموج

او شجر در لبس و در الباس بود
چونکه نار شعله در الماس بود
نه غروب او را مصور نه طلوع
نه فروغ او را مقدر نه فروع
اصل ثابت بود در یوم ازل
بس مطهر از حدود و از علل
فیض او ظاهر ز آیات صمد
اسم او بس مستظل اندر احد
حد و تحدید و شئون ماسوی
جمله در قید اضافات عدی
چونکه فیضش لا یحد و لاعد است
نقطهٔ سرّش برفعیت مد است
وصف و تعیین و عیان شد منوجد
مدّ و تمدید زمان از وی ممدّ
در مقام وصف تعبیر بیان
شد مشعشع از حروفات بیان
در عناصر هیکل با استواء
گشته ظاهر از مقام لا بهاء

تا مقام قدس عزّ با بهاء
ان مقام لامقامی در بناء
جمله را مصبوغ صبغ الله کرد
جمله را مشهود وجه الله کرد
الله الله این چه قدر است و چه شان
شد مظهر از حروف کن فکان
طیر طوبائی نظر کن با صفاء
تا که مشهود تو آید ابها
این همان مشکوة باشد با بهاء
زو مشعشع گشته کل ماسوی
این همان مصباح نورانی بود
کز فروغش جسم روحانی شود
حامل او بود مرآت بهآء
در کنوز غیب اندر پردها
کوکب دری معبر در بیان
نور رخشان در سموات عیان
در حجابات ثناء بودی یشآء
از یکاد کاد در شان نشاء

طلعت حق است با عز و وقار
در مقام لن ترانی شد دیار
هیکل با استواء با ضیاء
در تلجلج در تبرج با بهاء
در تنطق آمد از جذب ودود
جملهٔ ابواب مغلق را گشود
با ندای با صفای هات لک
می زداید زنگ کفر و ریب و شک
بس اشارتهای پی در پی عیان
گشته از او مبتدر اندر زمان
هان نگر ای طیر طوبائی ببین
صدق قولم آشکارا بالیقین
نار سینائی بفوران آمده
نور فارانی است تابان آمده
اسم اعظم او مظهر در عیان
گشته واله کون و هم امکانیان
جلوه گر بر کل اسماء آمده
جملهٔ اسماء را رهبر شده

الله الله این چه نور اهتزاز
گشت ظاهر از فعال بی نیاز
گوئیا شد سرّ وحدت آشکار
یا دیار لن ترانی شد دیار
یا حجاب منخفق شد مرتفع
گشته طالع وجه غیب ممتنع
یا احد در جلوهای با بهاء
در مرایای صمد با عزّ و هاء
یا که احمد گشت نازل از سماء
شد مشعشع از جمالش وجهها
یا علی در کرّه و کرت شده
یا عیان اسرار در رجعت شده
یا مفطر شد سماء منفطر
مکفهرات سنائی مستمر
یوم موعود است یا سرّ شهود
از مقام لامقامی رخ نمود
رمز مستور است یا اسم نهان
از حجابات ثلثه شد عیان

رمز مکمون در کمون لامکان

ساز اندر مصدر تمکین عیان

آدمی را سوی جنت باز آر

در مقام صدق عزت باز دار

نقطه مستور در احجاب نور

کن عیان او را بایات ظهور

گشت نازل حکم رب العالمین

بهر تطهیر عماء از واصفین

حرف ناریه که در استار بود

در حجابات هویت نار بود

وقت اظهارش رسید و نور شد

ماسوی از جلوه اش بر طور شد

عالم نور از بروزش شد عیان

شد برون از پرده آن سرّ نهان

از فروق خفق عکس وجه او

شمس حکمت با قمر شد روبرو

عکس ظل نابود و ناپیدا شدند

جملگی بر ساحل دریا شدند

آدمی را او باعیان شد دلیل — نوح را او وارهاند از کرب و حیل
پس شعیبی را نمود او باخبر — از رموزات نهانی سر بسر
ماسوی را از سوی شد رهنما — برد[۹] موسی را بطور اصطفا
عیسی مریم ز نفحش منوجد — عکس او شد ماسوی را بس ممدّ
احمدی را باعث وجد ظهور — بود او را اصل تبیان سرور
ای خداوندم بحق حقّیت — وارهانم زین شئون کتّ و مت
پس به بینم غیب وجهت در عیان — جان خود قربان نمایم در بیان
یا رب ای قیوم رب العالمین — حشر فرمایم بقوم صالحین

(۱۱)

در تغرد آی ای طیر عمآء
در شرر انداز اوراق ثناء
بازگو از سرّ های لم یزل
از رموزات نهان لا مثل
آر از پرده برون وجه بها
منصعق گردان ز جذبش ماسوی

طیر طوبائی نگر دیگر نگر   تا به بینی وجهه غیبی شرر
سرّ فطری آشکار آمد عیان   از مقام امر محبوب العیان
لیک بعد سیر ابراهیم او   در مرایای ثلث بی گفتگو
چونکه او شد منقطع از ماسوی   یافت او سرّ فطوری از عمآء
هان نگر ای طایر طوبی مقام   بار دیگر در زجاجه بالنظام
کیست کز نار خلّت شد کلیم   در مقام صدق ایفاء مستقیم
نوش از جام صراحی بازگو   کیست این مه طلعت زیبای رو
آمده بر طور با جذب و سرور   ذکر و وردش یا حبیب و یا غفور
طائر طوبی بیار از جذب او   تا که باشی سرّ او بی گفتگو

(۱۰)

یا علی سرّ خدای لم یزل   انکه او لا مثل باشد در مثل
لم یلد شانش بود در ابتداء   یولدش ناخوانده کس در انتها
پس احد ذات عزیزش دان و خوان   سوره توحید در این داستان
اصل وحدت را بناء بنیان او   سرّ جذبت را عیان اعیان او
در ذوات آمد مثالش جلوه گر   برد یکسر ماسوی را سر بسر

پـاک فرمایـد ز نـورش ماسـوی　　پـس نمایـد جلـوهٔ کیهـان خـدای
در تغــرد آیــد از جــذب ودود　　گویــد الحمــد هــو رب الوجــود

(۹)

طیر طـوبائی نگـر با عزّ و فـر　　تا چــه بیــنی بار دیگــر از نظـر
کیسـت ایـن زیبـا نگـار مسـتوی　　باشد او در فتق و رتقش بس قـوی
عالمی از شور وی انـدر خـروش　　ســینهٔ آدم ز حــــبّ او بجــوش
نـوح را او در بـدر از خـود نمـود　　تا کــه دادش آنچــه او را بــود بـود
سرّ ابــراهیم باشــد جــذب او　　بانی کعبـــه شـــدی از امـــر او
ســنگ نازل از ســماء اجتـذاب　　طــائف او آمــد ز امــر آنجنــاب
تا کـه یابنـد جمـله ذرات وجـود　　اینکه او معبود و غیرش نیست بود
هـان نگـر ای طـائر طـوبی لقـا　　تا چـــه یابی از رمـــوز ابتهـــاء
مبـــتلا گردیـــد ابـــراهیم او　　بــس تمـام آمـد عیـان بی گفتگـو
از کلامــات خداونــد بیــان　　عشــره آمــد نــزد او در عیــان
باشد این عشـره کلام از انتظـام　　در مقـــام نـــزف تطهـــیر انام
تا شـوند ایشـان قبـول کردگـار　　پـــس بیابنــد سرّ غیــبی آشــکار

۲۰

هان بگو سرّ افاقت در کجا است
امر مرموز قیامت از کجا است
آن مگر دیدی جمال احمدی
یا بیان نطق حال احمدی
های های ای مایهٔ جان جهان
بینمت هشیار بعد الالفیان
بعد حمد کردگار لم یزل
بازگو از داستان ما اجل

(۸)

هو

بلبل طوری بتغرید نوا
باز آی با جذبهای با صفا
ریز در جام بلوری مشک ناب
تا بیاشامد جناب مستطاب
پس عیان بیند ز عکس کاسیه
جلوهٔ محبوب را او جهریه
محو فرماید ز لوح با نضار
غیر را تا که به بیند در دیار
آشکار آمد عیان سرّ حبیب
نیست دیگر غیر تا باشد رقیب
آرد او بیرون ز قمص آستین
جوهر جذّاب ربّ العالمین

گوی حمد کردگار لم یزل
ذات پاک احمد است او لاعدل

در مقام وصف حق حمد آمده
اسم مطلق وصف مطلق آمده

در مقام نزل او اندر سمآء
احمد آمد وصف او اندر مرآء

باخبر از سرّ غیب آئی بیا
حمد احمد شد بتنزیل ندآء

قامت حمد آمد از وی در ظهور
بس ملمع شد بایات طهور

آیهٔ نور است شاهد بر بیان
جلوهٔ طور است بر اعیان عیان

روح اهل روح از وی شد فیوح
عالم عالم از نضارش در شکوه

هان قلم شو با خبر اندر رقم
قد اریک[8] صعق سکران ایقلم

منصعق گشتی ز اسم احمدی
منطرح گشتی بنمط سرمدی

۱۸

پاک کن خود را ز اغبار کدر
وارهان خود را ز احجار مدر
تا که بینی وجه مطلب عیان
از مقام عزّ ربّ کن فکان
جمله عالم بشور و اهتزاز
عرش آمد با توحّد با عزاز[7]
جمله اعراشیان بس مستعدّ
طرهٔ امکانیان در کدّ جهد
هان قلم مسکور بینم در عیان
اوفتاده در نماط کن فکان
گوئیا وجه خدائی در ظهور
گوئیا رنّ نوائی در طهور
یا قلم یوم افاقت آمده
یوم تطریز قیامت آمده
در مقام نطق و استنطاق آی
در بیان کشف استغراق آی
عالمی واقف نما از سرّ حق
از رموز غیب و از لیل غسق

شمس عزت زو نماید اقتباس
حفظ فرماید قوابل ز انطماس
یا ربا عرشت بود ماوای او
یا الها وجه تو رضوای او
از حروفش عالم منوجد
از عکوسش حور و رضوان مستمد
حاء باشد حبّ وجهت ای اله
میم برمجدیّت[5] مجدش گواه
دال او تربیع ارکان[6] آمده
از سناء عز نمایان آمده
جمله عالم بوصفش در ثنآء
حضرت آدم ز وصلش در بقاء
یا ربا جز حمد تو ناید عیان
از مقام عزّ فعل کن فکان
قمص بینم حمد را بس مشترق
زو فرّ هر جمله آیات سبق
بشنو ای سامع ز آیات ثناء
تا که گردی آگه از سرّ بداء

طـیر طـوبائی نگـر در منظـره
تا چـه بیـنی از صـفای منظـره
شـعلهٔ حمـد است شـعال آمـده
وجهـه حمـد اسـت فعـال آمـده
در مقـــام شرق اشراق جـــمال
او نمـــایان از مـــرایای فعـــال
هـــر مقـــامی از مقامـــات بهـــاء
مینمایـــد وجـــه او در آن ضـــیاء
هـر یـک از الـواح بینم مظهـرش
ز او نمایـــد سرّ وجـــه انـــورش
در عـــماء بـــین هـــواء رائقـــه
در ســـماء آیـــد غـــمام بارقـــه
ارض از اشراق او در اشـــــتراق
عـــالم عـــالم از بهـــائش در شراق
الله الله ایـن چـه وصـف با صـفا اسـت
جمـــله ذرات از وی در ثنـــا اســـت
بـدر سـان بینم بـدوران مسـتنیر
وجـه او انـدر مطـالع مستسـیر

۱۵

اول از حمد احد شو نغمه گر
عالمی افکن ز نور او شرر
زانکه حمدش مایهٔ جان آمده
اول از هرشئ باعیان آمده
عالم لاهوت از وی منوجد
قصبهٔ یاقوت از جودش ممدّ
ملک عزت زو مقرر در نیاء
اوج رفعت زو مقطع در عماء
زانکه حمد آمد خدا را وصف پاک
آینه آسا لقاء وجه پاک
ذات حمد سرمدی ناید بوصف
قطع راه وصف او را عین وصف
باشد او بیرون ز اوهام و ظنون
می نیاید وصف او اندر فنون
وصف او باشد بتبیان انقطاع
نعت او آید بدوران امتناع
زانکه باشد وصف حیّ لم یزل
ظل حق ناید بظل ظل مدلّ

يا اله الحـــق يا رب المجيـــب　　يا سميع الدعوة من لهف الكريب
قــد اناجيــک بســـرّ عونــک　　قد انال فرصتی من هيبتک
کم مـتی اطـرح بتيـه الانقلاب　　کم متی تشـهد دعائی لا تجاب
حقــک الحــق الحقيــق يا اله　　خلّص الـزاء مـن الکـرب البلاء
و ارفعيهـــا يا الهـــی بالنـــدآء　　و اسـکنيها فی نمــاط الانمــا
و اشربيهــا مــن کئـوس خمريــه　　و اطعميهــا مــن طعــام حقيّــه
کم مــتی يا رب تشــهد حالهــا　　و تحـــب قيلهـــا و قالهـــا
حــق الحــق ثم صــبری يا اله　　حـــذا بحقـــی يا اله يا اله

(٧)

طـــير طـــوبائی بتغريـــد ازل
باز آی وارهـــانم از ملـــل
باز گـــو از سرّهـــای باهـــآء
باز آر از رمزهـــای باصـــفاء
زان زجاجيّـــات عطـــرانی بيـــار
زان ســـنائيّات فـــارانی بيـــار

١٣

یابد آن حیّ کریم ذوالجلال　　ای که تو داری تمنای وصال

از مقام امر لابد در عیان　　بهر تو چشمان حق بین در کیان

بعد او با عین او بالا شدن　　بر فراز ذروهٔ اعلی شدن

دیدن آنجا آنچه او نادیدنی است　　پس شنیدن آنچه او نشنیدنی است

هان ایا غافل ز اسرار قدر　　از شنیدن از روات و از خبر

نایدت آن حالت حقی پدید　　تا بیابی لذت قربی عیان

بایدت تقطیع از کل سوی　　طرح افتادن چه میّت در مناء

بایدت صادق بدن در ادّعا　　تا که یابی راه بر آیات ما

سنت حق گشته جاری از ازل　　اینکه غیر او نباشد در مثل

حاکی و جاذب بنمط اقتدار　　او است خالق او است بارء کردگار

انبیا بودند جمله در خروش　　سینها از جذبهٔ وحدت بجوش

آمدند از بهر تنزیل بداء　　لا اله الا رب العرش العماء

هیچیك خود را ندیدند ای عزیز　　داعیون بودند از رب عزیز

در رساندن حکم را مرسل شدند　　عاری و طاهر ز عیب و غل شدند

لیک تر بودی لسانشان از ازل　　هادی و مرشد بود رب ازل

هر که را باید بیاید با صفاء　　تا به بینند وجههٔ کیهان خدای

آنکه او ناچیز صرف آمد عیان　　در طلب آمد ز افک افکیان

نبودش ره بر بساط کردگار　　منطرح افتد بتیه غم دچار

آنکه دم زد در مقام معرفت　　اینکه آوردم شئون معرفت
سوخت از ناریت شرکی بآن　　اوفتاد از آن او از آسمان
غیر تو نبود تو را عارف کسی　　وصف تو جز ذات تو ناید کسی
ذات پاکت عاری از وصف ظنون　　او مطهر از شئونات بطون
اینکه آمد از قلم نور نداء　　اینکه غیرت نیست مشهود از عماء
مطلبم باشد عیان سرّ قدر　　آنکه از وی نار و نوری در شرر
آنکه او را نفس خود خواندی عیان　　بدع فرمودی بامر کن فکان
پس مطرّز گشت از اطراز نور　　ناطق آمد از ثنائت یا غفور
در مقام تنزیه آمد عیان　　حالاً و قالاً بانوار بیان
الله الله از جلالیات او　　از شعاعیات با اجلال او
عالم ابداع از وی در بروز　　آمده کاشف بارماز رموز
هر که او را دید از خود وارهید　　حق را بی پرده و بی ستره دید
محو آمد از جمیع ماسوی　　طرح افتاده بطرز انّما
ایها السامع ز آیات جلال　　هان شنو تغرید جذبائی[٤] بجال
وانکه چشم تو نیاید در مقام　　قابل دیدار حیّ ذوالاکرام
بایدت تطهیر از کل سوا　　بعد او تنزیف از کل عدی
بعد او نابود صرف لاعیان　　آمدن تا باب بیت لامکان
در تضوّع در مناجات و دعاء　　تا بیاید جذبهٔ صافی بهاء

چون توئی مقصودم ای ربّ جلیل — وارهانم ای خدا از کید ایا وجه جمیل
غیر تو نبود مرا یار و نصیر — زانکه امرم از تو باشد یا قدیر
حق من باشد بنزد تو نهان — هان برون آر از مقام کن فکان
می نمی بینم حق خود یا اله — درکف مخلوق تو یا سیداه
زانکه ای محبوب وهاب منیع — آفریدی بیاوردی بدیع
پس بجدّ و جهد خود ای کردگار — یافتند لاشئ صرفی در دیار
چون بکرات ای خداوند بدیع — آنچه را دادی بافضال منیع
رحم فرما بر من ای ربّ رحیم — نصر فرمایم خداوند قدیم

(٦)

ای خداوند عزیز ممتحن[٣] — قادر و قیوم و حیّ ذوالمنن
ای که جز ذاتت ندارد او وجود — او است بود و ماسوی نابود بود
باشد این از عالم اول عیان — ای که غیرت نیست مشهود العیان
آنکه غیرت دید یا غیب الغیوب — سوخت در آن و فتاد اندر لهوب
لیک رؤیت یا الها نیست او — اینکه یابد راه در وی گفتگو
ذات پاکت عالی اعلا است او — از جمیع وصفها اعلی است او

۱۰

آیهٔ باهیمنه آید نزیل — از مقام امر حیّ لاعدیل
آیهٔ کو باشد از یوم ازل — ثابت و راسخ مبرا از علل
مشترق از نور او کل سوی — منقمص از عکس وجهش انبیاء
جملگی خاضع ز نزدش جملگی — از مقامش ظاهر آمد بندگی
از ازل مستور در بناء بداء — نامده از عالم وحدت بهاء
نزل انزال نزال نزلیه — فضل افضال فضال فضلیه
پاک بودی از همه شان و شئون — نور وی ظاهر ز امر کاف نون
جمله ذرات از وی در بروز — جمله آیات از وی در رموز
یک نفس گر غافل آیند ماسوی — منعدم گردند فی الحان از سوی
جملگی بر کون او باشند مقر — از رشاحیّات جودش با اثر
عارف آمد آنکه را اندر بیان — یافت سرّ وحدت از رب العیان
دید او اسرارها اسرارها — پس شنید او رازها آوازها
جمله عالم پر از انوار دید — کاس خمری را بلا اخمار دید
دید آنرا او نادیدنی است — یافت آن سرّیکه او ناگفتنی است
محو شد از ماسوی او سر بسر — درفتاد اندر بساط با و بر
یا ربا ای قادر حی عطوف — جز توام نبود دگر ربّ رؤف
یاب از فضلت که گریان آمدم — از تقعّر زار و حیران آمدم
جمله کون و مکان یا کردگار — تنگ بر من گشته از موج شرار

۹

حمد هو حبیب حق لیس هو الا هو
قد لمع من اللماع کل سوی بطول و عرض

(٤)

ای قلم برخیز با شور و شرر / ریز در الواح از سرّ قدر
آیهٔ مخفیّه در اطراز نور / در تلئلاء در تشعشع از ظهور
گوی از آیات لاریب خدا / آر از پرده برون اسرارها
تا که گردد حجت کل را تمام / بر جمیع مایحرک بالذّمام
جملگی یابند سرّ مستتر / جملگی واقف باسرار قدر
شاید آنکه باید از رشحات نور / در تظهّر آید از جذب غفور
وارهاند جمله اوهام و ظنون / پس بیارد حکم خود از کاف و نون

(٥)

ای مغرد بر غصون ناریه / آتی از آیات عز خافیه
گوی از اسرار غیبیّ نهان / تا برون آید رموز کن فکان

یک نظر از نظار طرف تا که بیایدم نزیل
از طرف دیار حی پس برباید او غرض
نیست مرا سوای تو جاذب و مجذاب ای حبیب
نیست مرا عدای تو لا بسماء و لا بارض
یاب ز فضل بدع خود تا که شوم مخلعت
آمده از سماء عز طرز بها بطول و عرض
وانگهی ایجبیب من یاب ز فضل بیکران
بار امانتت ادا آمده از مقام فرض
فرض نباشدم عیان جز که بیایدم بدان
از شرف قوام حی با شرف ضیاء محض[٢]
دائم اله اقدم آید او بداویه
از طرف عراقیه با رقم رقاع خط
رو که مرا است او نصیر آن نصر الهیه
نصر بود ز او مرا لمح عیان و عین فرض
بهجتم ار نیایدم بایدم آنکه شایدم
وصل صله ز تو مرا او است یقین عین فرض
حق حقیق بارئت نازلت آمد آن صله
نیست ورا سوای حق تا که نمایدش بفرض

۷

پس فتاد او در نهایت زار و رنجور و ضعیف
در تغرّد با حبیبش خفاِ خفئان غم مخور
خیز از جا طاهره آمد عیان سرّ شهود
موسی عمران نگر در طرف فاران غم مخور
عیسی مریم نگر نازل ز چارم آسمان
احمدی در کرکره آمد با عیان غم مخور
بهجتم دریاب اسرار فطاری در سطر
یاب در یاب انرا کو در ستاران غم مخور

(۳)

از کشش نهان تو بایدم آمدن بعرض
کز نظر عیان تو سجده مرا است عین فرض
انت اله اقدم یاب ز فضل بدع خود
مانده ام و فتاده ام لیس سواک لی غرض
آمده سوی کوی تو جمله حروف با ضیاء
از جذب عیان تو پاک شده ز هر مرض

هان ایا محبوب ناظر در مرایای کمال
درنگر پس در نگر با نصر احسان غم مخور
سنت حق را نباشد شان تبدیل طری
آید ان سنت باعیان تازه رخشان غم مخور
آدمی بنگر که در خلوتگه خاص اله
بود با حوّا بسی طرّاب و فرحان غم مخور
ناگهان گردید نازل زاسمان با اضطراب
منطرح در سطح غبرا زار و عریان غم مخور
تا که دریافت او همان کو یافت بد در نزد او
نفس او حق غیر او موهوم و بطلان غم مخور
هم چنین نوحی بدی در نوحه از مرئی رثی
تا رسیدش امر شد دریا بطوفان غم مخور
هان نگر از شطر کعبه بانی کعبه نگر
آمده با جذب فطّاره باعیان غم مخور
ساخته کعبه مربع تا که آرد در ظهور
سرّ تعریف معرّف ز او باکوان غم مخور
خواست از جا تا که قربان آورد نزد حبیب
حی داور را عیان دید او بقربان غم مخور

٥

آمدت ای جان من بشری نزیل از کردکار
از تـراب آمـد عیـان تقـویم ارکان غم مخـور
هـان نگـر مجمـوع املاک سماوی در نـزول
پـر شـده عـالم ز انـوار نیـاران غم مخـور
عرش بنگر در نهایت مرتفع در ارض طا
وجهـه حـق طـالع از سرّ الخفیقـان غم مخور
در نگـر محبـوب در منظـر بنظـر کردگـار
یاب ان سنت که لا تبدیل غیر آن غم مخور
اولا صـنعش تمـام و امـر وی با انتظـام
ظاهر آید از طراز عزّ و احسان غم مخور
پس لاجل کمل و تکمیـل و کـمال اکتمال
در تزلـزل آیـد ان ابـداع منـان غم مخـور
در سطیح ارض غبراء با تبلبل با خروش
در طلب آن حی داور رجع فطران غم مخور
تا کـه از تـدویر وقـر پـر تـدهّر وارهـد
یابـد آن سرّیکـه او در سرّ خفقان غم مخور
ناگهـان آیـد ورا نصـر بـدیع از کردگـار
رجـع فرمایـد الی اعـلای رضـوان غم مخـور

(٢)

آیدت آن بایدت از شطر رضوان غم مخور
تا بدت آن شایدت از وجه سبحان غم مخور
گیر از ما منظره ای محو از سودای ما
در نگر در عزّ و فر در روی تابان غم مخور
هان شنو از ما تو آیات خداوند عزیز
نازل آمد از چهارم رکن ارکان غم مخور
اولی او بود دارای توقّدهای نار
اوفتاد از اوج اعلی در بیابان غم مخور
سوخت او مجموع عالم را بصطلات بدیع
گشت ناپیدا ز انوار لمیعان غم مخور
ثانیش چون اولش لیکن چه ماه صافیه
جاری از انهار ناری در نیاران غم مخور
ثالثش چون ثانیش در جذب اشراق ضیاء
در تروّح در تنشّط همچو صبیان غم مخور
از مقامات ثلثه از صفایای قبول
در خفا اندر خبا ای شمس رخشان غم مخور

یا الها بس سرادقها مرفع از جلال

جلوها از طرفها در طرف فاران آمده

آسمانها یا الهی در تنصر در صفا

در مقام امرشان دوار نصران آمده

اف بر این ناسوتیان الاف اف ای کردگار

زانکه بر ایشان بفرط ظلم و طغیان آمده

یا الها حق با تحقیق این شاهنشهان

یا رب از فضلی که او بداع منان آمده

یا الها نیست تقصیری در آخر حب تو

بایدش تا آیدش آن کو ورا جان آمده

نیت[1] او چون رب محبوب قدیم لم یزل

ماسوایش نزد او معدوم و حرقان آمده

یا الها حق با تحقیق خود ای کردگار

یا رب از فضلت مریضی کو تو درمان آمده

٢

از شررهای لهیبیه بسوزد او تمام

زو نماند قدر ذر بل کل حرقان آمده

یا الها این چه عالم در بروز آوردهٔ

جمله ارباب عزت ذل طرحان آمده

یا الها گشت مشهودم باین طرف نظر

آنچه ز او آتش مرا در کل بنیان آمده

یا الها شهسوارانی عیان در بحر نار

هر یکی را وصف حق آیات قران آمده

یا الها قدرشان ارفع ز تنزیل نزول

شانشان یا ربّ اعلی در همه شان آمده

اهل فردوس اند مستشرق باشراق از آن

نور اعظم کو مر ایشانرا ز رضوان آمده

یا الها جمله عالین ستاده صف بصف

ذکرشان برکرد شا سبوح دیان آمده

بس کروبین ز انوار بهاشان در خروش

جملگی در کرسی عزت ثنا خوان آمده

این طریحی کو فتاده در مقام انطراح

جمله عالم بوی چون موج طوفان آمده

(١)

ای ز فضلت عارفانرا روح الایمان آمده
ذکر تو مرصادقانرا نور تبیان آمده
جملگی یا ربّ اعلی شانشان در هر مدار
در تطیر تا مقام قرب رضوان آمده
از تشرقهای وجهیه ببلج اضتواء
تا مقام فوق او ادنی باحسان آمده
هر یکی را باشد آیات الهیّه بجیب
او مجلی بر صُعَیق دشت فاران آمده
هر یکی را مفتخر از تاج عزّ کردگار
در مقام قرب حق الله گویان آمده
هر که را لطف الهیه شمیل آمد ز فضل
تا مقام قربشان الله جویان آمده
یا الها ای بدیع الصنع رب کردگار
این چه عالم کز بروزش نار نیران آمده
هر که را جذبت محیط آمد بجذب خفیهٔ
او محاط از چهار جانب تیر باران آمده